Additional Praise for *Hearts Touched with Fire*

"With customary eloquence and wit, David Gergen offers us invaluable insights from his decades of observing, researching, teaching, and practicing leadership. His book is an indispensable contribution to our understanding of how to create the ethical and effective leaders we so badly need."
—**Drew Faust, President Emerita of Harvard University**
and the Arthur Kingsley Porter University Professor

"David Gergen's breakthrough book is a commanding call to the new generation of leaders to make this world better by discovering their True North and pursuing a moral purpose. No one has done more to prepare and mentor this generation than David has. His rich stories about leaders are not only inspiring, but offer meaningful lessons for every leader."
—**Bill George, Senior Fellow, Harvard Business School**
and author of *Discover Your True North*

"A a wonderful leadership manual, drawing on dozens of insights and anecdotes from David Gergen's decades-long career. It provides us with a moral compass, showing how we can find our True North and stay the course. It is an essential, highly enjoyable read."
—**Klaus Schwab, Founder and Executive Chairman, *World Economic Forum***

"David Gergen has studied leadership for decades—as a White House adviser and as an educator—and has now written a masterpiece on the subject. I highly recommend this book for all who care about leadership in decades ahead." —**David Rubenstein, Co-Founder andCo-Chairman of**
The Carlyle Group, author of *How To Lead*

"When it comes to leadership, David Gergen has seen it all. He has spent a lifetime observing, coaching, learning from, and reflecting on both the individuals and the larger context of which history is made. In *Hearts Touched by Fire*, he draws on this deep understanding to offer a critical series of insights and lessons about how great leaders are made—from the inside and out—and what this means for our own high-stakes moment. Served up with short, compelling stories of leaders past and present, this book is a must-read for everyone who aspires to achieve a worthy mission, especially the young men and women, the world over, who are now beginning to make their impact felt and known." —**Nancy Koehn, Historian**
and James E. Robison chair of Business Administration
at Harvard Business School, author of *Forged in Crisis*

ALSO BY DAVID GERGEN

Eyewitness to Power

HEARTS TOUCHED
TOUCHED
with FIRE

HOW GREAT LEADERS ARE MADE

DAVID GERGEN

SIMON & SCHUSTER

New York   London   Toronto   Sydney   New Delhi

Simon & Schuster
1230 Avenue of the Americas
New York, NY 10020

First Simon & Schuster hardcover edition May 2022

For information about special discounts for bulk purchases, please contact
Simon & Schuster Special Sales at 1-866-506-1949 or business@simonandschuster.com.

The Simon & Schuster Speakers Bureau can bring authors to your live event.
For more information or to book an event, contact the Simon & Schuster Speakers Bureau
at 1-866-248-3049 or visit our website at www.simonspeakers.com.

Interior design by Ruth Lee-Mui

Manufactured in the United States of America

1   3   5   7   9   10   8   6   4   2

Library of Congress Control Number: 2021951610
LCCN 2021948152
ISBN 978-1-9821-7057-8
ISBN 978-1-9821-7059-2 (ebook)

TO GRANDCHILDREN

Gabriel, Amira & Hannah
Maya & Liam

For future lives of service and leadership

Contents

Introduction

We begin this story in Sweden, where a schoolgirl of eight years of age began her journey toward becoming one of the most influential leaders in the world. Early stirrings of her ascent started during her primary school years, when her teachers showed films about the degradation of the world's environment: plastic junking up oceans, starving polar bears, raging forest fires.

Most classmates listened, were momentarily concerned, and then moved on. Greta Thunberg listened and obsessively dwelled upon our impending doom. Her classmates went about their day; she retreated into herself and became severely depressed about how little adults were doing to mitigate the damage. She began skipping school, barely ate, and wondered if the world would survive its current course.

At home, she began speaking with her parents about the climate, reading reports, and watching films. Her Asperger syndrome, she often says, became a source of power—in her weeks at home, her laser focus enabled her to build an encyclopedic knowledge about the environment. She began testing her powers of persuasion on her parents, knowing she could be convincing but not sure how to make herself heard. She worried she was too small to make a difference.

Then in February 2018, an unrelated tragedy struck some five thousand miles away. In southern Florida, a gunman armed with a semiautomatic rifle stormed through the halls of a high school in Parkland, killing seventeen and wounding seventeen more. Survivors were devastated.

Rather than wallowing in grief, an emboldened cohort of students turned their suffering into action. Meeting at first in small numbers on their parents' living room floors, students launched Never Again MSD, an organization committed to tougher gun laws. They were determined that such a tragedy should never strike another community. In the days after the shooting, they took to the airwaves and to social media, demanding background checks and other measures of gun safety.

Young people across the United States became energized and inspired as they watched Parkland students walk out of classrooms, protesting weak gun laws. The students were plain in their language and unapologetic in their goal: They needed parents to end their complacency and finally act. Their protests quickly spread. Inspired by the Freedom Riders of the 1960s, they traveled the country to stir people up. Week after week, the momentum of their movement grew. It reached a peak when the students spearheaded March for Our Lives, a student-led demonstration that attracted some 1.2 million marchers in 880 events across America. It was the biggest anti-gun protest in American history, as millions shamed adults for their inaction.

From afar, Greta watched the Parkland students galvanize a following within a few short weeks. She was struck by the power and attention that could be attracted by a single defiant act like skipping school, an action many Parkland students adopted. Most of the Parkland activists—students like David Hogg and X González—were seventeen and eighteen years old, just a bit older than Greta. Before Parkland, they were normal kids; after, their world was upended. In response, they became national—and global—activists. They began to mobilize the country against its toxic gun culture.

Greta was amazed by their successes and inspired by their tactics, so she began to follow suit. Her protest—a walkout modeled after one staged by Parkland survivors—was small in scale at first. She stood outside the Swedish parliament with a painted sign reading "*Skol-strejk för klimatet*" ("School Strike for Climate"). She was fifteen. No one joined her, and many passersby pitied what seemed futile efforts. The next day, however, a few people joined after social media started buzzing. And the next, even more came. Soon enough, supporters regularly showed up. She stood there every day for five months until the Swedish elections, as she had promised.

Her internet presence continued to expand, fueling coverage in the national and international press. Her solitary act of defiance soon drew an estimated 4 million people into the streets for the Global Climate Strikes, the biggest single day of climate protests in history. *Time* magazine named her Person of the Year, and the UN invited her to speak to the General Assembly. She was once again scorching toward adults: "You are failing us," she charged. "But the young people are starting to understand your betrayal." Three years after her initial strike in Sweden, Greta doubled down on her attacks at Italy's Youth4Climate summit. Instead of taking action, she described thirty years of empty promises as a bunch of "blah, blah, blah." Greta Thunberg and the Parkland students are not alone, of course, in mobilizing thousands—and sometimes millions—to follow their leadership. Stories abound in which protestors are demanding greater social and economic justice. In some countries, we should acknowledge, the protestors are on the side of authoritarians, but in most nations they seek freedom.

In Pakistan, for example, a young girl in her teens became a voice for the education of other young women. At age fifteen, she was so threatening to the Taliban that they ordered her killed. Soon after, as she was riding a school bus to her home in the Swat Valley, three men stopped the bus, demanding to know which was Malala, and shot her in the face. She was perilously close to death. Somehow she not only survived but found the inner strength to continue her campaign to this very day. Her leadership in human rights has been so compelling that she was awarded a Nobel Prize for Peace, the youngest honoree in history.

In America, young women—especially Black women—have pressured the country's leaders into embracing a progressive agenda. Tarana Burke, a young Black woman born in the Bronx, became a social activist at age sixteen. Tired of being harassed and assaulted, she started the MeToo Movement at thirty-three, taking to social media to "empower through empathy." She wanted a safe platform where women could confide their private stories of sexual harassment and violence. In 2017, *Time* magazine proclaimed her one of its People of the Year. The day after Donald Trump's inauguration, supporters of MeToo built much of the momentum behind the Women's March, the biggest protest in American history on behalf of women's rights. Beyond that event, Burke's movement spurred a national awakening and reckoning on patriarchal sexual abuse, harassment, and power.

Several years after Burke coined MeToo, three Black women in their twenties and thirties—Patrisse Cullors, Alicia Garza, and Opal Tometi—created the social movement that came to be called Black Lives Matter when George Zimmerman, the man who murdered a Black youth named Trayvon Martin, was acquitted. Avowed "Black Radicals," they initially drew venomous attacks from the right. But when Americans saw the television clips of George Floyd's dying moments some seven years later, they were horrified. Just as TV clips of the Birmingham sheriff unleashing dogs on Black children transformed the civil rights debates of the past, clips of Floyd's murder transformed the racial debates of today. Millions were stirred into supporting Black Lives Matter protests across the country. What's more, the movement forced the country to confront its brutal racist past and present unlike any grassroots effort before it.

HOW LEADERSHIP IS EVOLVING

The journeys of Greta, the Parkland students, Malala, and the organizers of MeToo and BLM show just how rapidly leadership is evolving these days. We are no longer living in a world in which leaders are
formed only in our nation's most elite institutions, groomed in public
life, and take charge from the start. Those days are gone, and thank
goodness for it! Young people now are taking a multitude of different
paths to leadership, many up from the bottom. They are not afraid to
ruffle feathers, either. They speak up and stand up for causes that may
make some of us uncomfortable. Ultimately, we should welcome conversations that expose—in thoughtful ways—alternative perspectives.
We need fresh thinking as well as fresh energy.

Social media has given young leaders powerful new tools for making themselves heard by people around the world. In the past, young
leaders in institutions like Congress were expected to keep their eyes
open and their mouths shut. If you paid your dues long enough—say,
fifteen years—you might become a committee chairman, but even
then, the path to influence was uncertain. That was before Alexandria
Ocasio-Cortez, a part-time bartender with no experience in public
life, knocked off the fourth most powerful member of the Democratic
caucus and helped usher in a new progressive movement in America.
She was and remains a master of social media.

Of course, the internet and social media are a double-edged sword.
Yes, a strong personality, compelling ideas, and powerful rhetoric can
capture public attention in an instant, but anonymous figures can then
take to the internet to spread dishonest information, seeking to de-
fame and destroy you. As students of social media have learned, it has
become easier to gain power but harder to exercise it and much, much
harder to keep it. To lead in today's rapidly changing environment,
one must now be endlessly attentive and adaptive.

One more point about the past versus present ways of leading:
As emphasized here, emerging leaders today must be much more

adaptive than in the past, actively engaging with followers and their collaborators to meet changing demands. But great leaders know that even as you learn how to navigate in roiling waters, you must also hold firm to your own True North. Your junior officers, as I learned in the navy, must manage the engine room down below, but the captain must be topside, a steady hand on the tiller.

Although leadership is ever changing, some qualities and skills have eternal appeal across time and cultures. Leaders of today ignore them at their peril. Courage and character, for instance, have been prerequisites for great leadership since the classical Greeks and Romans. Euripides defined character as "a stamp of good repute on a person." That definition fits as well now as it did in the fourth century BC. Similarly, Winston Churchill's observation about courage still fits. "Courage," he said, "is rightly esteemed the first of human qualities . . . because it is the quality which guarantees all others." I worked for Richard Nixon and Gerald Ford and can attest that while both had courage, their characters were vastly different. One lacked character and was driven out by scandal; the other was a man of character who looks better and better through the rearview mirror.

Nations around the world have long embraced traditions of educating for leadership, but they have not always succeeded. In her book *The March of Folly*, the historian Barbara Tuchman raised the question of whether it is possible to educate for government. She concluded that many cultures have tried but have ultimately failed: the mandarins of China were rigorously schooled for administration but eventually gave way to corruption, incompetence, and an unquenchable thirst for power. So, too, the fate of the Turkish janissaries, Prussia after the Thirty Years War, Great Britain when its empire faded, and perhaps now the United States. All have tried to prepare leaders for good government; all wound up badly. "Aware of the controlling power of ambition, corruption and emotions," she wrote, "it may be that in the search for wiser government we should look for the test of character first. And the test should be moral courage." The problem, she then continued, may not be a matter of educating officials "as educating the electorate to recognize and reward integrity of character and to reject the ersatz." Courage and character will always be foundational for emerging leaders. We shall return to them often in the pages ahead.

WHY THIS BOOK

Some years ago, I started writing this book in my imagination. I was reaching that stage in life that Erik Erikson called "generativity." Erikson was a renowned twentieth-century psychoanalyst who created a development model identifying eight key stages in one's life. Generativity, he declared, was the seventh. By it he meant a stage when an older person shows "a concern for establishing and guiding the next generation."

When I left Washington for university teaching in 1999, I had definitely hit that stage. I was immensely grateful for the opportunity to have worked for four presidents in the White House—three Republicans (Nixon, Ford, and Reagan) and a Democrat (Clinton). But I had grown disillusioned with the direction in which our politics was headed and wanted to pass on to the next generations the key leadership lessons I had stockpiled from half a century in the public arena. Here, at the Harvard Kennedy School, we launched the Center for Public Leadership, which I directed or co-directed for nearly two decades.

Someday, I dreamed, I would write a book about leadership that shared my thoughts. But my twenty-year relationship with CNN was just starting up, while teaching and director responsibilities were seemingly unending, not to mention speaking engagements and other obligations in public life. In other words, life always seemed to get in the way.

In the past years, however, my dream—to help prepare a rising generation of new leaders—has taken on great urgency. Who could have imagined that our democracy—and long-standing democratic traditions around the world—might be on the brink of collapse?

Who could have imagined that serious observers would be debating whether we are heading toward a civil war? But here we are. It feels like we are driving along a cliff in the middle of the night with our lights out. We all know it, but we can't seem to stop it.

It's time to face a stark reality: It's time for the people driving the bus to return the keys. We have been at the wheel for the past thirty years, and it has not worked out so well. Now it's time for new, fresh leaders to step in. Those of us who are older still have vital roles to play—preparing the young for leadership roles, passing on lessons we have learned, trying to smooth the path ahead. Some of our top universities are now offering successful programs for older Americans to help them launch new careers, often in the nonprofit sphere; other universities should pay heed.

But let's be clear: much of our future now rests upon an infusion of fresh blood into our civic life. We need new, talented leaders who are looking for paths forward, not obsessing over past differences. As Winston Churchill said upon forming a new coalition government at a crucial moment in World War II: "Let personal quarrels be forgotten and let us keep our hatreds for the common enemy." The United States desperately needs new leaders who put country before party, unity before division.

This is an especially ripe moment for a historic passage of the torch. Millions of Baby Boomers and alumni of the Silent Generation are starting to leave the stage, to be replaced by Millennials (born between 1982 and 1996) and Gen Zers (1997–2009). Together, these younger generations represent 140 million people, over 30 percent of our population. They are the biggest and most diverse cohort in our history—and will soon be the most powerful. From among these millions, surely we can identify, recruit, and support hundreds of thousands who can now work together to save the country.

I have been privileged to work with a wide array of these emerging leaders: sailors, young military officers, public servants, White House staff, journalists, social entrepreneurs, and of course, students.

What distinguishes the best of the younger generations, I would suggest, are three qualities: their resilience, their civic engagement, and their idealism. Think for a moment of the trials they have encountered in just the first decades of the twenty-first century: the terrorist attacks of 9/11; two devastating recessions; once-in-a-century fires and floods; growing racial inequities; mass shootings of students; endless wars; a runaway national debt; the presidency of Donald Trump; a deadly global pandemic; and the breakdown in our politics and civic culture.

That's an astonishing list. And it doesn't count how many times Millennials and Gen Zers have lost their jobs, seen their debts explode, moved back home, and felt their future threatened. One might expect they would retreat from public life—and a good many have—but most of them have shown enormous resilience and spunk. They remain unbowed by tough times; some 80 percent between the ages of eighteen and twenty-nine feel they hold the power to change the country for the better. Some 60 percent "feel like they're part of a movement that will vote to express its views."

They are already becoming engaged in our civic culture too. A survey by CIRCLE at Tufts University found that in 2016, just 5 percent of those between eighteen and twenty-nine had participated in a protest demonstration; by 2020, that figure had shot up to 27 percent. Another Tufts University survey found that in the 2020 election, voting by college students exploded from 52 to 66 percent. As we have seen repeatedly among today's students, that voting tilted heavily Democratic, by a 61 to 37 margin in the 2020 presidential race. Meanwhile, the number of Millennials running for Congress between 2018 and 2020 jumped a whopping 266 percent! And new political stars like Pete Buttigieg, Alexandria Ocasio-Cortez, Adam Kinzinger, Seth Moulton, and Mikie Sherrill have already started to change our political discourse. While I don't share his politics, I also respect a former student, Dan Crenshaw. He is an ardent conservative who put his life on the line for his country—and paid a price, losing an eye in combat in Afghanistan.

At a time of so much cynicism about public life, it is encouraging as well to see many of the young maintain their idealism. A Deloitte survey has found that college-educated young people are increasingly telling prospective employers they won't accept a job offer unless their company is committed to good citizenship. Their idealism encourages them to embrace a liberal policy agenda: climate change, public option or government-run health care, student debt relief, marijuana legalization, and criminal justice reform.

Many Millennials and Gen Zers readily embrace protest marches because they believe older generations have failed to address environmental issues, the wealth gap, and inequities on the basis of both race and gender. Older generations have sometimes paid lip service to these issues, yet the rising generations are inheriting the miscalculations, inaction, and problems gone unsolved by their parents. The young are rightly angry that the American dream may end for them, that there is no pot of gold at the end of a rainbow. There are thus built-in tensions between past and current generations, with the latter wondering why they should take leadership lessons from the former. Good question. There were some first-class leaders in the past who stood out years ago and remain role models today: people like John Lewis, Ruth Bader Ginsburg, and John McCain, whose profiles kick off the first chapter of this book.

I am aware that I come to these issues as an older white male who has benefited from many privileges in life. While I grew up on a dirt road in the segregated South, I was blessed with a strong, supportive, and well-educated family. My dad was chair of the math department at Duke for a quarter century, and my mom was a lovely writer. I was unquestionably afforded certain opportunities that might not have been available to those of a different socioeconomic status, gender, or race. I have tried during my adult years to be sensitive to the views of others who have not been as fortunate, though I am sure I have fallen short at times here. I owe special thanks to the young people who served as early readers of this book; they helped me think more carefully about the differences among us, challenged my thinking, and helped me understand how we might heal the country in years to come.

THE ARC OF THIS BOOK

Some years ago, I heard Bill Moyers of PBS describe a hike he had taken in Africa. In a gathering darkness, he and his team came upon a tribe encircling a campfire. Every short while, a different member of the tribe would stand up, gather two or three logs, and throw them on the fire—keeping everyone warm. Moyers made the point that our life together in communities should be like that, with each of us contributing two or three logs to keep the fires going.

That's my hope in this book: to contribute my few logs. We are in a time of immense volatility in our national life, when crises are hitting us from all directions. It is increasingly clear that we need an infusion of strong new leaders to help us navigate safely. Through stories and reflections upon my half century in the public arena, I would like to share with you what I have learned about the development of young, passionate leaders—and why I am encouraged.

True leadership and change come through action. On that note I offer not only practical advice but tales of other defining leaders who have kept the campfires burning.

Over many years of teaching, I have been influenced by the work of Joseph Campbell, a prominent professor of comparative mythology and religion. In a study of myths and origin stories shared by societies across cultures and time, he discovered that one of the strongest shared myths is that of the hero's journey. In essence, the hero leaves home to slay a dragon. By confronting challenges and fears on the way to the dragon, the hero undergoes a series of metaphorical "deaths" from which he recovers and then returns home with a new set of sensibilities and values.

Campbell believed that most human lives resemble a hero's journey. "Our life evokes our character; you find out more about yourself as you go on. And it's very nice to be able to put yourself in situations that will evoke your higher nature, rather than your lower," he told Bill Moyers in a six-part PBS television series that drew on his work. Every one of us faces both inner and outer struggles: choices and soul searching we undergo in pursuit of a better inner self, and external experiences we face as we interact with others along the way.

This book, drawing from Campbell, views the development of a leader as occurring in two parts: an inner journey and an outer journey. It's an adventure that leaders begin when they are young and continue the rest of their lives. As the late Warren Bennis, a leadership guru and great friend, has argued, becoming a leader is fundamentally the same as becoming a fully developed person. You can have companions along the way, but ultimately you must make the journey yourself.

This book opens with a consideration of some ancient chestnuts in the field. Does leadership really matter, after all? Why do we need great leaders? What are their most important qualities or traits? What values have endured over the centuries and which have evolved over time? The answers provide a foundation to everything that follows.

The book then plunges into its first major part: your inner journey. How does a leader first become self-aware and then achieve self-mastery? It is not enough just to be smart and talented. Richard Nixon was one of the best strategists I have ever met, but he had demons inside of him that he never conquered, and eventually they did him in. You must become "author of your own life," as Warren Bennis once said. These early chapters explore the internal work you must undertake to identify your values, scattering some tricks and tips to help you as you embark on your adventure.

As much as we might wish otherwise, almost every rising leader experiences harsh, unexpected blows—crucibles, as they are usually called in leadership literature. A near-death experience, a collapse of your personal or professional life—they come in many forms. The next triplet of chapters explores how such hardships may impact your inner journey—and how, with the right outlook, some of our most celebrated leaders have emerged stronger. Crucibles have the potential to instill in us great moral purpose and an opportunity to solidify our goals.

The second part of the book will turn to your outer journey—the transition as you move from internal preparations for leadership to rubbing up against the outside world. We will explore how you might build relationships with others on your team and, increasingly, how well you work and play with others outside your immediate circle. As you will see, developing your awareness of others and your mastery of social skills is a close counterpart to your awareness and mastery of self. Questions abound in your outer journey: How do you manage your boss? Build a crackerjack team? Master the basics of public persuasion? Deploy social media? These are the tools and skills you need to make a leap to true leadership.

The third part of the book is an extension of Campbell's two-part journey. Once you have worked on your internal mastery and encountered the outer world, you must be ready for action. You do not become a good leader by studying under a lamp, pursuing a third or fourth academic degree. You must avoid "a snare of preparation," as Tolstoy put it. You must be in the arena itself.

The early days of a leader can be a time of danger, certainly one of failure. We will address the darkness that can come when a leader veers off course, abandons their True North, and self-destructs. In an increasingly volatile world, new leaders must exercise constant vigilance. You must learn to exercise leadership in a crisis—preparing when you can, then acting smartly when the crisis hits. This project would not be complete without addressing three of my favorite, but often overlooked, aspects of leadership: learning from history, a wicked sense of humor, and the creation of an integrated life so that you have joy as well as passion. You will find toward the end of the book's twenty key takeaways, an executive summary for people on the run. If you check them out now, perhaps they will encourage you to read the rest of the book. I hope so.

In conclusion, we will turn once again to the central argument of this book: America is experiencing one of its worst crises since the beginning of the republic. While the next few years are likely to be rough, we can be much more hopeful about the long run if we remember who we are, if we take heart from our past, and if we prepare young generations for lives of service and leadership. We must unleash their idealism. As Martin Luther King Jr. once observed: "Everybody can be great . . . because anybody can serve. You don't have to have a college degree to serve. You don't have to make your subject and verb agree to serve. You only need a heart full of grace. A soul generated by love."

PART ONE

YOUR INNER JOURNEY

ONE

HEARTS TOUCHED WITH FIRE

He could have ducked.

His father was a prominent physician and intellectual, his mother a major abolitionist, his family well connected. So when President Lincoln issued his first call for volunteers in the Civil War, Oliver Wendell Holmes Jr. could have easily ignored it.

Instead, he dropped out of Harvard College and signed up as a first lieutenant in the 20th Massachusetts, putting his life on the line for the sake of his country. He answered the call. In battles that followed, Confederate bullets struck him down repeatedly—at Ball's Bluff, Antietam, and Chancellorsville. In one battle, he was shot in the chest and barely survived; in another, he was shot in the neck and left for dead.

But as his biographer Mark DeWolfe Howe has written, those grievous wounds did not diminish his life. They instead shaped and strengthened his public leadership for the next seventy years. Even as he witnessed so much death and destruction, his inner steel hardened, and his aspirations for America grew. He rose to become one of the nation's most influential and eloquent jurists, named to the Supreme

Court by Teddy Roosevelt and serving until FDR reached the White House.

Some years after the Civil War, in a speech on Memorial Day in 1884, Holmes described how military service had inspired his generation. "As life is action and passion," he said, "it is required of a man that he should share the passion and action of his time at peril of being judged not to have lived. . . . Through our great good fortune, in our youth, our hearts were touched with fire. It was given to us to learn at the outset that life is a profound and passionate thing."

"In our youth, our hearts were touched with fire."

What a glorious way to capture what so many young men and women have experienced in one era after another in committing themselves to civic life, seeking to create a fairer, more just, and more peaceful world. Life will hold perils, but in devoting yourself to the service of others, you find a satisfaction that transcends your troubles. As many have discovered, service and leadership are inextricably bound together. Indeed, leadership at its best is service to others.

BUT DO LEADERS REALLY MATTER?

In one generation after another, down to our day, we have seen the joy and inner peace that comes to leaders who work tirelessly to serve others. Think of Jane Addams in the late nineteenth and early twentieth centuries, creating Hull House to serve as many as two thousand women a week; she was the first American woman to win a Nobel Prize. Or the many creations of Albert Schweitzer in the first half of the twentieth century, including the hospital he built in Africa, at Lambaréné. Schweitzer believed that "the purpose of human life is to serve, and to show compassion and the will to help others."

Think too of the work of Frances Perkins in New York in the 1920s and 1930s, a creative force behind the New Deal. Or Eleanor Roosevelt, who opened doors for scores of women in midcentury and served as the chairperson of the drafting committee of the UN's

Universal Declaration of Human Rights. Or Gandhi, King, Mother Teresa, down to John Lewis and New Zealand leader Jacinda Ardern of our own time. All commanded universal respect. As we will see in the pages ahead, the way men and women exercise leadership continues to change—we have, for example, largely discarded the Great Man theory of centuries past in favor of more collaborative and diverse leadership—but the need for leaders of courage, compassion, and character has not only remained essential but has grown exponentially.

For centuries, historians and social scientists have debated whether leaders matter to the unfolding of the human story. Origins of the study of leadership can be found in ancient Greece, Rome, and China. In more modern times, the Western school of thought has been driven by historians, moral and political philosophers, practitioners, and most recently, social scientists. Different scholars bring with them their own approaches: Historians tend to focus on lessons from high-profile leaders from the past, while practitioners apply their own experiences and insights to leadership analysis. In the past several decades, as thinkers like Warren Bennis worked to solidify "leadership" as an academic discipline in its own right, social scientists have increasingly dominated the field of leadership research, applying an objective, "value-free" lens in understanding what constitutes effective—or ineffective—leadership.

Although leadership studies were initially focused on the qualities of leaders, the discipline has taken on explaining increasingly dynamic forces at play between leaders and their followers. How do leaders effectively navigate a world in which their values and culture may not align with those of their followers? What role do followers play in the efficacy of a leader? If a man exercises power in an immoral or evil way, should he still be called a leader? How can one voice seek to empower and advocate for a diverse cross section of interests? As we continue to understand the nuances of human behavior and expand our understanding of who can become "a leader," questions related to what constitutes good leadership have multiplied.

At the crux of it all, however, is one central question: How great an impact can one person have on the arc of history? As the historian Arthur Schlesinger Jr. pointed out, many eminent thinkers have believed that individuals are only the pawns of larger forces, such as God's will, fate, and historical inevitability. In *War and Peace*, Tolstoy argued that if there had been no Napoleon, a different French general would have invaded Russia, slaughtering all in sight. Individuals, Tolstoy wrote, are but "the slaves of history." He belonged to what has been called the determinist school of thought—a set of beliefs stretching back to gods and goddesses on Mt. Olympus and stretching forward to Marx, Spengler, Toynbee, and, indeed, Nazism.

In one of my favorite essays, "Democracy and Leadership," Schlesinger made the counterargument that determinism at its core denies human agency as well as human responsibility. When an individual murders another, we hold him accountable for his act unless he is judged incapable of distinguishing right from wrong; we don't give him a free pass. We believe each of us is responsible for our own behavior. Each of us has our own agency—for good as well as bad. And so it goes with leadership: Each of us can choose to make a positive difference.

In 1931, Schlesinger wrote, a British politician visiting America crossed Park Avenue in New York City after dinner, looked the wrong way, and was struck down by a passing car. "I do not understand why I was not broken like an eggshell," he later said. Fourteen months later, an American politician was sitting in an open car in Miami when a gunman fired at point-blank range. Had the gunman's arm not been jarred by a nearby woman, the politician would have died; as it was, the man next to him perished.

Schlesinger posed this hypothetical: If history had played out differently, that British politician could have died that night in New York. So too could that American politician have succumbed to his bullet wound in Miami. If those two men, Winston Churchill and FDR, had died on those days, would history have been any different? You bet!

Every serious person believes that neither Neville Chamberlain nor Lord Halifax—the alternatives to Churchill—could have given voice to the British lion as Churchill did during the war. Similarly, no one believes that Vice President John Nance Garner, the Texan who said his office was "not worth a bucket of warm piss," could have led us through the Depression and the war as FDR did.

Our greatest leaders have emerged from both good times and, more often, challenging ones. They are those among us who, in our darkest hours, stir us with hope and provide us with a clear vision for the days ahead. Often they remain calm at the helm when facing a crisis; they can right a sinking ship. In a pinch, the very finest among them make the difficult calls, calls that can ultimately alter the course of history. Through courage and character, they motivate others to follow their lead; one single person can inspire the masses to act, to change the world for the better. Individuals still matter, especially in leadership.

ARE LEADERS BORN OR MADE?

Experts disagree whether the qualities and talents of effective leaders are in their DNA. When Dwight Eisenhower was a kid, others automatically looked to him in organizing their touch-football games; he wrote later that teenage teams were his training grounds for leadership. Abraham Lincoln had less than a full year of formal education, but his words still ring true with us a century and a half later. It certainly appears that some people are born gifted—or, as Warren Buffett likes to say about his investment savvy, he was lucky to have won life's lottery.

You may have been born with some natural advantages, but if you want to excel as a leader—to go "from good to great," as Jim Collins puts it—you have to work steadily over a long period of time. Frequently, personal development depends heavily upon your own patience and persistence. It is only through first mastering your own intentions, coming to understand your values, and then leading increasingly large groups of followers that one can truly become an effective leader. The journey is not straightforward and is sure to be full of failures large and small, but leading can prove to be one of life's most meaningful endeavors.

HOW SHOULD WE DEFINE LEADERSHIP?

Students of leadership also argue over how it should be defined. That's because the practice of leadership draws primarily upon subjective, hard-to-measure qualities like character, compassion, empathy, and the like. It is more art than science. Or as Supreme Court Justice Potter Stewart famously wrote in a 1960s case, obscenity is hard to define but "I know it when I see it." Or perhaps you might compare leadership to jazz: The art, as Miles Davis suggested, is how to play the silence between the notes.

Altogether, students of leadership have found over two hundred definitions of leadership. Many of them are similar. A number touch upon the ability to inspire others. Ronald Reagan, for example, thought a great leader is "one that gets the people to do the greatest things." A slightly different school of thought emphasizes the selfless nature of leaders. Lao-tzu famously said, "A leader is best when people barely know he exists; when his work is done, his aim fulfilled, they will say: We did it ourselves." Likewise, Nelson Mandela thought it better to empower others, leading from behind and allowing them to celebrate the fruits of their labor. Others home in upon personal traits, common among them courage, vision, and integrity. Today there is a school of thought emerging around the idea of leaderlessness—a concept that emphasizes collective action and shared roles rather than a single individual guiding the masses. We will return to this subject in pages to come.

The definition that I find most compelling, however, and use in classrooms comes from the Pulitzer Prize–winning author and historian Garry Wills. In a book written a quarter century ago, *Certain Trumpets: The Nature of Leadership*, he presented biographical sketches of individual leaders, weighing how followers shape their leaders. Sorting out distinctions, Wills offered this definition of a leader: "one who mobilizes others toward a goal shared by leader and followers."

Traditionally, scholars have agreed that there are three main elements to leadership: the leader, followers, and context. Each matters. We spend most of our time focusing on leaders and overlooking followers. But as Garry Wills recognizes, the qualities of followers heavily influence the success of leaders. For example, the French Revolution and the American Revolution both sought to strengthen the liberty of their peoples and both occurred at relatively the same time in history. Why, then, did the American Revolution succeed and the French fail? Thomas Jefferson believed that Americans had long experience in self-governance beforehand while the French people had lived under the thumb of the monarchy and the church. Americans were culturally ready for independence; the French were not. A former colleague of mine, Barbara Kellerman, has written a valuable book on followers that I recommend.

Similarly, the context in which a leader finds her- or himself will also shape what that person can get done. In his recent studies of leadership, political scientist Joseph Nye has pointed out that in 1939, Winston Churchill was a washed-up leader. The British public was then clinging to hopes of a negotiated settlement with Germany and saw Churchill as impulsive and militaristic. But within a year, as the Nazis marched across France and threatened to invade Britain, Churchill was seen as a savior. The context had changed, summoning him into action.

I would offer one amendment to the traditional view that leader, followers, and context are the three key pillars of leadership. In my experience in various White Houses, there is always a fourth element: the goals. A leader will be much more successful if she chooses goals that are doable and are aligned with the values and interests of her followers. In the early Reagan years, for example, Reagan's chief of staff, Jim Baker, distinguished among three types of goals for a president: easy, difficult, and tough but doable. Easy ones, he said, should be left to the departments to secure; difficult ones should be allowed to ripen; tough but doable are the stretch goals we should embrace. That perspective was a key to Reagan's success. Stretch goals like the massive reform of Social Security and the overhaul of the tax system—both requiring significant bipartisan participation—came to define his presidency. On occasion, other presidents have overstretched and failed. It's essential to find the right balance if you want to leave a positive legacy.

ENDURING VS. EVOLVING STANDARDS

It is fascinating to look back upon earlier times and to recognize how leadership has evolved over the centuries. A major theme of this book is that the capacity to adapt to a rapidly changing landscape is one of the most important skills a leader needs today. Even Ben Franklin, the most innovative of the founders, might be lost in today's culture of globalization and digitalization.

Yet as one looks more closely, it seems equally important—perhaps more important—that a leader also embrace standards that have endured for over two thousand years. We know that personal character has been essential to leadership since classical Greece and Rome. The ancients believed, as we do now, that a person's inner values and strengths were key determinants of their ability to practice principled leadership. Equally essential have been courage and honor. One can read Marcus Aurelius and Plutarch and learn as much about leadership as you can from any text of modern times.

I would be remiss if I failed to address an unshakable notion of leadership in America: that of a man on a white horse, strong and fearless, rescuing his followers from looming disaster. Richard Nixon reportedly watched the movie *Patton* no less than nine times. He loved the portrayal of a bold leader swearing at his troops on the eve of battle. General MacArthur played to that tradition too, as did Donald Trump in his presidential campaigns.

In truth, when darkness falls across the political landscape, democratic nations often call upon and sometimes need a visibly strong person. Witness the call to Churchill in May 1940. But over the years, scholars have moved away from individual strongmen and toward leaders who are collaborative and welcome partners. Instead of a lonely singular figure brooding over a decision, a favorite depiction of Barack Obama the night bin Laden was captured shows him in the Situation Room surrounded by half a dozen advisors. We will find repeated examples of collaborative leadership in the pages ahead.

Indeed, throughout this book you will find sketches of leaders whose lives shed light on the arts and adventures of leadership. In that spirit, let's look at three contemporary leaders whose lives underscore the idea that even though standards have evolved, the values we cherish have endured over centuries. What we see is that each leader had to adapt to the context of their times, resorting to different strategies for success. But equally so, we see striking commonalities in the way they thought and acted. Importantly, as leaders, they shared many of the same basic values.

Leadership of Conviction and Humility

In Pike County, Alabama, most people were poor, Black Americans were still picking cotton, and memories of slavery remained fresh almost eight decades after the Emancipation Proclamation. That was the world into which Robert John Lewis was born in 1940. It is hard to imagine that one day, a leading historian of our time, Jon Meacham, would write of that child: "He was as important to the founding of a modern and multiethnic twentieth- and twenty-first-century America as Thomas Jefferson and James Madison and Samuel Adams were to the creation of the republic in the eighteenth century."

The family roots of Robert John Lewis—he took the name John later in life—were sunk deep into Alabama soil. His great-grandfather was a sharecropper, as were his descendants; he had been born into slavery decades before and, despite emancipation, soon found himself a victim of racism and Jim Crow laws and regulations. John grew up pitching in to help his family's farming efforts. He watched as his mother toiled in the fields only to be paid $1.40 per four hundred pounds of cotton—about two days' work. In 1944, John's father had saved up enough money to buy a small plot of land. "Working for somebody else all your days, and then to have a little something you could call your own, it was bound to make you feel good," John's mother said. Perhaps in those early moments, John realized the importance of perseverance and just how sweet a little bit of freedom could taste.

When not in the fields, some of John's fondest childhood memories came from his engagement with Dunn's Chapel A.M.E. He thought he would become a preacher and took to practicing on his own. Lewis said that when his parents asked him to take care of the family's livestock, "I literally started preaching to the chickens. They became members of this sort of invisible church or maybe you want to call it a real church." He sometimes attempted baptisms and conducted funerals for chicks that had died, reading Scripture aloud and delivering a eulogy for those lost. It didn't always work out so well for the chickens. When he was five or six, a baptism went awry. He feared he had held a chicken too long underwater, drowning it even as he was trying to save its soul. Luckily, the chicken had its own resurrection of sorts and, after a few minutes in the sun, revived and wandered away. Might his experiences have helped John become a better preacher? I imagine so. With those chickens, he honed his powers of persuasion, developed a sense of empathy, and better learned the Scriptures.

John's other memories were not so rosy. While he loved school, he rode there on segregated, weather-worn buses and saw WHITES ONLY signs posted. He knew that segregation and Jim Crow laws were wrong. Injustices became even clearer one summer when he visited relatives in Upstate New York. There he had freedom to shop alongside white shoppers, ride an escalator, and see neighborhoods filled with people of all backgrounds. He began to understand how oppressive his home state was.

In 1956, as a sixteen-year-old, John began to form his own values. By chance he was sitting by his radio when Dr. Martin Luther King Jr. delivered a rousing address. In many ways, his remarks reminded Lewis of his own thinking: King proposed to intertwine faith and nonviolent protest to make the world more equitable. "When I heard his voice," said Lewis, "I felt he was talking directly to me. From that moment on, I decided to be just like him." John Lewis had found his role model and mentor.

Inspired by the actions of movement leaders around him, Lewis began to hear a call—a call to action. He made his way to Nashville to study at the tuition-free American Baptist Theological Seminary, where he became a disciplined student and increasingly embraced King's social gospel. At nineteen, he joined a group of peers walking into Harvey's Department Store in Nashville, where they took seats at a segregated lunch counter. The store's manager asked them to leave, and they did, but they continued to protest peacefully in Nashville day in and out. That February 1960, they got word that if they continued, they would be met by white mobs and violence. They persisted. Lewis took his seat at Woolworth's and was immediately heckled, hit in the ribs, and thrown to the floor. Instead of arresting the vigilantes, the police arrested Lewis for "disorderly conduct." He did not resist but made his way to the paddy wagon singing the anthem of the civil rights movement, "We Shall Overcome."

The mayor released the protestors from jail, but that did not quell the unrest. News of their efforts began to spread across the country. A twenty-year-old Lewis was increasingly at the forefront of the civil rights movement. Clashes became more frequent as protestors staged a full-fledged boycott of Nashville's stores and white agitators threw dynamite at the home of an NAACP lawyer. After a five-thousand-person march, the mayor of Nashville conceded and ordered the city's lunch counters desegregated. Lewis was experiencing his first victory for nonviolence. His bruises, his nights in jail, his exposure of deep-seated racism—those were badges of honor.

The rest of the story is familiar to Americans of the civil rights era. Lewis and a companion had a near-death encounter when a manager locked them in his Nashville restaurant and began to spread toxic insecticide throughout. "I was not eager to die," Lewis said later, "but I was at peace with the prospect of it." As demonstrations continued to trigger violent responses, Lewis was arrested and beaten time and again. He became one of the original thirteen Freedom Riders who made their way south to test the staying of two major cases in the Supreme Court.

His accomplishments by the age of twenty-five were stunning. He became the face of a new generation of young leaders who embraced nonviolence and refused to accept systemic racism. In rapid succession, Lewis helped found and then led the Student Nonviolent Coordinating Committee (SNCC); he helped organize and was a final speaker at the famous March on Washington in 1963; the following year, he led the march over the Edmund Pettus Bridge in Selma, where his skull was bashed in; and he participated in meetings between civil rights leaders and Presidents Kennedy and Johnson that prompted the passage of the Voting Rights Act of 1965. Lewis was arrested some forty times—all this before he began a second career as a leader of Democrats in the U.S. House of Representatives. He served there for thirty-three years.

John Lewis was usually soft-spoken and humble, but he was a leader of conviction. His courage and commitment were unmatched in his generation. For John, as for any great leader, life was devoted to a cause much greater than himself. He was driven not by personal interests or ambitions, but by ambitions for his fellow man. "John would not just follow you into the lions' den," said a fellow protestor, "he would lead you into it." He died a national hero.

Leadership of Grit and Ambition

In the very years when Lewis was solidifying his commitment to non-violence, a young law student was waging battles of her own. Ruth Bader Ginsburg did not face the bloody protests that Lewis did, but she experienced harsh resistance all her life as she struggled to achieve equal rights for women. Ginsburg was no icon at a young age—like so many other leaders, she seemed destined for obscurity. But like them, she developed a steely determination and an inner will that were a springboard to greatness.

Well before she became a jurist of national acclaim, Ruth Bader was a diligent student in Brooklyn, New York. From a young age, her mother, Celia, had encouraged her daughter to "love learning, care about people, and work hard." She expected Ruth to attend college and took her to the neighborhood library, where Ruth pored over classics like *Little Women* and *The Secret Garden*. Later, when Ruth reached James Madison High School, her intellectual appetite allowed her to succeed in all fields—she was popular and an excellent student, and she belonged to both the orchestra and twirling squad.

Life in the Bader household was not always easy. While she juggled her many commitments, Ruth quietly watched her mother's losing battle with cervical cancer. After school each day, Ruth would commute an hour on the subway to visit her mother at Beth Moses Hospital and eat dinner before the hour-long return home. Four years after her diagnosis, Celia succumbed to the disease. Her husband was so overcome with grief that he had to shutter the doors of his retail store, and Ruth was left to coordinate a new place for him to live. At the time, she was just seventeen. Though her mother's illness and death took an emotional toll, she confined her feelings to herself and did not let her academic or extracurricular performance slip. Her mother had long instilled in her the importance of a first-class education, and Ruth wanted to make her proud. That she did. Ruth's success in managing it all in trying times would be a challenge for any person, let alone a young woman, but she somehow pulled it off, preparing herself for even more trying times ahead.

This grit would become characteristic of Ginsburg as she faced one seemingly insurmountable challenge after the next. Ruth went on to Cornell, where she enrolled as an undergraduate. At that time, men tended to seek an education and women were encouraged to seek a Mrs. degree. Fortunately, Ruth excelled academically and was lucky enough to meet her future husband, Marty. A couple of years later, just as the newlywed Ginsburgs were beginning to start their family, Ruth would follow in her husband's footsteps and enroll at Harvard Law. As a starting law student—just one of nine women in a class of about five hundred—she had a fourteen-month-old daughter at home along with her beloved Marty, who was a year ahead of her. Amidst the hubbub, leave it to Ruth to make the *Law Review*.

In her second year at law school, life dramatically worsened when Marty was diagnosed with testicular cancer. At the time, chemotherapy was not yet available, so he needed massive doses of radiation. Suddenly Ruth once again faced serious family challenges—but this time as a mother, a wife, and a graduate student. As Marty underwent his treatments, Ruth enlisted classmates and friends to take notes for him while she kept up with her own work. After their daughter went to bed, Ruth stayed at the dinner table through much of the night, studying for her courses while also typing Marty's third-year paper. Yet again, her abilities seemed almost limitless as she thrived academically—her peers at the *Law Review* noticed no change in her work, even saying they did not know of her husband's illness—while she continued to prioritize the health and happiness of her loved ones.

I should note that after studying the lives of many leaders, my students always rank Ruth's efforts during those dark days as among the most memorable—and most admirable—they have encountered. She has become a constant source of inspiration.

In her third year of law school, Ruth transferred to Columbia to remain close to Marty, who had taken a job in New York. By her graduation when she was twenty-six, she had overcome two harrowing experiences. Her years to come would prove no easier, as she entered a profession still dominated by white males. She finished at the top of her class but did not receive a single job offer. (Sandra Day O'Connor experienced similar discrimination when she graduated at the top of her class at Stanford.) Ginsburg eventually did secure a clerkship with federal judge Edmund L. Palmieri, but not without some backroom pressure by a law school professor. Getting started, she once again proved her impeccable worth ethic and built a strong rapport with the judge. Speaking of her time spent in the clerkship, Ginsburg said she "stayed late sometimes when it was necessary, sometimes when it wasn't necessary, came in Saturdays, and brought work home."

At each new turn of her career, Ginsburg approached her work with a commitment to excellence. After her time clerking, the director of Columbia Law School's Project on International Procedure asked her to become a research associate on a book about the Swedish legal system. Not only did she tackle the work head on, learning Swedish at a rapid pace, but she was also promoted. Her boss later said of the judge, "Ruth is basically a reserved person, quiet but with a steely determination. When she sets her mind to do something, she does it and superbly."

A few years later, as one of two female law professors at Rutgers, she had her second child without missing a beat at work. Indeed, she hid her pregnancy until the last minute and quickly returned from maternity leave, resuming a full-time schedule. Meanwhile, her father-in-law had an auto accident and moved into the Ginsburg household. Ruth became exhausted but again persevered. Had she not had that inner fortitude, it is doubtful the world would have ever heard of her.

All this happened before Ginsburg had begun her rise to leadership in the legal profession, especially in advancing the rights of women. She was a co-founder of the ACLU'S Women's Rights Project, in many ways rivaling the key leadership role that Thurgood Marshall had played in the NAACP on behalf of civil rights for Black Americans. Soon enough she was appointed to a judgeship at the U.S. Court of Appeals in D.C. and then was offered a seat on the Supreme Court by President Clinton. I was working for the president in the White House at the time and remember well how many distinguished men and women rallied to her appointment; Clinton himself was immensely impressed. Her long years spent leading the country toward full rights for women were key to that appointment, giving her a platform to move a nation. She first transformed herself and then began to transform the country.

Ginsburg's presence on the Supreme Court continued to solidify the place of women in the legal profession. However, it would be her actions on the Court that would cement her place in American history as a true champion of equality and human dignity. Her record on the Court includes precedent-setting decisions regarding equal opportunity, access to reproductive care, and fierce dissents on any challenges to a woman's right to choose. In her confirmation hearing she famously stated, "The decision whether or not to bear a child is central to a woman's life, to her well-being and dignity. . .When government controls that decision for her, she is being treated as less than a fully adult human responsible for her own choices."

Labeled the "high Court's counterweight" by her friend and conservative colleague the late Justice Antonin Scalia, Ginsburg was not afraid to dissent when recognizing an injustice. Though the minority opinion, these words of dissent were as impactful as any decision. For example, she fervently dissented against the majority in *Ledbetter v. Goodyear Tire* (2007), in which an Alabama woman sued for back pay to account for the years of wage discrimination she faced as her male colleagues were paid significantly more for performing the same job.

Though the lawsuit in front of the Supreme Court was unsuccessful, Ginsburg's words of dissent were recognized by the U.S. Congress through legislation known as the Lily Ledbetter Fair Pay Act of 2009.

Indeed, while serving as a Supreme Court justice until her death in 2020, Ginsburg was a pillar of the Court's liberal block, protecting the rights of women, defending affirmative action and equal voting rights, and chipping away at legal barriers to equality. In fact, even before her time as a federal judge, Ginsburg had famously argued in front of the Supreme Court that gender discrimination hurts not only women but men as well: In *Weinberger v. Wiesenfeld* (1975), she asked the Court to strike down a Social Security provision that deprived widowers of survivor benefits after the death of their spouse. Her accomplishments in the realm of equal rights feel endless, and it is certain her impact on society will be. Overall, Ginsburg's rise above gender discrimination and her work in front of and on the bench, as she strove tirelessly toward a more equitable future, demonstrate leadership of true grit and ambition.

Leadership of Character and Honor

Reflecting upon the past few decades in American politics is a dispiriting exercise. Not since the Civil War have our elected officials been so deeply divided, our populace split in blind loyalty along partisan lines, often unwilling to acknowledge the opponent on the other side. What began at the turn of the twenty-first century as infrequent cooperation has culminated in a landscape where many of our public officials are willing to sacrifice their own ideals—and those of their country—for the sake of party or ideology.

While the atmosphere was one of increasing viciousness, one man emerged who was widely respected by both sides. He was lauded by staunch conservatives and progressive liberals for his character and commitment to country. That man, of course, was John Sidney McCain III.

John was born at the Coco Solo Naval Air Station in the Panama Canal Zone into a family with deep ties to the military: His father, John Jr., was a lieutenant at the time, and his grandfather John "Slew" was a four-star admiral in the navy. The McCain we have come to cherish in our national memory—the Vietnam POW who suffered harrowing captivity, returning home to honorably serve in the U.S. House and Senate until the day he died—might seem the natural descendant of two lifelong military heroes. One can imagine that a young McCain, groomed well and inspired by his elders, fell quickly into line, making all the appropriate preparations one should in his years leading up to service.

Reality, as it turns out, departed sharply from this idealistic image. Young McCain was no teacher's pet. In school, he often lacked motivation. At Episcopal High School, he was known to occasionally pick a fight or make an illicit excursion into neighboring Washington, D.C. Despite his schoolboy outbursts, McCain took one matter extremely seriously: honor. When he played football, one of the members of the team had refused to sign a training pledge and then proceeded to miss practice. His mates wanted to kick him off the team, but McCain stood up and told them the boy had done nothing wrong. Ever an independent spirit, McCain made it clear that the boy had never signed the pledge and had therefore never broken his promise to the team. I guess he was already a talented speaker, because his coach ended up listening to him and didn't punish the other boy.

As he made his way through life, McCain left behind a stream of mischief and troublemaking. His rebellious nature followed him to the Naval Academy. There, he accrued so many demerits that his classmates wondered if he might be expelled. Instead, he served his time, once joking that he had marched enough extra duty on weekends to have walked "to Baltimore and back many times." But he graduated by the skin of his teeth in 1958, ranked fifth from the bottom of his 899-person class.

Just nine years later, America found itself in the throes of conflict with North Vietnam, and McCain shipped off for duty flying A-4 Skyhawks. Months into combat duty, he experienced a moment that would forever shape his life. He was shot down over Hanoi and forced to eject himself from his jet, breaking both arms and a leg in the process. Upon landing, he was swarmed by a group of North Vietnamese, who pulled him from a lake, bayoneted him in the groin, smashed a rifle butt against his shoulders, and took him back to the Hoa Lo Prison—more commonly referred to as the "Hanoi Hilton." He was left largely untreated, floating in and out of consciousness as his weight dropped to almost a hundred pounds; his fellow POWs did not think he would make it.

Several months into his captivity, the North Vietnamese realized he was the son of a four-star admiral in charge of the Pacific Fleet. The Viet Cong decided to offer him release; despite months on the brink of death, McCain refused. He would not violate the Code of Conduct for Prisoners of War, which said POWs ought to be released in the order in which they were captured. Shortly thereafter, his captors—angered by his refusal to be released—beat and tortured him for four straight days. On the fourth, he broke, making a false confession that he was a "black criminal" and an "air pirate." The days following were sheer emotional torture for him, full of guilt. He later wrote: "I felt faithless, and couldn't control my despair . . . All my pride was lost." McCain's fellow POWs knew his confession held no real ramifications; decades later, when the tapes were released, many POWs defended McCain from those who disparaged his faithful service, emphasizing the great sacrifices he made for his fellow countrymen.

Finally, in 1973, McCain was released along with his American compatriots—in the order which they had been captured. He returned home carrying the pain of a five-and-a-half-year imprisonment; Americans captured in Vietnam suffered the longest bouts of imprisonment of any POWs in our history. Even so, McCain's independent streak, honor, and inner fire remained intact. He was only

thirty-seven years old when he set foot on American soil again, ready
to launch his next chapter of public service.

McCain's political rise is a familiar tale. The young veteran
began his political exposure as a naval liaison to the Senate, where
he built lasting friendships with young senators from both sides of
the aisle. When he failed a flight physical in 1980, he officially retired from the navy, running for, and winning, his first congressional seat shortly thereafter and then moving on to represent Arizona
in the Senate. He got into legal trouble during the savings and loan
scandal of the mid-1980s; he was accused, alongside four other senators, of interfering in a federal banking regulations investigation on
behalf of Charles Keating, a longtime friend and campaign donor.
McCain, however, quickly acknowledged and accepted responsibility for his mistakes. Voters largely forgave him. Though he often
became the voice of his party—culminating in his 2008 Republican
nomination for the presidency—McCain maintained his honor and
integrity in office, bowing only to his own beliefs and commitment
to country.

As Michael Lewis pointed out in "The Subversive," McCain paid
little heed to D.C. norms or political posturing. Once, when serving as chairman of the Commerce Committee, McCain had to leave
a hearing early. He whispered something in the ear of Democrat
Ernest Hollings and gave him the gavel. Hollings said to McCain,
"John, I'd be delighted to take it, but some of your colleagues might
object," to which McCain replied, "Screw that." He treated his colleagues across the aisle just as he would his closest allies. His legislative record showed the same: He was a pioneer in passing bipartisan
campaign finance reform, demanded humane treatment of prisoners,
and, most memorably, vetoed the Republican "repeal and replace" of
Obamacare in the late hours of the night—one of his parting acts of
independence.

At his core, John McCain was a man of honor, honesty, and decency. He certainly had a rebellious side, and coming home from

Vietnam, he was no plastic saint. But he always tried to remain true to himself and to his word. He was also the first to admit to his mistakes and missteps: During his 2000 presidential campaign, he refused to condemn the flying of a Confederate flag in South Carolina but, upon reflection, returned to the state to apologize. Notably, when a woman at one of his 2008 rallies loudly criticized Obama as an "Arab," McCain interceded to tell her she was wrong. Most important, he was a man of his word and of his promises. From those days on the high school football team to the Hanoi Hilton to his vote to keep millions on their health insurance, McCain stuck to his guns and brought honor to those he served. He died an American hero, not for his politics, but for his unwavering character and candor in public life—old-fashioned values that have proved to be still relevant to leaders today.

WHERE JOURNEYS INTERSECT

Lewis, Ginsburg, and McCain come to us from all walks of life—different upbringings, politics, backgrounds, and goals. Yet we can also see commonalities among them that defined their coming-of-age years and prepared them for lives of service and leadership. It is these commonalities that we find time and again as we explore the development of young leaders. Among those that stand out here:

Each Felt Called to the Public Arena

McCain, born to a family with a storied military past, understood what it meant to give himself to his nation and its ideals. He followed his twenty-three years in the navy with a different kind of service: thirty-six years in the U.S. Congress. Lewis was appalled by the oppression of his kinfolk in this country; when his activist work waned, he too took up a second career in the House of Representatives. As Ginsburg launched herself into a profession dominated by men, she came to understand just how critical it was for genders to be treated equally. Each of these leaders stopped asking what they wanted from life and began asking what life wanted from them.

Their Journeys into Leadership Began Early

Though still learning self-discipline, McCain in his early twenties became an informal leader of his Naval Academy class when he stood up for them against upperclassman bullies. He was unafraid to confront those with more power than he had. Lewis was only nineteen when he began organizing sit-ins in Nashville. At age thirty, Ginsburg was beginning her career as one of the first female law professors at Rutgers. Though each continued to grow as the years passed, all three showed leadership promise in early adulthood that would come to define them later in life.

Each Had to Summon Inner Courage

The journey of each was adventurous—and sometimes even quite dangerous. Lewis was frequently beaten up and was lucky to survive his encounter on the Edmund Pettus Bridge. After McCain was shot down over Vietnam, he endured years of pain, suffering, and torture in the Hanoi Hilton. Ginsburg, though she did not face physical danger, held her head high as she entered a world in which women had no place.

Each Stumbled but Came Back Stronger

Lewis was knocked down early but refused to change course and eventually prevailed. Ginsburg, despite graduating at the top of her class, struggled to secure a single job offer after completing Columbia Law School. McCain, early in his naval career, established a reputation for recklessness and partying, but he eventually became a role model for the young.

Each Began Sorting Out and Embracing Core Values Early On

All three were defined by more than their successes in the field. They were recognized by the values they came to embody: Lewis for his dedication to cause and humility, a soft-spoken approach that disguised his inner steel; Ginsburg for her ambition and perseverance in the face of repeated obstacles; McCain for his unwavering decency and candor. Leaders often start with an excess of narcissism, but what separates the good from the bad is that the good acquire a deep, abiding loyalty to their team, their community, and their mission. Lewis, Ginsburg, and McCain all embraced that sense of ambition for others.

Each Found a True North

Through their struggles, each of these leaders not only sorted out their values but discovered an internal moral compass that helped them navigate hard, complex choices, remaining true to their values and their followers. From the day he stood up for his fellow football teammate, McCain would be bound by his honor and unwilling to bend to the interests of those around him. Lewis kept his eye on his North Star for over half a century. Ginsburg, from her early days at the ACLU through her final hours on the Supreme Court, remained a fierce supporter of women's rights.

They Were All Idealists to Their Core

A person who wants to spend a lifetime giving back to others needs a serious dose of idealism to stay the course. In the case of these three leaders, all had these virtues in abundance. All expanded their horizons and brought devoted followers with them. Their commitment was not to self but to a higher truth. And no matter how harsh reality became, they stayed the course, unwilling to sacrifice their fundamental values and vision. John Lewis said of the battle for equal rights, "Do not get lost in a sea of despair. Be hopeful, be optimistic. Our struggle is not the struggle of a day, a week, a month or a year, it is the struggle of a lifetime." In their own ways, McCain and Ginsburg also lived by that ideal. They never gave up the fight.

More broadly, the experiences of these three contemporary leaders help to underscore key themes of this book. All three found different roads to leadership, but as they grew older, their inner and outer journeys began to converge. The process of becoming a leader, as Bennis has stressed, is indeed much like that of becoming a full person. They discovered as well that the ways leadership is practiced are rapidly changing, and to navigate the shoals, one had best steer by a moral compass. All three also suffered through unrelenting struggles as they came of age. Yet as they looked back, they realized, as did Oliver Wendell Holmes Jr. two decades after the Civil War, "Through our great good fortune, in our youth, our hearts were touched with fire. It was given to us to learn at the outset that life is a profound and passionate thing."

TWO

BECOMING THE AUTHOR OF YOUR OWN LIFE

It is a privilege for any American to work in the White House. Having worked there for four administrations from both parties, I feel quadruply honored, and to the extent I have a legacy, it will doubtless start there. But in truth, my greatest satisfaction in public life came many years earlier, when I was in my early twenties and still in college.

I grew up in North Carolina, and in 1963 I heard a call to service from our new Democratic governor, Terry Sanford. Terry was our state's John Kennedy, a fresh, charismatic leader who wanted to create "a New South," recognizing and promoting the civil rights of Black Americans. His message appealed to me, and I signed up to be an intern in his administration during the summer between my junior and senior years in college. At my request, the governor's office assigned me to work for a new initiative of Terry's: creation of the North Carolina Good Neighbor Council, the public role of which was to create biracial councils across the state where Black and white leaders of their communities would work together on public education and jobs. Their unstated role was to help keep interracial peace.

That was one of the smartest requests I ever made. Within days, I reported for work to David Coltrane, the council director. Dave had been a farmer who served as a hardheaded state budget director. More to the point, he had been a staunch segregationist until he had a conversion and became an outspoken pioneer for civil rights. I came to love the man.

His full staff consisted of one secretary. He turned me into his chief policy advisor, communications director, and driver. I spent the next three summers "driving Mr. Dave." From one town to the next, we crisscrossed the state, meeting at night with civic leaders of both races, persuading them to sit down together. We weren't always successful, but they often shook hands, and over time, we could see a turning away from hatred and violence.

The ones who deserve by far the most credit for racial progress in the state were, of course, the young Black Americans who began sit-ins years earlier in Greensboro and Nashville, marched and rode buses across the South, and were punished with jail time and beatings—young heroes like John Lewis. They not only brought down many barriers against Black Americans but also lowered walls between poor southern states and the rest of the country.

Our adventures in the Council were not without danger. The Klan was extremely active in our state, especially in the southwest, home of the Grand Dragon. One of my best friends from high school—he was white—was spending one of those summers as an associate pastor in a Black church. He and I agreed that we should attend an open Klan rally near Salisbury—I to better figure out why these people were so full of hatred, he to make an audio recording and share it with his parishioners, perhaps to make them feel less threatened.

Two additional white friends joined us, and as soon as we drove into the parking field next to the rally, we saw the first signs of trouble: The state cops who greeted us on arrival had disappeared. In their places stood big, burly, brown-shirted Klansmen keeping "order." As the crosses were lit, Klansmen began clustering around our little group. One seized the tape recorder. Others spit out threats. As the rally ended, we walked back toward our car and discovered a large, menacing crowd surrounding it. They let us get in, but quickly began banging on the windows, rocking the car, climbing on the roof, and cursing us. They swore we would never attend another rally. Our imaginations called to mind what had just happened in Mississippi to James Chaney, Andrew Goodwin, and Michael Schwerner, three valiant men—two were white and one was Black—who came to demonstrate and had disappeared. Their bodies were later found; they had been beaten and tortured.

It looked as if we had no escape. I urged my friend at the steering wheel, "Turn on the ignition and start driving slowly, slowly into the crowd. It's our only choice." As our car crept forward, the crowd still beat up on it but gradually made way. Quickly, however, they jumped into their own cars, and that began a mad chase after us down darkened highways. After what seemed forever, they began peeling off and we made it safely home, still shaking. Had we been Black, our fates would surely have been more grim.

That night taught me some lessons. Stand up against forces of oppression, push back against evil, take risks, but don't be reckless. I had been reckless. Showing up in the middle of their rally was like waving a red flag at a bull—that was dumb. Find out how folks unlike yourself live their lives, but don't toy with them. Don't treat them like animals in a zoo, as our visit had. Nothing could excuse their virulent racism and hatred, but under their hoods, the men I saw that night appeared to be mostly working-class folks down on their luck who were searching for their lost dignity.

Those summers crystallized thoughts about my own inner journey. I had always been curious about ways that societies and their leaders cope with the biggest challenges of their time. I knew deep inside that that's where I wanted to spend my professional life—in the public arena, where big things happened, the arena where one might make a positive difference. I wasn't sure *what* I wanted to be, but I knew *where* I wanted to be.

As I learned, you don't have to be in the White House or even in Washington, D.C., to be at the center of action. With the federal government so paralyzed, the arena has changed. Power is no longer coming just from the top down; increasingly, it is coming from the bottom up. I often tell students interested in public service that unless they can find a special job in Washington, D.C., they should explore jobs back home in state and local government or in social enterprises, nonprofits, or mass organizations that seek change; that's where the action has been in recent years. There is also much to learn from taking a position at a fast-growing start-up, in technology, or in the arts—each area has its own lessons to offer. One day, with growing pressure from young activists and from the Oval Office, I hope the federal government will again become a magnet for a rising generation of change makers.

Looking back, I would like to think that the North Carolina Good Neighbor Council played a modest role in advancing civil rights. Certainly, it played a large role in my own life. There at a young age, I heard a call to service—a summons, really—and found the work enormously rewarding. The job was hands-on and allowed me to work in the trenches alongside people of all backgrounds; I felt a moral purpose and that I perhaps made a modest difference. As much as I have been blessed to work inside the White House, I was more fulfilled when I could work face-to-face with people on the margins and could see changes emerging.

SELF-AWARENESS

Through my early encounters with public life, I also began to understand another fundamental: that leadership starts from within. It's important to learn how the world works, but it is even more important to learn how you work. As the preacher Peter Gomes used to say, you must learn to lead yourself before you can serve others. In short, you must wrestle early on with your own self-awareness and your own self-mastery.

Each of us must discover for ourselves who we are, what we believe in, and what dreams we have for the future. Philosophers have agreed on that point since the days of ancient Greece. "Know thyself," commanded the oracle at Delphi. "The unexamined life is not worth living," Socrates said at his trial. Following Socrates, Plato explored the meaning of the Delphic maxim in half a dozen of his Dialogues.

In our own time, we continue to ask ourselves about our purpose. "Tell me," asked Mary Oliver in her poem "The Summer Day," "what is it you plan to do / with your one wild and precious life?" Hundreds if not thousands of essays about leadership have agreed that a clear understanding of yourself is the foundation upon which to build an integrated life. But those same essays are all over the lot about how to get there. In my experience, the people who have achieved the greatest understanding of their inner selves have been "reflective practitioners"—those who have welcomed a wide array of experiences, have read history and biographies with care, and have had a series of conversations with their inner selves, exploring ways to build that foundation. We certainly saw all of those traits in Lewis, Ginsburg, and McCain.

One of the best essays on leadership was published in 1999 by Peter F. Drucker, the foremost management guru of the twentieth century. "Managing Oneself" is still a must-read. Years ago, I spent time with Drucker and was struck by how many CEOs would fly across the country to sit for an afternoon with him. And they always came back.

To become self-aware, Drucker wrote, a person should ask herself or himself a set of basic questions:

What Are Your Strengths and Weaknesses?

Obviously, people are better at working from strength. The trouble, Drucker argues, is that most people think they know what they excel at but are usually wrong. Candid feedback thus becomes essential. For over two decades, before making a key decision, Drucker would write down what he expected to happen. Nine to twelve months later, he would compare the actual results with his earlier expectations. To his surprise, he found he intuitively understood technical people—engineers, accountants, etc.—but he had no resonance with generalists.

He found the feedback so informative that he urged everyone to follow that practice.

For a number of years, CEOs and other corporate leaders have tried a variety of other devices for achieving self-knowledge. One of the most popular a decade ago were 360s—multiple confidential assessments of your professional performance from subordinates, peers, and superiors, those who form the entire circle around you at work. These 360s are still useful, but as employees learned how to game them, corporations have experimented with other approaches. Some are as straightforward as Myers-Briggs testing and StrengthsFinders, which, of course, come with their own limitations.

In a much more ambitious effort to provide timely assessments, Bridgewater Associates, the hedge fund, asks its executives to sign and send their colleagues candid assessments of them within twenty-four hours of key meetings. Some have found that uncomfortable and have left the firm. Others swear by it and have moved up the ladder. In his bestseller of 2017, *Principles: Life & Work*, the founder of Bridgewater, Ray Dalio, presented a sprightly defense of the Bridgewater approach. Finding the right formula to achieve self-knowledge is thus a fluid undertaking. Whatever test you use, Drucker argues, you should learn several basic things about yourself:

How Do You Learn? Are You a Reader or a Listener?

I have found this question especially pertinent to presidents and CEOs. Some are voracious readers. Teddy Roosevelt perhaps holds the record: Historians tell us he often read a book a day as president. TR had a capacity to read and reflect similar to that of Jefferson and Lincoln, which made him a much better president. By contrast, Ronald Reagan was a listener; he absorbed oral briefings, but briefing papers were held to a page or so. To stuff him with facts and minutiae was a waste of everyone's time. It is important that you know how your boss learns, but it's even more important to know how you learn.

Where Do You Lie on the Introvert/Extrovert Scale?

Historically, introverts have been seen as less effective at leadership than extroverts. In 2012, Susan Cain wrote a popular book sharply disagreeing. An introvert herself, in *Quiet: The Power of Introverts in a World That Can't Stop Talking*, Cain challenged "the omnipresent belief that a leader's ideal self is gregarious, alpha and comfortable in the spotlight." That tradition, she argued, is a mistaken belief from the Greco-Roman world that men of action were better leaders than men of contemplation. Much of Jim Collins's bestseller *Good to Great* agrees with Cain. If you are introverted or quietly a loner, you should definitely read Cain and Collins as you venture forth. For those of you who lie somewhere between the two poles, understand how each personality type can help you succeed and play to those strengths. Many of us increasingly find ourselves lying somewhere along a continuum.

How Do You Respond to Stress?

As central as education and training are for young emerging leaders, the rubber hits the road when you are in charge of a group that is suddenly thrown into danger. Later in this book, you will read about James Stockdale, an American POW who was tortured and beaten during the Vietnam War. As he wrote in his memoir, *In Love and War: The Story of a Family's Ordeal and Sacrifice During the Vietnam Years*, you don't really know who the true leader of soldiers is until there is a crisis; it isn't the fellow with the most stripes on his uniform, it's the man who charges toward the enemy.

Shortly after becoming a rookie naval officer, I was sent to damage control school on Treasure Island, in the San Francisco Bay. We practiced and practiced putting out fires and plugging holes to save the Good Ship Lollipop. I thought I was well prepared until I was in charge of damage control on my ship and a serious fire broke out. I found that I feared for my life but my enlisted guys—all hardened by experience—coolly got the blaze under control. It was only after I had encountered more dangerous moments that I approached the leadership qualities of those enlisted men; they were fearless. If you want to lead, there is no substitute for getting your hands dirty and overcoming your fears. (By the way, damage control training turned out to be great preparation for life in the White House).

Are You a Good Number One but a Better Number Two?

Too often organizations promote a good deputy into the top leadership position without undertaking due diligence. Some people are terrific subordinates or chief operating officers but terrible at the top—and vice versa. As Drucker noted, General George Patton was America's top troop commander and a military hero in World War II. But when he was proposed for an independent command, General George Marshall, the army's chief of staff, vetoed the promotion. "Patton is the best subordinate the American army has ever produced, but he would be the worst commander," Marshall said. Drucker went on to point out that Marshall was probably the most successful picker of men in U.S. history. He was right.

Most of us sort out fairly quickly whether we are better managers, leaders, or something in between. In my case, I learned early in life that I am a poor administrator. I don't really enjoy shuffling papers, and I get bored too easily. As they say about Alaskan dog sleds, if you are number two or below, the scenery never changes. All of which means that I am a lousy number two. To the extent that I have strengths, they are more on the leadership side—building a team, imagining a common future, and executing to get there.

Many sociologists and social psychologists argue that people have multiple selves. In *The Presentation of Self in Everyday Life*, an influential work originally published in 1956, sociologist Erving Goffman drew an analogy of actors onstage: In different plays, they play different roles. Similarly, each of us tends to present ourselves to others in different ways, depending upon the context. So, it can be said, we have more than one self. My brother Ken, a leading social psychologist, believes that, indeed, who we are is defined to a significant degree by how others respond to us. These arguments can be complicated. The conclusion I draw is that in our early years, each of us experiments with different presentations of self to others, but in growing older, we come to recognize and embrace a core inner self. True North.

SELF-MASTERY

Self-awareness is a foundation for your journey, but for a potential leader, the secret to long-term success is to build upon your self-understanding in order to achieve self-mastery. Too many lack self-confidence or find the obstacles too big. They give up their quest too soon and ultimately fall short. But history shows many, many examples of others who persevered against all odds—and became authors of their own lives.

Before you can persuade others to follow, you must focus on building up your strengths, relentlessly improve your performance, and conquer your dangerous weaknesses. Again, there are no guarantees in life—but you won't know for sure how successful you will be until you give it your best effort. As ice hockey star Wayne Gretzky liked to say, "You miss 100 percent of the shots you don't take."

Focus on Your Strengths

Intuition will likely tell you that if you are strong in one area but weak in another, you should concentrate on fixing the weak one. That way, like a utility infielder, you can play more than one position. But experience has taught leadership authorities like Bennis, Bill George, and Drucker that you should instead focus on transforming your strong area into superstrong. It's a waste of time, they say, to focus on going from mediocre to just plain average. Of course, you must overcome weaknesses that are disabling. But as emphasized in this book, you will find that employers will be most favorably impressed if you have one to two super strengths. They will never fill a team of B+ players. Researchers at the Gallup organization, including Marcus Buckingham and Donald Clifton, have also found that encouraging one's unique strengths builds confidence and increases the desire to perform well.

We see this in many walks of life. A football team does not field a team of quarterbacks; it pulls together athletes who excel at one particular position, while displaying skills that fit many other aspects of the sport. Orchestras are put together in much the same way: Conductors look for individuals who specialize and have become world-class in a single instrument. Then they blend them, so that together they create a world-class ensemble. Even in large companies and organizations, we don't hire people who could perform well in any aspect of work, but instead hire those who provide expertise on one specific set of goals or responsibilities.

IDEO, the creative design firm, is renowned for taking the idea one step further. In their projects, they recruit and cultivate what have become known as "T-shaped people." The vertical bar represents the special skill that each person brings to the table. The horizontal bar represents the art of collaboration with others—across disciplines and across fields. CEO Tim Brown explains that it is essential to the firm to find people who have both—special skills and a collaborative nature. As a young, emerging professional, you should have that same profile—at least one area of great strength combined with the capacity for working and playing well with colleagues across the spectrum.

Relentlessly Improve Your Performance

Most young Americans are likely familiar with the tale of how Michael Jordan—who went on to become the greatest NBA star of all time—did not make his high school varsity basketball team until junior year. Very few athletes ever made the varsity team at Jordan's high school before they were in their junior year, but the fact that his high school coach did not see his promise early stuck with Jordan, who has repeatedly claimed that he was "cut" from that first team. (In reality, he was just placed on the JV team with the rest of the sophomore class.) Regardless of whether he was truly "cut," the lesson of this story is clear: Even if you do not find success on your first attempt, do not be deterred. Greatness comes through patience, discipline, and dogged practice. There is no better example than Michael Jordan himself.

Though blessed with incredible natural gifts, Jordan did not begin his college basketball career as a star player. In fact, his coach at the University of North Carolina, Dean Smith, called his freshman-year performance "inconsistent." What was clear from day one of his collegiate career was that he was one of the most determined players to ever grace the program. Early in his freshman year, Jordan made it known to assistant coach Roy Williams that he wanted to be not only the best player on the team that year but the best player in the history of UNC basketball. When Williams told him he would need to work much harder than he had on his high school team, Jordan responded, "I'm going to show you. Nobody will ever work as hard as I work." And he delivered.

Teammates recall that after grueling practices, Jordan would continue playing one-on-one with the team's top players to test his skills. He viewed practice not as a trial run but as fierce competition: Jordan turned it on constantly, always giving his top performance. This hunger for competition served Jordan well after he catapulted himself to the top of the UNC program and into the NBA. He said that during his rookie year with the Chicago Bulls, "My mentality was:

Whoever is the team leader of the team, I'm going after him." Each and every moment on the court was a challenge to best the man ahead of him—a mindset he continued even when he had reached the top. "I don't do things half-heartedly," Jordan said, "because I know if I do, then I can expect half-hearted results."

This is a behavior we see repeatedly in our finest performers. Bill Bradley, another basketball star—who later became a U.S. senator—began his playing career as too awkward, too gawky, and a poor jumper. Determined to become great, he created a weekly training regimen: three and a half hours of practice after school each day and on Sundays, eight hours on Saturdays, and three hours a day during the summer. He put ten-pound weights in his shoes so he could jump higher. And he taped cardboard to the bottom of his glasses so that he could dribble without seeing the ball. It paid off when he played at Princeton, then in Europe, and finally for a New York Knicks team that won two NBA championships. Winston Churchill practiced similar discipline in his studies: He is said to have rehearsed one hour for every minute of a public speech he was delivering.

Jordan, Bradley, and Churchill are the perfect embodiment of what Malcolm Gladwell describes in his popular book *Outliers: The Story of Success*. Gladwell set out to discover how talented people become world-class successes. Conventional wisdom, as he points out, is that high-end performers are born with huge innate talent and effortlessly float to the top. His research shows, he argues, that the story is actually quite different: that opportunities and extraordinary effort are what lift people from being very good to becoming "outliers." He found that some people get a lucky break in life, seize it, and then apply themselves. The more interesting aspect of Gladwell's work focuses on the way talented and lucky people then become world-class: They work incredibly hard at improving their talent. "Practice isn't the thing you do once you're good. It's the thing you do that makes you good," writes Gladwell.

In particular, Gladwell argues for the validity of what he calls a

"10,000 Hour Rule." Drawing upon the academic work of psychologist K. Anders Ericsson, he points to several examples: Mozart famously started writing music when he was six, but his early works were not outstanding, and some may have been written by his father. By the time of his first masterpiece at age twenty-one, however, he had been composing concertos for ten years. In some ways, claimed the American music critic Harold Schonberg, the man we think of as a child prodigy "developed late." Similarly, the Beatles weren't exactly overnight sensations, as Gladwell points out. They reportedly performed live in Hamburg—usually in all-nighters—over twelve hundred times between 1960 and 1964. That shaped their talent. A Beatles biographer, Philip Norman, says by the time they returned to England from Hamburg, "They sounded like no one else. It was the making of them."

"Ten thousand hours is the magic number of greatness," Gladwell concludes. Just to break that down: To reach 10,000 hours in 10 years requires about 1,000 hours a year, 19 hours each week, and 2.75 hours each day. "The people at the top don't work just harder or even much harder than everyone else. They work much, much harder." Elsewhere, the virtuoso Vladimir Horowitz is quoted as saying, "If I skip practice for one day, I notice. If I skip practice for two days, my wife notices. If I skip for three days, the world notices."

In a related study, *Talent Is Overrated: What Really Separates World-Class Performers from Everybody Else*, a columnist for *Fortune*, Geoff Colvin, adds an important caveat to Gladwell: Mere experience or spending prodigious amounts of time on an activity is not a predictor of success. (I should know—that describes my golf game.) What counts is learning how to practice in a more productive way. Take marathon running, for example. The best high school time in a marathon now beats Olympic gold medalists of a century ago by some twenty minutes. Why? Not because they are somehow better people, says Colvin, but because they train more effectively. He calls it "deliberate practice." In a nutshell, here are the key recommendations Colvin makes to convert excellence into world-class excellence through deliberate practices:

- Design your practice to improve performance: Joan Sutherland practiced various trills for many, many hours. A young Tiger Woods would grind balls into the sand and then hit one after another out of a sand trap.
- Focus on correcting errors: "Try again. Fail again. Fail better," as Samuel Beckett urged.
- Never become complacent: Set a distant target but realize you will often fall short, experiencing what Martha Graham has called "divine dissatisfaction."
- Seek continuous feedback: Chess masters, as Colvin notes, practice by studying the games played by the greatest stars; a student chooses a move and then sees what play the champion made.

As we saw with Michael Jordan and Bill Bradley, smart practice enables you to read a context better and quicker than others. A quarterback is better at making a split-second decision. When his passenger plane lost power shortly after takeoff, Captain Chesley Burnett "Sully" Sullenberger, calm and well trained, brought off the "Miracle on the Hudson," safely landing and saving the lives of 155 passengers and crew members. Three Navy SEALs, given only a second apiece, fired and killed three Somali pirates preparing to execute Captain Richard Phillips. Their years of deliberate practice made them extraordinary.

The first mountain you have to climb as a young developing leader is the one inside you. Until you become self-aware and then work toward self-mastery, you are likely to be drifting through life. As William James famously advised, "Seek out that particular mental attribute which makes you feel most deeply and vitally alive, along with which comes the inner voice which says, 'This is the real me,' and when you have found that attitude, follow it."

THREE

YOUR GATHERING YEARS

The journeys of people in their young adulthood are often called their "coming of age" years. Others have called them the "promising years." Still others, the "gathering years." No matter the label, there is agreement among scholars that your experiences between leaving the nest and taking full flight are among the most formative, passionate, and adventuresome in life. Much depends on how wisely you embrace them.

We have seen how self-awareness and self-mastery are stepping-stones in personal development. To enter full adulthood, one must come to grips with both. As Erik Erikson has argued, it is difficult to move on to the next stage in life until you have worked your way through the one you are currently in.

But it is also true that even as you come to know who you are and have conquered your most glaring weaknesses, you haven't yet completed your journey toward leadership. Self-awareness and self-mastery, as it turns out, are necessary but simply not sufficient. To realize the great promise of young adulthood, you must cast your net more widely. You should be in the early stages of launching your career. You need to find mentors, coaches, sponsors, and role models who will open your eyes and possibly open doors. You need to sort out your values and principles. And ultimately you must create your own moral compass—your True North.

LAUNCHING YOUR CAREER

"Tell me, what is it you plan to do / with your one wild and precious life?" Remember that quote from the poet Mary Oliver? It is worth keeping in mind as you sort out your career path and learn how to succeed in the job market. How well you navigate those questions could shape your future for decades to come.

It is a lot easier to determine what you don't want to do than to decide what you do want. That was certainly my own experience: I wound up just fine, but I took lots of twists and turns—and made some mistakes—before getting there.

Like many teenagers, I thought I would become a professional athlete. I was tall, lanky, and could throw a good fastball. But that dream shattered when I reached high school. In the six months before freshman year, I had grown like a bean pole—perhaps as much as six inches—and I had lost my coordination. Because of rain, the first day of tryouts for the high school baseball team was relocated to a gym. There, we split up into pairs of pitchers and catchers. I managed to throw a couple to the catcher, but my third pitch went horribly wild. It didn't come down anywhere near home plate. Instead, it careened off and went through a window—on the second floor! I knew instantly that my sports ambitions were dead.

Instead, I stepped up my commitment to the morning newspaper, agreeing to cover the high school football team on Friday nights. With pad in hand, I walked up and down the sidelines, taking notes. At halftime, I climbed a rickety ladder to a radio microphone to analyze the game so far. When it was over around ten o'clock, my dad drove me to the newspaper offices, where I would peck out ten to fifteen paragraphs on a typewriter. (I was too young to drive.) A senior editor would then help me edit and meet our midnight deadline. My dad would often drop me off at a football party afterward, but most of the girls had left by then.

Studying up on Grantland Rice, the premier sportswriter of his day, I became more confident and my writing more colorful. And I loved waking up Saturday morning to see a big spread and my byline. Years later, after college, law school, and the navy, I explored the possibility of going home to North Carolina, becoming a real journalist, and even running for office. But opportunities arose in the White House, and that ended my North Carolina dream. I will always be grateful to the many older journalists who mentored me in those early years, making our work a source of play and adventure.

After my undergraduate years at Yale and its college daily—where I spent endless hours among people I now count as lifelong friends— I had no clear idea what career or job I wanted to pursue. I wanted to make a difference—but how? There were too many choices and yet too few that appealed. Uncertain, I applied to Yale's PhD program in international affairs; on a parallel path, a young woman I was seeing was accepted by the architecture school. But the PhD program showed me that I just didn't have the temperament to spend two to three years in the stacks of the university library, so that dream—along with the girlfriend—disappeared.

Again, I floundered. By chance, the president of the university, Kingman Brewster, encouraged me to leave my studies in New Haven for law school in Cambridge. Persuaded and yet still tentative, I decided that I would apply to one law school, Harvard, but no other. That was rash, but it worked, and I headed north. To be honest, the first year at HLS was the most intellectually satisfying of all my graduate studies. You begin by thinking of yourself standing before a whiteboard. You read two or three related cases and put dots on the board representing the holdings. After more cases, more dots. The dots seem random at first, but around Thanksgiving, you begin to see patterns emerge—how one set of dots connects to another. No one else can figure them out for you; you must do it yourself. But how elated you feel when you can finally see the logic of the law.

Sadly, after a summer at a major Wall Street firm, I found the practice of law much less engaging than its study. I just didn't care that much which behemoth corporation won its case against another. I could see why those who reached the top of the profession liked to counsel CEOs on strategy, but who wanted to work for years in back offices, poring over documents and data, in order to get there? In comparison to my experiences trying to advance civil rights back home, the practice of law seemed too tame. It just didn't resonate. So strike off another career possibility.

Soon after law school, I was married in England to the woman who became the love of my life and has remained with me—not sure how she does it—for over half a century. Neither Anne nor I fully understood how our lives would change when, three weeks after our marriage, I reported to the navy's Officer Candidate School in Newport, Rhode Island. In this case, it took about twenty-four hours to know that the navy was not a career path, either.

While I knew I would be returning to civilian life in three and a half years, my naval experience was the best leadership training program I have ever encountered. After OCS and damage control school, I was put in charge of some fifty young men aboard a repair ship homeported in Southern Japan, the USS *Ajax*. Coming out of ivory towers and a life of privilege, I was given the opportunity to live, work, and grow among twenty-year-olds from working-class backgrounds. They didn't give a tinker's damn about me on the high seas, but those guys soon commanded my respect. They were serious sailors and were committed to our mission. To this day, I am proud that my enlisted guys gave me a rousing farewell—helped along with lots of libations.

Before signing up with the navy, I interviewed a series of Wall Street lawyers (including Richard Nixon), asking whether I should try to become a navy lawyer (JAG) or become a line officer. To a person, they urged me to become a line officer—that taking charge of fifty men (all men in those days) was far better preparation for leadership down the road. And if I practiced navy law, they said, it would take a year to unlearn what I had learned. That was sound advice. I have told countless students since that they should explore a few years of military service as a young officer as a way to strengthen their leadership skills. There are now a variety of other ways young people can also serve their country though programs like AmeriCorps, Teach For America, and City Year.

As Anne and I set out for my navy post in Japan, events began to unfold quickly. About eighteen months in, I submitted a formal request for transfer to Vietnam. I wanted to join *Stars and Stripes* as a correspondent in uniform. That's where the action was. But my skipper turned me down flat. He insisted I stay aboard the *Ajax*. Coincidentally, my law school roommate called from the White House soon after and asked if I would accept a transfer to Washington to work on draft reform. My skipper couldn't block that one, and within ten days, I was on a flight to D.C. I was entering a whole new exciting world.

What sense can be made from those twists and turns stretching back nearly sixty years? What insight or wisdom can be drawn for those in their twenties and thirties today, living in a rapidly changing, chaotic, and unpredictable world? What career advice? I sure don't have all the answers—and some of what I believe is undoubtedly wrong—but let me step back and offer eight tips distilled from my many adventures:

(1) Take Time-Outs

In my experience mentoring the young, I have found that students who take occasional time-outs from the standard academic track grow more fully than their peers. So I suggest to them that they explore a variety of short-term options: go abroad for a semester in a studies or work program; sign up for a summer research project with a favorite professor; take an internship in a political campaign; work in a soup kitchen or homeless shelter; or volunteer to work on climate change. The possibilities are endless.

I especially recommend they also explore a commitment to a service organization for a year or two. If you truly want to make a difference, there is no substitute for living and working among those on the front lines. I have learned most when I have had the opportunity to invest in getting to know communities outside my own; it is through building relationships with those beyond your bubble that you can begin to see the world in a clearer light.

Of course, it may seem that a service year or even a short timeout is unaffordable, especially if you already have sizable debts. But if you search around, you will likely find there are a good many service jobs that are beckoning these days. They won't provide much, but programs like the Peace Corps, AmeriCorps, and many others will pay you modestly and make your debt more manageable. They also strengthen the civic life of this country and they are increasingly effective in combating climate change.

I must also note the rise of experiential learning and the investment our educational institutions should make in the field moving forward. When I was on the board at Duke University, the university created DukeEngage. The program brought students and faculty together to spend a summer immersed in communities at home or abroad, where they would work to address issues most crucial to the people they were serving. It has been an enormous success and has made Duke even more of a magnet. Today experiential learning opportunities are available at a wide array of institutions and range from co-op programs to semesters of service in underserved areas.

(2) Choose Jobs That Align with Your Passions and Values

I once accompanied a group of two dozen Kennedy School students on a trip to Washington. There, Samantha Power, a Kennedy School faculty member at the time and the current administrator of USAID, organized a visit with then Senator Obama. One student talked of his career plan, including the jobs and places where he planned to work. Obama immediately jumped in. Don't try to map out a five- to ten-year job plan for your career, he said. Instead, work with passion on a cause that matters to you, and you will find that new jobs start knocking on your door. That was excellent advice. Ironing out what you like to do in life and what gives you meaning will lead you to the right jobs, even when you aren't looking for them. It is far easier to excel in a position aligned with your passions and values than in a role that brings prestige but conflicts with your inner purpose.

(3) Perform Every Task—No Matter How Small—with Excellence

Within weeks of my graduating from Harvard Law, my navy superiors had me down on hands and knees, cleaning latrines with a toothbrush. Was that humiliating? Ya think? But it was also darn good discipline. You must learn how to follow well before you can lead well. And superiors notice when you also try hard—that's when they start giving you more responsibility. Humility is your friend; arrogance is your enemy.

(4) Look for Stretch Jobs

Find work that demands more of you than you have ever imagined. That way, you will develop not only your humility but also a quiet self-confidence that you can handle anything thrown at you. At times you will fail in ways both small and large, but it is from stumbling that we grow both personally and professionally. Please note: When your learning curve flattens out, start exploring for a new job in which you can continue to grow. Your gathering years should be your growing years. I have long been blessed with a small team in my inner circle—a top research assistant and a top executive assistant. They work closely by my side and we learn from each other. But they stay for only two years so they can continue their upward journeys. They have remained family for years after.

(5) Understand Your Value to an Organization

As James M. Citrin and Richard A. Smith write in their book *The 5 Patterns of Extraordinary Careers*, a majority of executives begin their careers with a good education, a lot of ambition, and precious little experience. They come to see that their value to an organization is derived from two elements: the value of their potential and the value of their experience. You start with high potential value and low experience; over time, your long-term potential goes down, but your experience goes up. The trick is to grow the value of your experience faster than you diminish your potential. Doors will then open up that you never imagined.

(6) Spot Those with High Promise and Join Forces

Leadership guru Ron Heifetz and I once had an opportunity to interview the former prime minister of Singapore Lee Kuan Yew when he visited our campus at the Harvard Kennedy School. He was then much celebrated. I asked him what his secrets were in transforming Singapore from a dirt-poor place into a world-class country. He compared himself to a sheepherder who visited a litter of new pups. After examining each one carefully, he would spot two or three who could be champions. Those were the ones he groomed. And so it is in spotting future leaders: You need to develop a good eye to see their promise. They can become your friends for life and important members of your personal network.

(7) Accept That You Will Make Big Mistakes Early On

We all do. But don't let that get you down. In his memoir, a man widely considered to be one of the best CEOs of the twentieth century,

Jack Welch, recalled his experience at General Electric three years into his first job. A twenty-seven-year-old Welch was managing a GE facility when an explosion on his watch blew off the top of one of its buildings. Top management summoned him to headquarters. He thought for sure they were firing him. Instead, his boss walked through what happened with him, asking questions along the way. Then he told Welch, "Everyone makes mistakes; just make sure you learn from them." Welch wrote: "He was coaching me—[he] couldn't have been nicer." Bottom line: Make your mistakes early in life, dust yourself off, go forth with better judgment.

(8) Keep a Parachute in the Closet

No matter how well you perform on a job, there is a serious possibility that one day you will lose it. You may be fired, or you may decide you have had enough. Either way, you should have a Plan B: sufficient funds to tide you over and a network of friends who can help you emotionally and professionally. Some say you should have at least two months rent. In the mid-1980s, after he had bought *U.S. News & World Report*, the new publisher, Mort Zuckerman, asked me to serve as its top editor. I had some journalistic experiences over the years but nothing as serious. Thankfully, Mort brought in a world-class journalist, Harold Evans, as my coach.

I knew that I probably wouldn't last long—Mort had a history of letting editors go pretty quickly. As a backup plan and with his approval, I signed up as a commentator at *The MacNeil/Lehrer NewsHour*, partnering with Mark Shields, who became a dear friend. I thought if I could just last two years at *U.S. News*, I would have the credentials to go on in journalism. Thank goodness I had that backup plan. When *The Washington Post* leaked a story that ABC was talking to me about a management job, Mort had reached his limit, and within days, I was gone. But Anne and I had the funds to survive for at least two months, and soon enough, other offers came in. Mort and I eventually put our differences behind us and became good friends. One of his next editors served for a couple of decades and brought the internet version of *U.S. News* to solid profits. It was a win-win-win.

About that same time, I was among a handful of men who attended a private talk that a former governor of Texas, the inimitable Ann Richards, gave to about two thousand women. Her main theme was straightforward: Men had learned long ago how to keep "F-you money" when their lives fell apart, and Ann urged the women to do the same: have enough money to walk away from a bad boss or a worse marriage. That will keep open your path to freedom and dignity.

FINDING MENTORS, COACHES, AND ROLE MODELS

For over two thousand years, mentors and coaches as well as role models have been central to the development of young leaders. The examples are legion.

- In the fourth century BC, King Philip II of Macedon invited Aristotle to tutor his son Alexander the Great. Curious by nature, Alexander studied under "The Master," as Aristotle was called, for seven years and was enormously influenced by him. On his subsequent travels, Alexander kept under his pillow a copy of the *Iliad*, marked up by Aristotle, along with a dagger.
- Ralph Waldo Emerson mentored Henry David Thoreau, introducing him to Transcendentalism. Emerson also used his influence to promote Thoreau's work and gave him access to a piece of property on Walden Pond, a decision that triggered Thoreau's greatest work.
- Having grown up in rural Kansas and after finishing low in his class at West Point, Dwight Eisenhower seemed destined for a mediocre career. But then a tour in Panama under a legendary

mentor, Fox Conner, changed Ike's trajectory. On his next assignment, Ike finished at the top of his class at the Command and General Staff College and was on his way to a brilliant career.

- In recent American politics, when Alexandria Ocasio-Cortez and other progressive women were elected in 2018, Congresswoman Pramila Jayapal took them under her wing and helped to propel them into lives of promise and power. They are rapidly changing the face of our politics.

There are many, many others who deserve recognition as well. One of my favorites is a remarkable woman from Tennessee: Patricia Summitt. Over her lifetime, she shone as a coach, a mentor, and a role model—a trifecta. She is now gone, but her legacy lives on.

In 2016, when she died from the early onset of dementia, Pat Summitt left behind the winningest record in NCAA Division 1 basketball history at the time and a women's sports environment that was changed for the better. Her greatest legacy, however, lies with the generations of women she coached and mentored, making them better athletes and better leaders. In an industry dominated by men, she now holds her own among the greatest coaches in history—people like Vince Lombardi, John Wooden, Casey Stengel, and Coach K.

Summitt grew up on a dairy farm with three older brothers and a sister in Clarksville, Tennessee. Her father was tough on his children and would never accept excuses—traits inherited by his daughter. She played at the University of Tennessee at Martin and a few years later became head coach of the Lady Vols at the Knoxville campus. At the time, prospects for her teams were dim, but she became a transformational coach, earning eight NCAA championships and no less than a record-breaking 1,098 NCAA victories.

In 1998, *Sports Illustrated* published a revealing profile, drawing heavily from the experiences of one of Summitt's star players,

Michelle Marciniak. At age thirty-eight and heavily pregnant with her first child, Pat insisted on taking a private aircraft to keep her date with Michelle, a top high school recruit at the time. Just prior to the meeting, Pat's water broke, but she insisted that she honor her commitments and sat down with Michelle. Pat rattled through recruiting materials until nature would no longer wait—she was heading into labor! Michelle and her dad drove Pat to the airport so she could fly back to Tennessee to give birth there. She arrived just in time.

Summitt would serve as coach, mentor, and role model for Michelle and many other players. As her parents had taught, Pat insisted on absolute excellence on and off the court—no excuses. Everything had to be earned, not given. Her players even had to sit in the first three rows of their classes, and she kept tabs on all parts of their lives. She was a master at dispensing tough love, berating her players in front of their teammates and punishing them brutally for poor, lackadaisical performances. After a devastating loss in Cleveland, Mississippi, she had the bus drive her players back to Knoxville for over eight hours straight, no bathroom stops allowed.

But even as she became famously ruthless on the court and in the locker room, Pat acted as a maternal figure to her players off the court. The author of the *Sports Illustrated* article, Gary Smith, aptly described her dual theory: "When you sit in her office [as a player] she leans toward you to connect . . . the flesh around those piercing eyes wrinkling in concentration, and invariably asks what *you* think the team needs. And then, as you're getting ready to leave, asks if *you* think her beige shoes go with her white skirt."

As good mentors so often do, Summitt fostered a desire among her players to do mentoring of their own. A total of sixty-two women who played for her went on to coach basketball teams or hold administrative roles at high school, college, or professional levels. In her final years, President Obama awarded her a Medal of Freedom—the nation's highest civilian honor—and after her untimely death, he observed: "For four decades, she outworked her rivals, made winning an attitude, loved her players like family, and became a role model to millions of Americans, including our two daughters."

It is hard to overstate how much difference a dedicated, first-class coach, mentor, or role model can make in molding the leaders of tomorrow. No matter how many classes in management and leadership young people take, there is no substitute for person-to-person relationships with older people who have learned the arts of navigating through rough seas.

The word *mentor* became popular through Greek mythology. Heading off to the Trojan War, Odysseus asked his friend Mentor, then in old age, to look after his son Telemachus while he was gone. Thus "mentor" became a verb in the English language with its own meaning: to impart wisdom and share knowledge with a younger colleague.

In our own time, mentorships have acquired an expansive use. In business, leaders have often turned to mentors, as Richard Branson did when he was trying to get Virgin Atlantic off the ground. "I wouldn't have gotten anywhere in the airline industry," he said, "without the mentorship of Sir Freddie Laker." Similarly, members of the Young Presidents Organization (now known as YPO) are expected to find a personal coach when they first become CEOs. In sports as in politics, star performers look for coaches and mentors.

Mentors bring a wealth of practical insights to the conversation. Typically, the best of them provide a voice of wise, balanced judgment, and they spark the ambitions of their mentees. Repeatedly, I have found the counsel of mentors, coaches, and role models invaluable in opening my eyes and often opening doors. They also provide an extra set of eyes for mentees, helping them see things they may miss and avoiding blind spots. A few years ago, a delegation of top British police officers visited the Kennedy School to explain how they had dealt with domestic terrorism. Based on past successes, they assign one veteran officer to head up an operation but ask a second to stand at his side, watching intently and then whispering in his ear possible course corrections. It works!

When it comes to the issues of both mentorship and sponsorship, gender and race play roles that cannot be ignored. Far too recently, when top positions in a corporate world long dominated by men were beginning to be filled by women, there was a sense among women at the top that they had to overcome insurmountable obstacles to achieve their successes—and that was certainly true. Many worked like crazy to get to the top. As a popular saying goes, "Ginger Rogers did everything that Fred Astaire did. She just did it backward and in high heels." I was surprised to learn, however, that once these women reached the top, many hesitated to extend a hand back down to help younger women advance. As a few told me, they felt that because they overcame such difficulties in achieving their own success, it was only right that the younger generation similarly struggle.

As someone who has benefited greatly from older, wiser men who mentored me up the ladder, I am happy that times have changed and talented, more senior women often provide great mentoring for younger women. A 2017 study by the business management firm Heidrick & Struggles found that women mentorship is in fact growing among younger generations. Of workers over sixty years old, only 14 percent reported having been mentored by a woman leader. That number grows to 35 percent for workers aged fifty-one to sixty and is an impressive 46 percent for those aged twenty-one to twenty-five. The survey suggests not only that more women are rising to positions of power, but that they're finding their voice as leaders as well. I'm sure the rising generation of women leaders would now agree with Madeleine Albright, who once said: "There is a special place in hell for women who don't help each other."

Interestingly, the first female self-made millionaire was well ahead of her time in recognizing this necessity. At the turn of the century, when Madam C.J. Walker, a female Black entrepreneur, built her cosmetics empire, she made sure to assist other Black women along the way. She developed schools across the country to train Black women to sell her product, and by 1919, as many as twenty thousand agents had joined her company. These agents bought Walker's product wholesale and could use whatever profits they made to build their own branch of the business. Walker once said, "I am not merely satisfied in making money for myself, for I am endeavoring to provide employment for hundreds of women of my race."

THE ROLE OF SPONSORS

She might not have realized it at the time, but Walker was providing an early form of sponsorship to her employees. Just as it is essential to build a network of support, it is equally important to find—or become—a sponsor. Mentorship and sponsorship are related but different. A mentor is someone who helps a mentee develop key skills. A sponsor is an active champion of a person within an organization, pushing for that person's recognition and promotion. Obviously, the mentor may become a sponsor too. In both cases, the junior person develops loyalty to their mentor or sponsor.

While sponsorship resembles mentorship, the explicit responsibility of a sponsor to advocate on your behalf—and protect your back—makes a crucial difference in advancement. Herminia Ibarra, a professor of organizational behavior at the London Business School, and Nancy M. Carter and Christine Silva, top researchers at Catalyst, a nonprofit that works with businesses to expand opportunities for women, wrote in the *Harvard Business Review* that women and men are "mentored" at the same rate, but women are significantly under-"sponsored" and are subsequently not advancing at the rate of their male peers. Similarly, Sylvia Ann Hewlett, a leading expert on sponsorship and diverse leadership, found in 2012 that only 8 percent of people of color had sponsors, compared to 13 percent of white people.

Unlike mentorship, where you can enlist someone to become your mentor, sponsors typically choose their own protégés. Unfortunately, not everyone wants to play the role of sponsor. If leaders of an organization truly believe in diversity, they should recognize that it is as much their responsibility to advance the marginalized as it is the responsibility of the marginalized groups themselves to create close bonds in the workplace. In a world still dominated by men, there are more Fortune 500 CEOs named James or Michael than there are women who are Fortune 500 women. Not a single Black woman made the 2020 list. We are simply not making the progress we anticipated only a few years ago.

Mentorships and sponsorships can play a key role in advancing the careers of marginalized groups. These relationships move beyond elevating the opportunity and advancement of the marginalized. Cumulatively, they bring more women and people of color into visible roles at the top, changing our perception of what it takes to be a leader and improving the ways in which organizations become infused with diversity of thought and experience.

Even so, research shows that to this day, employers are more likely to hire candidates similar to themselves or with similar backgrounds. Having attended the same college or university or growing up in the same zip code can provide huge advantages to job seekers. That is especially true when an organization or field of endeavor has no firm set of criteria for evaluating candidates.

Iris Bohnet, a professor at the Kennedy School, along with academic colleagues, found revealing evidence of the effect of discrimination. In the 1970s, women composed less than 10 percent of musicians in U.S. symphonies. In an experiment since then by Bohnet and colleagues, orchestra directors began placing all candidates behind a curtain so that hiring teams could no longer see their gender. The intervention in audition design has had telling results: women today have become about 40 percent of members of U.S. symphonies.

The lesson is clear in this and other experiments: When leaders in organizations actively work to lower barriers for women and people of color, they can deliver wonders—but leaders have to believe wholeheartedly in the mission.

PINNING DOWN YOUR CORE VALUES AND PRINCIPLES

Each of us has our own story of experiencing the world and distilling from it a set of values and principles that guide our behavior. One challenge that arises as you sort out your values is that there are so darn many of them. We all want to be honest, courageous, happy, responsible, respectful, compassionate, empathic, fair, curious souls who are devoted to the creation of a better world. We call those personal values. Among our loved ones, we want to be loving, kind, caring, honest, and present. Let's call those family values. At work, we value professionalism, integrity, trustworthiness, vision, collaboration, competitiveness, and mutual support. Call those professional values. In our public or political life, we would like to believe that we support freedom, equality, justice, unity, diversity, mutual respect, and goodwill. Those are our civic values. And, quietly but persistently, most of us also value money, power, influence, and fame. Perhaps we should call those our "get real" values.

Together, that represents more than thirty different values. How can anyone live a life fully committed to each of them? The answer is that you can't. There are too many, and many of them often conflict. For example, out of your caring for the world, let's say you start working for a world-class nonprofit. It's a terrific organization, but over time, your constant travels threaten your marriage. Which matters more to you—your career or your family? Or you sign up to work as an assistant to a powerful congressman—a dream job until you find he is a terrible boss and is in office for all the wrong reasons. Are you prepared to walk? Graduating from a premier business school, you are offered a high-paying job on Wall Street, but you know that five years from now you won't be able to go back home and run for that office you once dreamed of. Which path better fits your values? After finishing college, you are presented with an entry-level position at a top-tier technology company or the option to start up a business of your own. Will you go with prestige or take a risk?

Those aren't the only questions you need to resolve in your early years. If you want to make a difference in the public arena, you must also wrestle with the way that values can collide there. Let's assume that in your mind, you are pledged to liberty and equality. Both are noble aspirations. But what you learn over time, as James O'Toole has written, is that if you pursue a society with full, absolute equality— guaranteed services and income to all, a thicket of government controls, high taxes—you will lose lots of liberty. If, on the other hand, you seek complete liberty—no rules, regulations, taxes, or affirmative action—you will lose lots of equality.

Clearly, one of the highest priorities in public life is to strike a fair, thoughtful balance between liberty and equality—just as we should strike balances between individualism and community, capitalism and socialism, centralization and decentralization. As Americans, we speak as if we have "shared values," but in reality we don't. Unfortunately, the country's current leaders are so polarized that it has become well nigh impossible to bridge differences across the aisle. That's why, I repeat, we so urgently need a new generation of leaders—men and women who can stop litigating the past and start a new, fresh chapter in our national life.

Once a leader has her values sorted out, she is in a good position to sort out her principles. In effect, your principles are the way you translate your values into action. A few examples:

Value: Concern for others
Principle: Create a work environment that consistently looks
              after your team

Value: Equality of opportunity
Principle: Equal pay for equal work

Value: Set an example for others
Principle: As leader, always take the first hit

Emerging leaders often have such busy lives that there is little time to step back—or, as Ronald Heifetz has argued so well in his books, to go up on a balcony and watch yourself on the dance floor. But taking time out of each day for personal reflection or meditation is, as so many have discovered, an important passageway to sorting out what you believe. When we remove ourselves from the bustle and continuous stresses of everyday life, we can begin to see the bigger picture, sort out our larger goals and ambitions. It also pays off to be mindful of your daily life and ongoing projects. Perhaps you can try to keep a gratitude journal; it will help when you hit rock bottom—as, one day, you might.

When our daughter Katherine converted from Christianity to Judaism, I wasn't quite sure what to expect. As it turns out, her life was enormously enriched—as was the life of our entire family. One of the joys we found was the tradition of Shabbat—Friday dinner and a Saturday given over to family, friends, quiet contemplation, and gratitude for life. I wish I had discovered that earlier. Buddhism encourages similar practices. There are lessons here for all of us trying to make sense of a jumbled world.

Bottom line: The years of young adulthood are an ideal time to sort out what values and principles you want to embrace in life. They will evolve over the years—but you will find, time and time again, that you will be well served if you have a set of values and principles uppermost in your mind as you navigate through life.

CONSTRUCTING YOUR OWN MORAL COMPASS

For the past several decades, America has endured a series of massive leadership failures, stretching from our corporate and nonprofit sectors to our public life. In mid-2020, over 80 percent of our fellow citizens said we are spinning out of control.

Into this breach has come an effort in the business community to push for a course correction, moving away from old forms of leadership in favor of a different approach. "No longer," says Bill George, a principal player in this effort, "should leadership be about developing charisma, emulating other leaders, looking good externally, and acting in one's self-interest." Those didn't work out so well in the 1990s and early 2000s, as he points out. Instead, leadership should be about authenticity, honesty, openness, emotional intelligence, collaboration, and systems change. This school of thought is called "authentic leadership" or "Finding Your True North." Leaders in all sectors have come around and now affirm that every leader should construct their own moral compass. The best leaders of tomorrow will be those who stand for something bigger than themselves.

So what does it mean to practice authentic leadership? Simply put, you as a leader must rely upon your own internal, moral values and principles in tackling difficult leadership choices. It is easy to honor your values when life is going well. But when a crisis strikes and tough calls are needed, you must be able to decide which values are most important, which must be sacrificed, and what trade-offs may be required. It is especially necessary that you reach deep inside yourself to lead from your heart as well as your head.

After a long and successful career in business, Bill George has become a leading pioneer in leadership studies—a worthy successor to Peter Drucker, John Gardner, and Warren Bennis. One of Bill's favorite quotes comes from the Buddhist spiritual leader Thich Nhat Hanh: "The longest journey you will ever take is the eighteen inches from your head to your heart."

To be authentic, a leader should be transparent and open to others, comfortable in disclosing vulnerabilities, and consistently honest. The person who appears in public places should be the same person behind closed doors. You should take inspiration from other leaders, but not try to be their copycats. Be yourself. As Steve Jobs said, "Don't let the noise of others' opinions drown out your own inner voice."

Leading today has become high-stress work; authentic leaders try to stay grounded and welcome the support of family, community, and friends. Authentic leaders also need a high degree of self-knowledge as well as self-mastery. In business and in civic life, leaders naturally like the extrinsic rewards of compensation and recognition, but intrinsic rewards—having meaning in your life—are ultimately more fulfilling. Summing up, George writes, "Authentic leaders have discovered their True North, align people around a shared purpose and values and empower them to lead authentically to create value for all stakeholders."

Herminia Ibarra, an authority on professional development at the London Business School, raises an important counterpoint about authentic leadership. Authentic leadership, she writes, requires you to be true to yourself—but which self? "We have many selves, depending on the different roles that we play in life," she says. As contexts change, so must leaders. When things are going well, a leader can be collaborative, creating round tables where all voices are heard. But when an emergency strikes, the team leader must put on the cloak of command, making decisions in rapid-fire order. So too must a leader display confidence to others that often masks his own inner doubts. In the darkest days of World War II, General Eisenhower said the head of an organization should "reserve for" his "pillow" any "pessimism and discouragement." As the needs of your followers change, you must adapt and adjust your own leadership.

Critics of authentic leadership sometimes take its advocates too literally. They claim, for example, that if you are a jackass in private, the only way you can be truly "authentic" is to be a jackass in public. That, of course, is BS. Rules of common sense and etiquette apply as much to authentic leaders as to more traditional ones. If you are a damn fool, you need to clean up your act.

A more serious question is the place that role models should play in the lives of authentic leaders. I am a strong advocate of role models— as we have seen, they stretch all the way back in history to Aristotle becoming an intellectual role model for Alexander the Great. It is also true that changes in context may require a leader to wear a new mask.

FDR is a prime example: He started his presidency as "doctor recovery" and ended as "doctor win the war." He once told Orson Welles, "Orson, you and I are the two best actors in the country.

So how to reconcile the importance of role models with the need to be authentic? Bill George and I have discussed this on several occasions and agree that an emerging leader should study closely the lives and lessons of role models but should not try to copy them. Be yourself; don't try to be someone else. Listen to your own inner voice.

One should not try to be an exact copy, of course. Even if you wanted, who could possibly copy Lincoln? Eleanor Roosevelt? Mandela? Or Golda Meir? But great leaders can provide a source of aspiration as well as inspiration. They can prompt you to look inward and begin developing the timeless qualities we see in the best of humankind. I would also suggest there is often a sequence in our lives— that in our teens and early twenties, we begin to learn through role models. In the years that follow, that knowledge—along with other experiences—becomes the basis for forming one's values and, over time, discovering one's True North.

In Bertolt Brecht's play *Life of Galileo*, the character Andrea says, "Unhappy is the land that breeds no heroes," to which Galileo responds, "No, Andrea, unhappy is the land that needs a hero." To me, Andrea has the better side of that argument. America is a land that has always relied upon heroes. Part of our problem today is that we have so darn few. Because our supply has declined so sharply in recent years, we have nearly forgotten what it is like to live among great men and women. They inspire; they give hope; they are role models.

In my mind, authenticity does not mean that every thought of a leader must be expressed. Nor does it mean that every emotion should be worn on your sleeve. Rather, authentic leadership demands that as you navigate, you stay true to your values and principles. In your mind and in your behavior, you hold steady your long-term destination. But as contexts change, you adjust your tactics. There is a difference between steadiness and rigidity. The world around us is changing so fast that even as you keep hold of your values and principles, your leadership must be nimble.

As for the critics of authentic leadership, one must ask: What would you put in its place? Authentic leadership is not a perfect solution, but it sure beats the alternatives. For leaders embarking on some of their most harrowing days, it is all the more important that they know and stay true to their values. The chapters to come will show that when put to the ultimate test, those leaders who emerge from difficult times with their compass intact are not only just admirable. They become our heroes.

FOUR

SURVIVING THE "FLAMING CRUCIBLE"

FDR, THE STRICKEN PRINCE

During a family vacation on Campobello Island, thirty-nine-year-old Franklin Delano Roosevelt awoke to a life turned upside down. As he swung out of bed and tried to make his way to the bathroom, his left leg buckled, and he fell to the floor. He had a fever of 102. By the next day, his right leg was in trouble too. He could no longer walk.

Doctors came and went, uncertain at first about what ailed him. But soon they reached a unanimous conclusion. An athletic man had come down with the most dreaded disease of his time: polio, a virus that at its peak killed or paralyzed tens of thousands in the United States each year. A vaccine was still three decades away.

Until the virus invaded his immune system, Franklin had led a charmed life. A pampered only child from one of the most prominent families in America, homeschooled on the banks of the Hudson River, editor of the *Harvard Crimson*, a cousin of one of America's most celebrated presidents, second-ranking civilian in the navy during World War I, a vice presidential nominee of the Democratic Party at thirty-seven, and a star who appeared destined for even higher office—Franklin seemed to have it all. His biggest failure, in his eyes, was his rejection by the Porcellian Club at Harvard. As one observer put it, his path through life was strewn with rose petals.

Yet to both family and friends, Franklin, for all his promise, also seemed superficial, self-centered, and vapid. Behind his back, family members called him "Bertie Wooster," a dithery character in a string of British novels portraying the idle rich. Teddy Roosevelt's daughter Alice thought he was a mama's boy, too closely tied to his mother's apron strings. After college, he followed Teddy into the New York State legislature; unlike his cousin, who "rose like a rocket," Franklin was seen as supercilious.

Thus it was not at all clear how Franklin would respond to the cruelties of polio. Would he retreat from public life, as his mother urged. Sara Roosevelt was a domineering woman who wanted him to come home and be under her charge. Or would he try to walk again and regain a position in public life, as urged by his wife, Eleanor, and longtime political advisor Louis Howe. Days passed without progress, and Franklin fell into a depression. God had forgotten him, he lamented.

Somehow, though, he reached deep inside himself, rediscovering not only his sunny optimism of the past but also finding an inner strength and determination that no one knew he had—not even Franklin himself.

And so began one of the most dramatic comeback stories in American history. Polio became the dividing line in his life—the pre-polio days and the after-polio days. He became a classic example of a public leader who not only rebounded from a knockout blow through resilience but also grew in character and compassion. He had met his biggest crucible in life—and won.

Strikingly, he failed in the mission he first saw as central. He believed that he couldn't run for office again until he could walk again, and he tried persistently. Day after day, he dragged himself forward; within a year, he was able to stand with the support of leg braces— each weighing seven pounds. He also found that the warm waters at a rehabilitation center in Warm Springs, Georgia, eased his physical and psychological pain. He so loved working with other polio sufferers, especially kids, that he bought the place and went there often. A film clip of him in the water with polio-stricken children is available online. It's moving.

But try as he might, it became clear over the next seven years that he would never again stand or walk unassisted. He seemed through with public life. His mama had won a round.

What no one foresaw was how Roosevelt would be transformed by this crushing blow—or perhaps more accurately, how he transformed himself. Optimism was in his genes, it seemed, and he turned it into an art form, inspiring others with a jaunty presence, listening to them with a new intensity, insisting that, as he famously said later in his first inaugural, "The only thing we have to fear is fear itself."

Before polio, Franklin was a snob; after polio, he was deeply compassionate and empathic about others who had endured suffering. Before polio, he was interested mostly in himself; after, he was devoted to the well-being of others.

One of my favorite passages about political leadership is contained in Ted Morgan's FDR biography. In a chapter titled "Stricken Prince," he wrote of Roosevelt that "although his legs remained withered, his spirit triumphed. It was this spiritual battle, this refusal to accept defeat, this ability to learn from adversity, that transformed him from a shallow, untested, selfishly ambitious and sometimes unscrupulous young man into the mature figure we know as FDR."

He changed perceptibly. His face broadened, and, through exercise; he built up a massive chest. He was proud of his strength, taking pride when he fought for two hours and eventually landed a 237-pound shark. But greater than the strength of his upper body was the strength of his character. He was much more patient than in earlier years. As president, he had an exquisite sense of timing, an ability to wait until an issue had ripened before striking.

He was also more reflective. When he was elected to a third presidential term in November 1940, in the middle of World War II, the British were desperately pushing him for military aid. His staff thought that as soon as the election votes were counted, he would surely begin a series of emergency meetings. Instead, he insisted upon spending several days aboard his presidential yacht in the Caribbean. The United States was officially neutral, and the opposition to giving Britain arms was intense. He needed time to think.

It was there, on a cruise in the Caribbean, that he came up with the brilliant idea of Lend Lease, a stratagem not to give arms to the Brits but to lend them. He also came up with a famous analogy that carried the day: If your neighbor's house is on fire and he asks to borrow your garden hose, you wouldn't bicker. You would lend it to him instantly. Perhaps the hose would be lost in the fire, but if so, the neighbor could replace it. Surely, he said, we can do the same for our embattled friends. Within weeks, Roosevelt had won congressional approval for Lend Lease and Churchill got his destroyers.

Craftiness was also natural to Roosevelt, and in his struggle with polio, he turned that into a high art, too. He believed it essential that the public not see just how devastated he was. But to win election as governor of New York and then president, he had to make lots of appearances onstage. How to solve such a conundrum? Why, create a visual mirage! His car would drive as close to the podium as possible. Hidden from public view, men would lift him and his wheelchair onto the stage, stand him up, and lock on his leg braces. Roosevelt would then hold a cane in one hand and, with the other, grasp the arm of a helper—often a son. Coming onstage, he would tilt up his head, break into a big smile, and while the audience was watching his glow, he would swivel—not walk, swivel—across the stage. He looked the happy warrior; what the audience couldn't see was that by the time he grasped the microphone, he would be sweating profusely, and his helper's arm would sometimes be bleeding from Roosevelt having dug in his fingers. And it worked! William Leuchtenburg, a leading Roosevelt historian, told me that as a college student he'd seen Roosevelt speak at a rally and had come away convinced that he could walk.

He could never have gotten away with it now, but in those days, FDR's openness with the press enabled him to persuade them to not print any photographs that showed his disability. The FDR library in Hyde Park—one of the best, as it is so modest—has thousands of photos of Roosevelt, but only three show him in a wheelchair. One of the reasons FDR won the presidency was a widespread belief that he had conquered his illness. Any man who can lift himself up from polio, it was said, could surely lift the country up from depression. Roosevelt knew exactly what he was doing.

"Crucibles" mold a public leader. For a long while, leadership scholars saw crucibles as a form of adversity and focused on ways that leaders cope with setbacks. More recently, crucibles have gained a spotlight of their own as biographers and others have come to see how much leaders transform themselves during key moments in their lives. There is no better example than FDR. As Doris Kearns Goodwin, the wonderful historian, wrote in her book *Leadership in Turbulent Times*, "Franklin Roosevelt's ordeal provides the most clear-cut paradigm of how a devastating crucible experience can, against all expectation and logic, lead to significant growth, intensified ambition, and enlarged gifts for leadership."

A SOLDIER'S FLAMING CRUCIBLE

One danger of leadership studies, and of writing this sort of book, is that most people will not become the president or prime minister of their country, much less FDR. So it is tempting to shrug at the example. But crucibles are more universal than something we include in stories of a great president to humanize him or explain his rise. Crucibles, as one scholar has put it, "may be found woven into the fabric of day-to-day life." A wife is unable to say goodbye to a husband as he dies from COVID-19; a father watches helplessly as his tiny daughter drowns; a Black mother is devastated when her twenty-five-year-old son is shot dead jogging through a white neighborhood by white men who say they mistook him for a burglar. A war ravages one generation after another. The human experience is such that each one of us will likely encounter acute suffering at one point or another. Whether it be the result of personal tragedy or national crisis, these events can allow us to reshape our visions of ourselves and the world around us. Shortly before FDR contracted polio, one of the world's deadliest wars had raged across Europe, leaving 20 million dead and hundreds of millions more grieving. World War I, in particular, was known for its goriness.

A French soldier wrote memorably about his time in the trenches and the struggles of returning home. For André Fribourg, a reservist in the army, the pain of watching his fellow soldiers die riddled him with doubt—about his country, the war, his role in it, and his purpose in returning home, where he had been a teacher. Everything he thought he had taught about and fought for was in doubt, and so too was his identity.

So Fribourg, like many before him, took to the page to capture memories and thoughts. Fribourg wrote the book, entitled *The Flaming Crucible: The Faith of the Fighting Men*, in an attempt to express the pain of so many, the danger his country had endured, and the efforts to save France. The writer who translated the book into English wrote of Fribourg:

Shattered in body, his sight and smell and taste almost gone, the schoolmaster returns from the war, to brood over the dead and the empty hollowness of his life. These are the dark hours, infinitely sadder than the terrible days and nights in the trenches. In the blackness, his soul is locked in the gloomy caverns of his heart. But gradually, the awakening comes. On the crowd whose apparent carelessness had at first chilled and shocked him, he learns to lean.

He feels about him kindly hands guiding his uncertain steps, and hears gentle voices. The walls of the cavern are rolled back; and his heart swells like an organ. He has learned that Faith alone accounts. He has been remoulded in the Flaming Crucible.

Though Fribourg's story is one of war, many have spoken about their personal hardship in a similar fashion. Paulo Coelho, a Brazilian writer and a colleague of mine on the Schwab Foundation board, was institutionalized in his teenage years because his parents hated his aspiration to become a writer. He became a songwriter instead but was arrested for criticizing the Brazilian government. Once released, Coelho did become a writer and has since published dozens of works in over eighty languages. He says of the life-altering moments he has endured: "When we least expect it, life sets us a challenge to test our courage and willingness to change; at such a moment, there is no point in pretending that nothing has happened or in saying that we are not yet ready. The challenge will not wait. Life does not look back."

Not surprisingly, one of our country's greatest writers and poets gave voice to a similar phenomenon of enduring terrible pain and doubt. Maya Angelou faced countless hardships, including the hatred of racists and the trauma of rape at a time when no one talked about the issue. Her spirit was equal to the test, and her words echoed the toughness of FDR when she wrote: "You may not control all the events that happen to you, but you can decide not to be reduced by them."

THE POWER OF CRUCIBLES

My dear friend Warren G. Bennis and his colleague Robert J. Thomas so popularized the importance of crucibles in the literature of leadership that they are now highlighted frequently, even indiscriminately, in tales of trial and triumph. "Why is it," they asked in the *Harvard Business Review* in 2002, "that certain people seem to naturally inspire confidence, loyalty, and hard work, while others (who may have just as much vision and smarts) stumble, again and again?"

The answer, they concluded after interviews with over forty CEOs and public figures, is in how leaders deal with extreme physical or psychological challenges—crucibles. They wrote: "One of the most reliable indicators and predictors of true leadership is an individual's ability to find meaning in negative events and to learn from even the most trying circumstances. Put another way, the skills required to conquer adversity and emerge stronger and more committed than ever are the same ones that make for extraordinary leaders." Every single one of the men and women they interviewed had experienced severe challenges somewhere on their journey and found them transformative.

In fact, the hero's journey—and the closely related journeys of leaders—lie at the heart of Western myths stretching back over three thousand years. Indeed, Homer's tale of Odysseus can well be considered the original crucible story. Odysseus was a pivotal figure in the Greek victories in the Trojan war, recruiting the Greeks' best soldier, Achilles, and coming up with the idea of the Trojan horse, allowing the Greeks to enter Troy and win the war.

But coming home after a long absence was a very different and difficult ordeal for Odysseus. Strong winds throw him off course, he and his men are captured by Cicones, and they have to defeat a Cyclops. Then hubris sets him back: Bragging of victory, he enrages Poseidon, the sea god, who makes the seas dangerous for Odysseus and his men. One adventure gives way to the next and Odysseus spends seven more years at sea. Finally returning to his island home of Ithaca, he faces yet another challenge: His wife, Penelope, after waiting patiently for him, is to remarry and has engaged her suitors in a competition for her hand. Odysseus, disguised, defeats the other suitors and at long last is reunited with his family and returned to his throne. In contrast to the *Iliad*, a bloody account of war and hubris, the *Odyssey* is a story that for thousands of years has given heart to leaders struggling to overcome profound adversity.

Since the days of Freud and Jung a century ago, psychologists have focused not only on the outer struggles of leaders but also on their inner emotional struggles. Early in the twentieth century, the psychologist and philosopher William James famously wrote of leaders forged in personal crises. "Emotional occasions, especially violent ones, are extremely potent in precipitating mental rearrangements," he wrote in *The Varieties of Religious Experience*. One way of being in the world gives way to another. James came up with the phrase "twice born" to describe individuals in such transformations. He believed that people who are twice born could achieve a "heroic level . . . in which impossible things . . . become possible, and new energies and endurances are shown." Doesn't that describe Franklin Roosevelt?

Of course, crucibles disrupt the lives of leaders in many different ways: childhood traumas that still haunt in adulthood, as experienced by Oprah Winfrey; the sudden, calamitous assassination of a loved one, as happened to Bobby Kennedy; or the pain caused by a loss due to more innocent causes, such as for Sheryl Sandberg, who lost her husband suddenly; the pain of facing dark, ugly racial prejudice, as was the case for Sojourner Truth, Shirley Chisholm, and Gandhi; long, lonely, and stupefying imprisonment, as was faced by Nelson Mandela, Dietrich Bonhoeffer, John McCain, and other POWs; and near-death experiences like that of Serena Williams, who almost died after giving birth to her child.

As noted earlier, perhaps the best-known modern crucible example comes from Pakistan, where a father instilled a love of learning in a young girl early in life. As she watched her father run his school in the Swat Valley, Malala Yousafzai took an early interest in education and before she could even speak would join her father's classrooms and imitate the teachers. When the Taliban began to control northwestern Pakistan, dancing and television were banned; most notably for Malala and her family, however, was the prohibition of girls from attending school. This was a devastating development, one that may have ended the educational endeavors of most young girls. Malala was undeterred and instead began campaigning for female education. She took to television and the Urdu platform of the BBC, asking, "How dare the Taliban take away my basic right to education?" She was only eleven years old when she published her first blog post online. Many would consider being stripped of your fundamental right a crucible moment in itself; Malala, in continuing her education under the Taliban and finding moral purpose through her advocacy, proved she could bounce back from hardship.

As said earlier, when Taliban fighters boarded her school bus, they demanded "Who is Malala?" and shot her three times in the head. She endured another crucible that was much more difficult to recover from. Her advocacy efforts had threatened her life; she awoke from a medically induced coma in Birmingham, England, facing weeks of surgeries, treatments, and therapies. She was lucky to have survived. When she had recovered adequately to return to school, she did not do so quietly; instead, she doubled down on her advocacy efforts, extending them across international boundaries to champion the cause of girls' education around the world. Her autobiography detailing her advocacy and subsequent attack drew international acclaim; in 2014, at age seventeen, she became the youngest winner of the Nobel Peace Prize. Today, she has come under greater scrutiny in her home country as the influence of the Taliban and other militant Islamic groups grows; provincial police have raided bookshops and schools carrying works that share her story.

Hardship came in waves for Malala. First she faced the oppressive rule of the Taliban, barring her from her passion on the grounds of gender alone. Like many women and people of color before her, she learned that the circumstances in which she was born created their own form of extreme adversity. Then, of course, she looked death squarely in the eye, only to emerge stronger. Undergoing such an experience is not an actual necessity for leaders, but for those who do have them, this sort of encounter can change their entire journey as a person and a leader. Personally, I have had formative losses and struggles but not transformative ones.

Crucibles, to be clear, often never completely leave those affected. Even if the obstacle is overcome, even if a leader snaps back and eventually grows from the experience, memory of that crucible can shape a leader's self-doubt and darkness for decades—indeed, until death. Consider Eleanor Roosevelt. She grew up with parents who were often indifferent to her welfare and frequently left her insecure and lonely. After she married her distant cousin Franklin, she stayed at home raising their five children. Then a thunderbolt struck: When Franklin, then a high-ranking official in Washington, came home from business in Europe, he was so sick that Eleanor had to unpack his trunks for him. There she discovered a packet of torrid love letters between him and Lucy Mercer, Eleanor's own social secretary. It took years of pain, but Eleanor eventually emerged stronger and became a champion of the downtrodden, people whom she would never have met were it not for that crucible experience. For decades, long after Franklin died, she was the most admired woman in America. But even as Eleanor forgave, she never forgot. After her death, a poem was found next to her bed. On it she had inscribed the year "1918," the year she discovered Franklin's love letters to Lucy Mercer. The poem was titled "Psyche," by Virginia Moore:

> The soul that has believed
> And is deceived
> Thinks nothing for a while,
> All thoughts are vile.
> And then because the sun
> Is mute persuasion,
> And hope in Spring and Fall
> Most natural,
> The soul grows calm and mild,
> A little child,

Finding the pull of breath
Better than death . . .
The soul that had believed
And was deceived
Ends by believing more
Than ever before

FIVE

THE KEYS TO RESILIENCE

Why do some public leaders crumble when faced with a crucible moment and why do others—like Odysseus, Franklin, and Malala Yousafzai—come successfully to grips and even grow? The father of positive psychology, Martin E.P. Seligman, and his colleagues have determined from their research that human reactions to extreme adversity tend to fall into one of three camps along a bell-shaped curve.

On one end of the spectrum are those who become hopeless—and for those who have experienced extreme trauma, this reaction is quite understandable. Lacking the help needed to recover, they fall apart in anxiety, depression, drugs, post-traumatic stress disorder, and, increasingly, suicide. They suffer from what Seligman and company have described as "learned helplessness"—a sense that they are stuck in life and are incapable of snapping out of it. Fortunately, those in this group are a minority and increasingly find themselves supported by networks of both family and professionals to guide them forward.

In the middle of the spectrum is a second group—a majority—who initially fall into depression and high stress but, after a period of time, begin to snap back to where they were. We call those cases resilient.

And then at the other end of the spectrum, says Seligman, "a large number of people show what's called post-traumatic growth." These folks typically go through hard times in the immediate aftermath of a traumatic event—even forms of PTSD—but a year later "they're stronger than they were before by psychological and physical measures." These are the people of whom Nietzsche said, "If it doesn't kill me, it makes me stronger."

The U.S. Army, which places a premium upon training officers and sergeants who are resilient and will grow from challenging experiences, reached out to Seligman some years ago and worked with him to create special training for those purposes. Thousands went through the resulting courses, reportedly with enthusiasm.

The marines, naturally enough, took notice. In the mid-nineties, all of the military branches were struggling to meet their recruitment goals. Three of them—the army, navy, and air force—decided to make life more comfortable for recruits (e.g., shorter deployments, more shore time, etc.). The marines, by contrast, decided to make it much tougher. They created a hellish final week called—appropriately— "the Crucible."

The marine corps took pride in demanding that after six hours of sleep and food, recruits work together in squads to endure fifty-four straight hours of physical, psychological, and moral trials with food and sleep deprivation and forty-five miles of marching. Coming up the last hill of the Crucible, the candidate becomes a marine. The result for recruitment by the services? The army, navy, and air force saw continuing declines in applications while the marines shot up. Twenty-five years later, the Crucible is still considered the defining experience of joining the corps. A sizable number of young people in America—more than one might suspect—clamor for experiences that require great bravery offer close bonds, and bring purpose to one's life.

Given our increasingly chaotic and dangerous world, it is not surprising that parents try so hard to protect their children. Even so, I often wonder whether we should encourage more hardiness among the young, more experiences beyond their comfort zone. Certainly, the many marines who show up in my classrooms, mostly in their early or mid-twenties, have emerged from their military experience with enormous self-discipline, a mental toughness, and abundant resilience.

In her final years, my mom helped me enormously on my own journey. She knew, I believe, that I had long harbored a fear of dying. I didn't want to talk about it, read about it, or think about it. But then she made a big gift: She taught me how to die. She didn't hide any of her decline; I saw every scary moment; I was there holding her hand when she passed. But she did it all with a grace and dignity that robbed her death of sting. It was a moment of beauty and awe. On that same morning, the first day of spring, one of her great-grandchildren was born, giving me a sense of the cycles of life—by the grace of God, one door closed as another opened. I no longer harbor those old fears. I became hardier.

By now we have a pretty good handle on the traits that make leaders more vulnerable to extreme adversity. We know that those who are deeply insecure and narcissistic will eventually come a cropper; the same for those with excessive ambition, a lack of character, cowardice, or lazy incompetence. No one wants to be in a foxhole with people like that.

But what are the most important traits for strengthening the resilience of public leaders and also spurring them on to personal growth? The research strikes me as inconclusive. But I do think that we can draw important lessons from personal experiences as well as from history, social science, and philosophy. From my own years in the arena, serving four presidents plus teaching for over two decades, I would suggest that beyond the obvious foundational qualities of all leaders—character, integrity, courage—there are four other key qualities that characterize men and women who have responded to their crucibles with resilience.

A SUNNY TEMPERAMENT

A few days after his first inauguration in 1933, President Franklin Roosevelt paid a courtesy call on Supreme Court Justice Oliver Wendell Holmes Jr. on his ninety-second birthday. The two men talked for an hour. After FDR took his leave, Holmes turned to an associate and said of Roosevelt: "A second-class intellect but a first-class temperament." Holmes had nailed it. FDR was not the smartest man in public life and, before polio, was unusually sheltered. But as we saw earlier, he had a sunny disposition that let him address his affliction with a good heart and inner confidence. He never conquered polio, but he wrote a new narrative about his life that not only transformed him but won him the presidency.

I saw how much an optimistic, positive outlook helped President Reagan not only survive but also flourish after he was nearly killed by a would-be assassin. The Gipper believed in the majesty of his office and never let his guard down. I was in the West Wing that fateful afternoon in 1981 when he was shot. His car pulled up to the hospital and he got out of the car on the far side. Standing up, he carefully buttoned his suit coat, walked around the car on his own, and only when he had reached the waiting doctors and was beyond camera range did he collapse in their arms. He just knew he could make it, and he didn't want the nation to see our president sprawled and vulnerable.

In the months when I found myself in meetings with him, Reagan was always upbeat. He was full of funny stories and especially loved one about two young brothers on Christmas morning. One of the boys was a grump. When his parents showed him a brand-new bike, the kid burst into tears, telling them that he was sure he would soon have an accident, the bike would be trashed, and he would be heartbroken. Frustrated, the parents took the other, optimistic kid to a separate room for a gift. Opening the door, all he could see were stacks and stacks of old newspapers. The kid burst into giddy laughter and tore into the piles, exclaiming, "There must be a pony in here somewhere!" I don't know how to measure it, but Reagan was another president whose first-class temperament helped him thrive as he recovered from his crucible.

ADAPTABILITY

It is difficult to remember any generations in American history that have lived through more collective crucibles than Millennials and Gen Zers. In the past two decades alone, as we noted in the introduction, they have come through horrendous terrorist attacks on our own soil, two of the sharpest economic recessions since the Great Depression, a pandemic that has killed hundreds of thousands of Americans, and growing threats to the planet itself. Many are also graduating from universities with heavy debts and uncertain job prospects.

In a world that is so volatile and chaotic, a capacity for adaptation has become indispensable. As Bennis and Thomas write, "Adaptive capacity, which includes such critical skills as the ability to understand context and to recognize and seize opportunities, is the essential competence of leaders." They cite the work of Harvard psychiatrist George Vaillant, who has spent his life analyzing the stages of development in the famed Grant Study. The first volume of his work, titled *Adaptation to Life*, found that people who aged most successfully had great adaptive capacity, continued to learn new things, and looked forward with eagerness and optimism, without being stuck in the past.

The life of Ida B. Wells was in many ways a constant story of adaptation. Born enslaved in Mississippi in 1862, she and her parents spent the early days of her life trying to make a living for themselves in the South after the end of the Civil War.

But misfortune soon struck: Both of Wells's parents died of yellow fever. Ida was the oldest child and was just sixteen years old at the time. Her church community decided the best thing to do was to split up and separate the children, finding foster homes for them. Ida, though, refused. She told those who had come up with the plan, "My parents [would] turn in their graves to know their children had been scattered," and she resisted continued efforts on their part to separate the family. She soon became a schoolteacher to keep everyone fed and housed.

That adaptability served Wells well on her rise to becoming, in the words of one journalist, "the unsung heroine of the civil rights movement." In fact, the launching of her greatest work may only have happened because she was willing to change course without hesitation or fear. In the 1880s, Wells returned to her hometown of Memphis to run a newspaper, *Free Speech*. There she began to champion the rights of Black Americans and began to investigate violence of white Americans against Black Americans. In 1892, a white mob lynched three Black men. One of them was the owner of the grocery store that was the heart of Memphis's Black community, and a dear friend to Wells.

Wells took to the pages of her newspaper, calling on Black citizens of Memphis to leave the city. Her voice was so respected that "scores and hundreds" did just that in the weeks that followed. When she ran an anonymous editorial that said that lynching was not about Black men's violence toward women (then the excuse offered by white lynch mobs), she placed her own life at risk. While she was traveling to New York, a mob broke into the *Free Speech* offices and destroyed them. And soon, when the mobs found out that Wells herself had written that anonymous editorial, they put out threats saying that if she ever returned to Memphis, she could well die.

Her career's work was in physical tatters; her investments were gone; her life was in danger; and her friend was dead. But this moment became a catalyst for Ida. She later wrote: "This is what opened my eyes to what lynching really was. An excuse to get rid of Negroes who were acquiring wealth and property and thus keep the race terrorized and 'keep the n***** down.' I then began an investigation of every lynching I read about. I stumbled on the amazing record that every case of rape reported in those three months became such only when it became public." She committed her life's work to exposing the harsh and gruesome truths of lynching.

And she did just that. She toured the country, telling crowds what she was discovering and writing an investigative series on lynching, *Southern Horrors*. According to *The New York Times*, the reporting techniques she pioneered in this effort remain central to the practice of journalism today. She also went to Britain to rally support for her cause. Frederick Douglass, one of country's greatest orators and most effective activists, wrote about Wells's pronouncements, saying, "There has been no word equal to it in convincing power. I have spoken, but my word is feeble in comparison." Later in her career, Wells helped found the NAACP and the National Association of Colored Women, while finding time to work in prisons. She called out the problem of mass incarceration long before most paid attention to it. It's no surprise that when lynching finally became a federal crime in 2020, the law was named for Ida Wells.

There's much more to say about Ida B. Wells—her bravery, her commitment to justice, and her intellect were all of the highest order. If she had not had such an ability to adapt willingly and effectively, though, our country would surely be a less just place. Rather than dwelling on the hardship she encountered in her life, she sought to make the best of her difficult circumstances and saw opportunity in the gravest challenges. Shifting terrain, grief, and unexpected misfortune did not deter Ida from pursuing a better life; instead, she capitalized on hard times as a chance to shed light on injustices. Most of us will never face difficulties like those posed to Wells and her family; we will, however, each confront unpredictable circumstances, many of which will seem insurmountable. The best among us will take such issues in stride, changing ourselves and our perspective to create light in the darkest of hours.

HARDINESS

In recent years, my colleague and friend Nancy Koehn, a professor of history at the Harvard Business School, has reintroduced me to Rachel Carson. I knew about Carson's work as an environmentalist. Her book *Silent Spring* was one of the most important of the twentieth century. But I had no sense of who she was really and how she became a case study in what New Englanders often call "hardiness." Others call it "perseverance." And still others—starting with Angela Duckworth—have popularized it as "grit." Duckworth posits that grit is a combination of passion and perseverance toward one important goal; her findings suggest it is a central trait of high performers across a variety of industries.

Call it what you will—hardiness, perseverance, or grit—Rachel Carson had it in abundance, and that made a huge difference in her impact. In 1960, she was in the midst of working on her latest book, an investigation into the growing dangers of synthetic pesticides widely employed in those days in American farming. That spring, her doctors for the third time removed small growths in her left breast. The tumors were sufficiently "suspicious" to justify a radical mastectomy, but the doctors recommended no further treatment. Sadly, that recommendation turned out to be overly optimistic, because within months, the Cleveland Clinic told her the cancer was spreading.

Rachel Carson then began a race against time. She was determined to finish her book but worried that she might not make it, and she was frequently racked with pain. As Nancy Koehn points out in her book on leadership, *Forged in Crisis*, Carson kept her darkest thoughts to herself. "I moan inside," she wrote in the margin of her notebook. "And I wake in the night and cry out silently for Maine [where she liked to spend summers]." While some days proved productive in her writing, she faced monumental challenges there too. "How to reveal enough to give understanding of the most serious effects of [pesticides] without being technical, how to simplify without error—these have been problems of rather monumental proportions," she told a confidant.

Perhaps miraculously, Carson finished her manuscript, but then she encountered yet another obstacle: When *The New Yorker* published three excerpts, it ignited a firestorm. Supporters rushed to her side. Supreme Court Justice William O. Douglas called her work "the most revolutionary book since *Uncle Tom's Cabin*." On the other side, though, the chemical industry led a charge to discredit her work as well as her. One industry chieftain suggested she was a front for Communist influences. Another said her teachings could return us to the Dark Ages, so that "insects and diseases and vermin would once again inherit the earth." Seriously ill, she hung in long enough to help set the wheels of government action in motion.

Knowing that death was rapidly approaching, she had a final walk along Boothbay Harbor with a close friend. Just after, Carson wrote: "We had felt no sadness when we spoke of the fact that there would be no return. And rightly—for when any living thing has come to the end of its life cycle, we accept that end as natural. . . . That is what those brightly fluttering bits of life taught me this morning [on our walk]. I found a deep happiness in it."

Nancy Koehn writes that "Carson's moment of forging—her crucible—stretched out for more than two years. This long, slow burn demanded, again and again, that she find her way back from the precipice of despair and then recommit to her mission." Nancy concludes:

> "Her ability to stay the course, finish her book, and exert enormous impact was fueled by her unrelenting dedication to a mighty cause." A quiet, reserved woman, Rachel Carson is seen to this day as the mother of the modern environmental movement. We are fortunate she stayed the course when waters became rough.

Carson teaches us that making change is rarely easy and almost always requires an unflappable commitment to the cause. In the face of adversity, great leaders are those who hold strong to their purpose and goals. There will be difficult days, months, and even years, but oftentimes it is through hardiness that we can recommit to our values and forge ahead.

As Peter Gomes, the late pastor at Harvard Memorial Church, often admonished churchgoers about adversity: "Get used to it; get over it; get on with it."

STOICISM

The Greeks and Romans of two thousand years ago have long since been eclipsed in science, technology, engineering, and many other fields, but I have found that their thoughts about life remain a vital source of wisdom for leaders today. In the 1990s, working in the White House, I accompanied President Clinton on a domestic flight aboard Air Force One. Clambering aboard, the president saw Ted Koppel, ABC's longtime news anchor, deeply engrossed in a short book. "What are you reading, Ted?" the president inquired. "Oh, a book called *Meditations*, by the Roman emperor Marcus Aurelius." "Ah," said Clinton, "so am I. In fact, I try to read it once a year." And Koppel responded, "I do as well." From his readings and from conversations with leaders like Nelson Mandela, Clinton found stoicism a helpful way to keep his emotional and mental balance when Republicans tried to drive him from office. Mandela counseled him to not let his enemies gain an upper hand over his emotions and mental balance.

I can hardly say I match them in their reading habits, but I do find that as I get older, I wish I had studied the Greeks and Romans more diligently when I was young. Their philosophers were practical men who frequently engaged with their followers in seeking wisdom and a good life. And their writings and colloquies heavily influenced America's founders, drawn as they were to Roman philosophers and to a school of thought called stoicism. As the historian Forrest McDonald argues, it was not enough that the founders miraculously defeated the world's strongest army; they then had to create a durable republic knowing that none had succeeded for long. To the founders, Athenian philosophers like Plato and Aristotle had little application, and even Locke and Montesquieu fell short.

Instead, the founders found guidance and hope in the stoics of the past—philosophers and statesmen like Seneca, Cicero, Epictetus, and Marcus Aurelius. Those men spoke about ways of life and leadership that had immense appeal on American shores. The stoics held that a people's actuating principle was public virtue—"virtue in the sense of selfless, full-time, manly devotion to the public weal," as McDonald writes. That public spiritedness prevailed during the Revolutionary War, as many made great sacrifices for the cause of independence, but there was rightful concern that in normal times, men would be driven instead by their passions, and that for public men, the ruling passions would be ambition and power, "the love of power and the love of money." Historically, stoicism has emphasized not only liberty and independence but self-command, a stern self-mastery, a putting aside of passions, restraint, keeping a firm upper lip, and a resolute devotion to honor.

In our own time, the story of James Stockdale—another POW in the Vietnam War—has sparked a much-welcomed revival of interest in stoicism. Before his imprisonment, Stockdale had spent twenty years as an American fighter pilot and was rarely out of the cockpit until his late thirties, when he enrolled in graduate studies at Stanford's Hoover Institution, specializing in national security. He was preparing, he thought, for a career at the Pentagon as a strategic planner. By his own admission, he soon found his studies a tad boring and decided that he wasn't cut out for paper shuffling in Washington. One day, by chance, he wandered into the philosophy area of the school and ran into the dean of humanities and sciences, Phil Rhinelander. That chance meeting opened up a new world for him.

Stockdale wrote a stirring account of the years that followed in *Courage Under Fire: Testing Epictetus's Doctrines in a Laboratory of Human Behavior*. It's an essay of some forty pages and is easily found on the internet. I would recommend it as reading to any aspiring leader. Born a slave in Asia Minor in 50 AD, Epictetus at fifteen was shipped to

Rome in chains. Treated brutally, he became lame in one leg and was auctioned off as a "cripple." Fortunately, he was bought by a Roman who came to admire his curiosity and mind, so that Epictetus was eventually accepted as a stoic philosopher in his own right.

"Stoicism," Stockdale concluded from his studies of Epictetus, "is a noble philosophy that proved more practicable than a modern cynic would suspect . . . Stoics belittle physical harm, but this is not braggadocio. They are speaking of it in comparison to the devastating agony of shame they fancied good men generating when they knew in their hearts they had failed to do their duty vis-à-vis their fellow men and God." Stoicism's demand for disciplined thought and brave behavior attracted only a minority to its standard, but, citing Will Durant's *Life of Greece*, Stockdale says "those few were everywhere the best . . . men of courage, saintliness, and goodwill."

Stockdale was soon put to a severe test of turning his thought into deed—his crucible moment. Returning from Stanford to active military service, he served three tours on aircraft carriers in the waters off Vietnam. On each, he brought the writings of Epictetus and kept them by his bedside. On September 9, 1965, as he wrote, "I flew at 500 knots right into a flak trap, at treetop level, in a little A-4 airplane that I suddenly couldn't steer because it was on fire . . . After ejection I had about 30 seconds to make my last statement in freedom before I landed in the main street of a little village right ahead. And so help me, I whispered to myself: 'Five years down there, at least, I'm leaving the world of technology and entering the word of Epictetus.'" Epictetus told his students "that there can be no such thing as being the 'victim' of another. You can only be a victim of yourself. It's all how you discipline your mind."

In the hands of his captors, Stockdale—like John McCain, who at one point was held captive two cells down from Stockdale—was treated to unimaginable brutality and hardships. He spent eight years in the Hanoi Hilton, where he was tortured fifteen times, was put in leg-irons and was locked in solitary confinement. Moreover, Stockdale

was the highest-ranking officer among the POWs, and under military
rules stretching back to the Korean War, he was in charge of all of his
fellow prisoners—a group that grew from fifty to some four hundred.

Through it all, he remembered that a stoic always kept two files in
his mind: one for those things that are up to him and within his power,
and one for those that are not up to him and thus beyond his power.
If you pay lots of attention to events beyond your power, you will ultimately have a life of fear and guilt; you must let those go and pay
attention only to those things within your power. When shot down,
he thought, he gave up his station as a wing commander in charge of
his fellow Americans and, in the eyes of his guards, became a criminal
and an object of contempt. Because he had no control over that dramatic change, he would treat it beyond his power—and therefore he
would suffer without letting his captors dominate his emotions and
thoughts. His stoicism gave him the power to put down fear and anxiety while enduring immense suffering.

The hardest moments came when the POWs "took the ropes."
Checking into the Hanoi Hilton required that a POW first visit an
interrogation room, where the guards demanded information and,
when it was withheld, brutalized their captive. New arrivals quickly
realized, in Stockdale's account, "that you can be reduced by wind
and rain and ice and seawater or men to a helpless, sobbing wreck—
unable to control even your own bowels—in a matter of minutes . . .
In a flurry of action [you can face fragilities like] being bound with
tourniquet-tight ropes, with care, by a professional, hands behind,
jackknifed forward and down toward your ankles held secure in lugs
attached to an iron bar, that, with the onrush of anxiety, knowing your
upper body's circulation has been stopped and feeling the ever growing induced pain and the ever-closing-in of claustrophobia, you can
be made to blurt out answers, sometimes correct answers, to questions
about anything they know you know."

Stockdale concluded: "These were the sessions where we were
taken down to submission, and made to blurt out distasteful confessions

of guilt and American complicity into antique tape recorders, and then to be put in what I call 'cold soak,' a month or so of total isolation to 'contemplate our crimes.' What we actually contemplated was what even the most laid-back American saw as his betrayal of himself and everything he stood for." Epictetus understood that long ago: "Look not for any greater harm than this: destroying the trustworthy, self-respecting, well-behaved man within you." Surprisingly, during his long years of captivity, Stockdale chose not to speak openly of stoicism to his fellow POWs; instead, he tried to inspire them through his own stoic leadership. Stockdale always gave Epictetus credit for his resilience and survival; he himself grew into a role model for his generation.

A sunny temperament, adaptability, hardiness, stoicism—these four qualities remain the hallmarks of those who successfully respond and ultimately conquer their crucibles with an inner resilience. There is no guarantee, of course, that if you have all four qualities, you will emerge as a promising, resilient leader; but if you lack them, there is a good chance you will wind up a loser. Let us look now at how leaders can not only rebound from adversity but actually find moral purpose from it.

SIX

TURNING ADVERSITY INTO PURPOSE

"The habits of a vigorous mind are formed in contending with dif-ficulties," Abigail Adams famously wrote to her son John Quincy during the bleakest days of the American Revolution. "All history will convince you of this . . . Great necessities call forth great virtues. When a mind is raised and animated by scenes that engage the heart, then those qualities, which would otherwise lie dormant, wake into life and form the character of the hero and the statesman."

Abigail Adams continues to speak truth to us 250 years later. Not long ago, the historian David McCullough told me he had decided to write a book about the exchange of letters between Thomas Jefferson and John Adams when they were both retired. But, as David read more deeply into their individual lives, he fell out of love with Jef-ferson and into love with Abigail. The result: his prizewinning biog-raphy of John that lifted the reputation of them both. Jefferson would not have been happy.

Abigail was also absolutely right in her clear-eyed view that tough times call forth strength and bravery from an alert citizenry. Time and again, public leaders knocked down repeatedly have rebounded and actually grown stronger. In many instances, those who were struck have also acquired a new moral purpose in their lives—in Abigail's words.

The lives of two contemporary leaders underscore her point.

THE HARVEY MILK STORY

No one could have foreseen the role that Harvey Milk would play on our national stage. He was originally a conservative Goldwater Republican who, after resigning from the navy in 1955, began his career in teaching and then became a stock analyst in New York. In his early years, he lived a closeted life. As a high school student, he played the traditional heterosexual athlete, fearful of the ostracism he would face as an openly gay man. His mother warned him in hushed terms of the danger gay men posed.

At seventeen, he was corralled with other gay men in a paddy wagon for being shirtless in Central Park; luckily, he was let off, but who knew what his fate would hold the next time? In New York, he lived in fear and led a double life, often living in private with men while playing the role of a Wall Street financial analyst for the outside world. Those years brought not a single crucible moment, but instead the continuous, grueling, and demoralizing experiences of living in a world you know does not accept you. For Milk, adversity came in the accumulation of experiences in which he was reminded he did not belong or was actively discriminated against.

As the 1960s and 1970s progressed, Milk started to take an increasingly progressive political stance, participating in anti-Vietnam protests and befriending a more progressive group of activists. He realized that he could no longer live in the closet, so he moved to San Francisco in the 1970s, opened a camera shop on Castro Street, the cultural epicenter of the San Francisco gay community, and began living life as an openly gay man in the heart of the city's emerging gay community. His small business was soon home to a revolution, as his charisma and sense of humor attracted the attention of the gay community. Harvey registered many other gay and lesbian Americans to vote and encouraged them to get involved in politics both as individuals and as a group—to make their interests and identities known to the world. He would greet his customers not with a sales pitch but instead with the question: "Are you registered to vote?" He pushed the then-groundbreaking idea that gay America deserved explicit representation—and, critically, that the person representing the community should be gay him- or herself, rather than simply an ally of the community. Soon enough, Milk was being referred to as the "Mayor of Castro Street" for his leadership in the neighborhood.

It did not take long before Milk became a controversial national figure. He toured the country from Buffalo to San Antonio, giving motivational speeches. "You gotta give 'em hope," he said. And for millions of gay Americans, Harvey Milk did just that. It wasn't easy. He ran for San Francisco supervisor in 1973, trying to be the first openly gay person to win major elected office in the United States— a glass ceiling that would not be broken until Elaine Noble was elected to the Massachusetts House of Representatives in 1974. Despite having few native connections to San Francisco, he attracted the attention of local voters through his commitment to liberal populist issues and his fiery oration. He was determined to be not only the gay candidate but also a candidate for all those who had been left in the dust by the California elite. His first campaign posters claimed, "Milk Has Something for Everybody."

When Harvey lost, he was undeterred. Assailed with vitriol and homophobia, tagged as a loser at the polls, he stood his ground, becoming ever more resolute. He had been criticized by gay leaders who had deep roots in the San Francisco community for being too radical and not waiting his turn to run; Milk did not care. He was steadfast in his commitment to his populist agenda and gay liberation. His convictions were unwavering; if anything, he doubled down on his efforts in response to fresh criticism. While his loss stung, he did win a respectable seventeen thousand votes—many of which came from the gay community. Understanding that he might need to take the next election more seriously, he cut his hair and persisted in his efforts to win elected office.

After the 1973 loss, Milk resurrected the Castro Village Association, which became one of the first groups in the nation to organize LGBT businesses. His focus shifted from voting to supporting gay business. He also launched the Castro Street Fair in an effort to draw business to the gay district, creating a road map for success for gay-owned businesses across the country. A whopping five thousand people attended that first fair, bringing business not only to the gay community but also to other shopkeepers on Castro Street; crowds exploded in years after. He also championed the causes of adjacent groups more formally, once famously striking a deal with the Teamsters; he supported their strike against the union-busting Coors Brewing Company by discouraging gay bar owners from selling the beer in exchange for the Teamsters hiring more gay drivers. As he wrote in a column for the *Bay Area Reporter*, "If we in the gay community want others to help us in our fight to end discrimination, then we must help others in their fights." The boycott worked; five of the six beer distributors agreed to sign the proposed union contract, and more gay drivers were hired.

In 1975, he ran again for supervisor, this time with the serious backing of his new union friends, but lost again—a second punch that would have knocked out most fighters. In his concession speech, he remained undeterred, saying, "We established a great amount of contacts. We will build upon those basics in the next two years." The support he garnered during the 1975 campaign led the newly elected George Moscone to appoint him as the city's first gay commissioner. As commissioner, he remained committed to the cause of helping gay Americans receive representation, so he ran for office yet again two years later. And in 1977, he finally won. He was steadfast in his commitment to a moral purpose, advancing the rights of the gay community and advocating for the interests of a broad coalition of marginalized groups.

That year, Milk stood up once again to those more powerful than he, fighting against Proposition 6, which would have required the firing of gay teachers in California schools. He managed to mobilize people too, as larger and larger numbers started coming to gay pride parades in California in opposition to State Senator John Briggs, who spearheaded the ballot initiative. Those who were typically engaged in more radical efforts rolled up their sleeves to volunteer for Milk's campaign. Thanks to the efforts of Milk and his allies, Proposition 6 was soundly defeated. It became a well-known victory at a time when, elsewhere in the country, politicians were successfully threatening the gay community.

Less than a year later, Harvey Milk was gunned down—yet another assassination that plagued the United States in the 1960s and 1970s. The mayor of San Francisco was killed as well in what appears to have been a toxic combination of hate and revenge on the part of Dan White, a fellow member of the board of supervisors whom Milk campaigned against reappointing.

Milk's funeral captured the impact he'd had on San Francisco's gay community and the city at large: More than forty thousand people showed up to honor and mourn him. In October 1979, a national movement inspired in part by Milk's assassination drew over a hundred thousand marchers to Washington. Harvey Milk came to be a martyr, icon, and inspiration for the budding gay rights movement in America. One of his former aides later wrote of him, "Harvey Milk was born into a world that didn't want him and left behind a world that discovered it would be difficult without him."

That statement is perhaps even truer today. In 2008, the city of San Francisco created a statue of Milk in the center rotunda of its city hall. Terminal 1 at the San Francisco airport is named after him, as are numerous other sites in California; popular films have been made about his life; *Time* magazine declared him one of the hundred most influential Americans of the twentieth century; and Barack Obama posthumously awarded him the Medal of Freedom, the nation's highest civilian honor. His example proved inspirational to millions who have come out of the closet and entered the political arena. He will always be in the pantheon of civil rights leaders. Few have had to work through as many inner and outer struggles as he did.

KATHARINE GRAHAM: A TWO-PART LIFE

As so often has happened in the lives of those who have suffered through extreme adversity, the life of Katharine "Kay" Graham can be divided into two halves. In her first, she seemed destined to play a relatively minor role in public life. But in the years after facing tragedy, she transformed herself into one of the most influential and admired women in the world, leading *The Washington Post* through what many would consider its golden era. Though she had several qualities that guided her forward, her rousing success was due in no small part to something she found deep inside her that is often the guiding light for leaders: a moral purpose.

I first came to know Katharine through my relationships with *The Washington Post*, stretching back to the early 1970s and my time as a speechwriter in the Nixon White House. In the midst of the Watergate scandal, *Post* reporter Bob Woodward would occasionally call, asking for White House guidance on a blockbuster story he and Carl Bernstein were about to publish. With Nixon's approval, Bob and I would talk. By day, I was hearing from my superiors at the White House that Nixon had done no wrong—that "Katie Graham and those people at the *Post* are just out to screw us." By night, Woodward would insist that Haldeman and Ehrlichman were lying. As it turned out, of course, my bosses were lying, and the *Post* was telling the truth. The cover-up worked better inside the White House than anywhere else—a lesson relevant to this day.

Years later, the Reagan White House and the press developed one of the most professional relationships we have seen—we treated one another with a high degree of respect. Kay Graham played a significant role in that. Things got off to an unexpectedly good start when Kay hosted a dinner welcoming the Reagans to Washington. They hit it off so splendidly that Kay and Nancy became lifelong friends. Importantly, the *Post* also dispatched two topflight journalists, Lou Cannon and Ann Devroy, to cover the White House.

Our chief of staff, Jim Baker, asked me to serve as communications director, one of the close, behind-the-scenes links to them. I wound up seeing them at least once a week, each side sharing what we could about what was going on. Neither side wanted to be cozy; both wanted a professional relationship. They asked of us transparency; we asked of them fairness—and for the most part, that's what we got. It helped that a conservative couple like the Reagans got along so well with a liberal hostess like Kay. The relationship between the West Wing and the *Post* certainly wasn't perfect, but it was one hell of a lot better than any we have seen in more recent years.

Soon Kay began inviting me to receptions at her home. Our relationship deepened over time, so much so that she wrote a warm, supportive note when I was under attack for joining the Clinton White House six months into his presidency. An invitation to a one-on-one lunch with Kay in her office followed, and we had a delightful time swapping stories. I could see why she had won over so many. I am grateful that I came to know her in the second half of her life, but to fully appreciate how she became Kay Graham, one needs to know about the first half, too.

Katharine was born during World War I and was raised in New York and Washington, D.C. Her father, Gene Meyer—a successful investment banker—purchased *The Washington Post* in the middle of the Great Depression. Both parents were preoccupied with their professional lives and gave Katharine little love or time. Her resulting lack of self-confidence was a burden for most of her life.

After completing studies at a nearby prep school, Madeira, she enrolled at another all-girls institution, Vassar College. She arrived a Republican, like her parents, but soon became a committed liberal. For her final two years of college, she transferred to the University of Chicago, where she was a liberal activist even as she studied the great books under Robert Hutchins. Katharine was tentatively spreading her wings. Upon graduation, she headed west as a cub reporter, covering unrest among longshoremen in California. It's hard to imagine her having lunches with Harry Bridges, a fighting labor leader targeted by U.S. prosecutors over thirty years, but she did.

Moving back to D.C. to help out with her father's paper, she met the man who became the center of her emotional life. Philip Graham had all the makings of a star: extremely bright, charismatic, witty, irreverent, and on the move. Coming out of Harvard Law, he clerked for two Supreme Court justices: Stanley Reed and the widely heralded Felix Frankfurter. In the words of one of the country's finest writers, David Halberstam, Philip was an "incandescent man."

Katharine fell deeply in love, and the two were married in 1940. It was a fateful decision. As has been said, she turned in her reporter's hat for a woman's apron, as expected of women in those days. In the years following, she became a devoted mother and wife as their family expanded, despite a miscarriage and the loss of a baby at birth.

Life with Phil often gave her joy, but even at its best it would be considered insufferable today. Looking back, she once observed, "I really felt I was put on earth to take care of Phil Graham . . . He was so glamorous that I was perfectly happy just to clean up after him. I did all the scut work: paid the bills, ran the house, drove the children. I was always the butt of family jokes. You know, good old Mom, plodding along. And I accepted it. That's the way I viewed myself."

When Phil returned from serving as an intelligence officer in World War II, Katharine's father gradually turned over to him—not Katharine, please note—responsibilities for running the newspaper. Phil directed the paper for seventeen years while Katharine was relegated to the sidelines so that she could be a good mother and wife. All the while, Phil became quite a dashing figure.

From the outside, it appeared they were an ideal couple. But dark forces had crept into their marriage. On some days, Philip could be brilliant and boisterous; on others, morose, depressed, quarrelsome, and even violent. To ward off despair, he drank to excess. One of Kay's friends described her as "patient Griselda," recalling the wife in Chaucer whose husband cruelly torments her while she remains submissive. In 1957, Philip had a mental breakdown that required his institutionalization. A few years later, late in 1962, Katharine learned of an affair he was having. When she confronted him, he told her of other flings. Soon after, Philip left Katharine to live openly in D.C. with a new paramour while also demanding a divorce. In her autobiography, Katharine writes that the world she had known and loved had disappeared.

As biographer Robin Gerber writes, Phil's descent gathered speed at a 1963 dinner for newspaper owners and publishers. Without warning, he strode to the microphone, denounced guests by name, identified a woman he alleged to be having an affair with President Kennedy, and then started to strip. He was soon returned to his psychiatric hospital. When released, he tried to give Katharine's share of company stock to his mistress.

The days that followed were likely hell for Katharine. But she hung on, trying to do everything she could to rescue her husband from madness. After six weeks in a psychiatric hospital, Philip persuaded doctors he was better, and they gave him a pass whereby he and Katharine could spend a weekend together at their 350-acre farm outside Washington. That Saturday, the couple lay down for an afternoon nap. Philip soon excused himself. A few minutes later, Katharine heard a terrifying blast of gunfire. Rushing downstairs and into the bathroom, she found Philip had turned a shotgun on himself. He was buried in a plot across the street from the couple's house, his grave visble from Katharine's window.

The curtain had come down on the first half of Katharine's life. In the days that followed, an army of friends and admirers rose to provide support. While she was deeply appreciative, Katharine kept her inner emotional struggles guarded. Historians and friends have remembered very few conversations with her about her calamity. She chose to master her emotions in her own way. "It was difficult to talk about," she once confided. "I just shut the door." On another occasion, she said, "What I essentially did was to put one foot in front of the other, shut my eyes and step off the ledge. The surprise was that I landed on my feet."

Ben Bradlee, who become one of Katharine's most trusted advisors, wrote that most of her friends and newspaper colleagues "secretly wanted her to sell the *Post*." It wasn't just that she lacked management and significant journalistic experience. Rather, she was a woman and housewife who would be entering a highly masculine, competitive environment. No woman had ever run a major newspaper in the United States. It would be better for everyone, many at the *Post* argued, if she stepped aside. "What most got in the way of my doing the kind of job I wanted to do was my insecurity," Katharine once observed. "[That] stemmed from the narrow way women's roles were defined, it was a trait shared by most women in my generation. We had been brought up to believe that our roles were to be wives and mothers, educated to think that we were put on earth to make men happy and comfortable and to do the same for our children."

Katharine did not think of herself as a feminist, but she also had more inner steel than the men knew. "When my husband died, I had three choices," she later recounted. "I could sell [the paper]. I could find somebody else to run it. Or I could go to work. And that was no choice at all." In her first meeting with her board, she announced that she wasn't selling the paper; she was running it. She made clear that she would hold the ultimate power over the paper's journalism and would be a co-partner in its business management.

She had to hide her fears in public. She was haunted as well by the impostor syndrome, as so many leaders are, but she insisted that she be in charge of her fate and the fate of her beloved newspaper. Her commitment to the *Post* and what it stood for quickly became the animating force in her life—both a product of her despair and the rock that helped her through it. Katharine was coming out of her crucible experience with a new purpose in life: to transform the *Post* into a world-class newspaper that would have impact and help change the world. She must have sensed that in transforming the newspaper, she might also transform herself.

Her transition to becoming a high-performing chief executive was sometimes rocky, and it took time. Major transitions in life always consume more time and energy than expected. But Katharine applied herself, and despite her lack of experience as a manager and leader, she started to perform as if she were a natural.

She quickly had ideas that paralleled those of leadership guru Jim Collins. In his book *From Good to Great*, Collins writes that the key for a CEO getting started is to get the wrong people off the bus and the right people on the bus and in the right seats. Katharine gradually got her executive editor, her editorial page editor, and her business manager off the bus and brought in her own team. She had an excellent eye for talent, as she proved with her recruitment of Ben Bradlee as her executive editor; she put talent above past friendships; and she not only gave her new talent lots of running room but also invested in hiring rising new stars like David Broder. Together, Katharine and Ben created one of the most formidable partnerships in the history of American journalism. It helped that her language could be as colorful as his.

Since her early years, Katharine had always enjoyed hanging out with journalists, swapping stories and gossip. Katharine made it a point to seek out members of her team and, importantly, listen to them intently. She learned from them how to run a newspaper; they learned from her a full-scale commitment to the cause. That gradual process in the 1960s of building a community and creating shared purpose, along with Katharine's own hardiness and adaptability, prepared her and her team for the momentous 1970s and the years that followed.

What happened in those following years is a long story, whose details are best saved for another time. In a nutshell: Two dramatic crises struck the *Post* out of the blue in the 1970s, each threatening the very existence of the newspaper. In the Pentagon Papers case, Katharine had to choose between two difficult options—to publish them or to hold them back. Either was dangerous. She put principle above profit, sticking to the highest standards of her new profession: She published. Vindication soon came as the Supreme Court voted in favor of publication. Thereafter, Ben Bradlee liked to say of Katharine, "She has the guts of a cat burglar." She didn't mind that—she didn't mind at all.

Barely a year later, a second saga began that proved even more crucial for her and her team. It began on a Saturday morning in June 1972 when her managing editor called her with an update on stories from the night before. There were two odd stories, he said: A car had crashed into one side of a house and then out the other while a couple was making love on a couch; and five well-dressed men had broken into the Democratic National Committee headquarters in the Watergate apartment complex. Reporters shared laughs over both stories. The *Post* assigned two of its rookie reporters, Bob Woodward and Carl Bernstein, to follow up on the Watergate story. No one knew where that might lead. Over the next two years, of course, it exploded into the biggest political scandal of modern times, forcing a president of the United States to do the unimaginable: resign from the highest office on earth. The good news from Watergate is that the checks and balances envisioned by the founders held; every institution and source of power worked toward the common good. No institution worked better than the one much reviled by the White House: *The Washington Post*.

It is hard to think of a more classic example than Katharine's of being pitched into a crucible—suffering, floundering, sinking—before resilience sets in and then, thankfully, one finds a purpose and a path toward generosity and wisdom. That was the Katharine Graham I came to know and admire.

To me, she represented one of the finest public servants imaginable. Her life in journalism was indeed an admirable form of service. It was not just a matter of upholding the First Amendment; it was about whether we value truth in our public discourse. In recent years, I have found *The Washington Post* far more trustworthy than more than one of our recent White House administrations.

The Katharine Graham I knew had the moral force, the charm, and the generous and gracious spirit that made everyone feel wanted. I didn't know her during the first half of her life, but—like so many others—I will always be grateful for the second.

THE NECESSITY OF MORAL PURPOSE

In the sixteenth century, a Spanish poet and mystic, John of the Cross, wrote a poem about an excruciating journey through the wilderness by a wandering soul. To this day, when terrible trouble strikes a friend, we talk of the friend experiencing a "dark night of the soul." Yet we forget that, in the poem, the soul eventually achieves its purpose: a mystical union with God. In the end, through long travails, the soul triumphs.

We have seen that story play out again and again in these pages as terrible, wrenching trouble has struck down its victims. Polio swept in overnight for Franklin Roosevelt and he never walked again; Ida Wells suffered one misfortune after another as white mobs tried to silence her; a spreading cancer forced Rachel Carson into a race against time; James Stockdale spent eight years in the Hanoi Hilton, where he was brutalized repeatedly; Harvey Milk could hear the footsteps approaching from would-be assassins; Kay Graham heard that terrifying gunshot. How many, many "dark nights of the soul" there have been.

But we have also seen each of these leaders rise to the challenge,

bouncing back through a determined resilience. And even more im-
pressively, each has reexamined life's possibilities and embraced a new
destination. From FDR to Kay Graham, they have grown in inner
strength, dedicating their lives to a higher moral purpose. They give
proof that William Faulkner was right in his Nobel speech seventy
years ago when he said that "man will not merely endure: he will prevail."

For centuries, philosophers, religious figures, poets, and historians
have urged mankind to adopt purposes beyond those of the individual.
Their wisdom continues to serve well. A few quotes give you a flavor.

From the Buddha:

> *Your work is to discover your work and then*
> *with all your heart to give yourself to it.*

From Thomas Carlyle, a Scottish historian of the 1800s:

> *A man without a purpose is like a ship without a*
> *rudder—a waif, a nothing, a no man. Have a purpose*
> *in life, and, having it, throw such strength of mind*
> *and muscle into your work as God has given you.*

From Oprah Winfrey:

> *If you don't know what your passion is, realize that one*
> *reason for your existence on earth is to find out.*

And from Helen Keller, who lost her sight and hearing after a bout of
illness at nineteen months and yet she became an inspiration:

> *Many persons have a wrong idea of what constitutes true*
> *happiness. It is not attained through self-gratification*
> *but through fidelity to a worthy purpose.*

For leaders, there is a critical difference between personal purpose—goals for oneself—and a higher calling, a moral purpose that inspires people to pursue service, activism, and politics. Milk, in experiencing discrimination himself and witnessing the hardship felt by his community, committed himself to advocating for those who were little seen in elected office. Kay saw that her newspaper not only remained in circulation but became the gold standard of journalism in her time. Though personal ambition is important in creating change, it is no substitute for finding a cause or a group to which a leader commits a life.

In recent years, psychologists as well as religious figures have begun focusing more intensively on how the embrace of a moral purpose changes people's lives. Their consensus is that, in most cases, having a purpose increases energy and satisfaction, provides motivation, and promotes resilience. It makes us more civic minded and strengthens our sense of citizenship. It also tends to counteract our destructive tendencies toward self-absorption. As the scholar William Damon has written, "Purpose endows a person with joy in good times and resilience in hard times, and this holds true throughout life."

One of the most interesting research endeavors is the Good Works project launched in 1996 by an array of scholars. One of its first fruits was a 2001 book by three prestigious psychologists, Howard Gardner of Harvard, Mihaly Csikszentmihalyi of Claremont, and William Damon of Stanford, titled *Good Work: When Excellence and Ethics Meet*. They found that when people embraced moral purpose as an ultimate concern, it gave them fresh energy and satisfaction when they reached their goals, and it gave them persistence when they ran into obstacles. They also discovered that for people to find satisfaction in a job, the work, among other things, must have a compelling mission and meet the highest standards of a profession. Otherwise, professionals turn elsewhere. One can imagine that moral purpose—and a love of their work—allowed both Katharine Graham and Harvey Milk to persist in the face of constant adversity as a woman and a gay man, respectively.

It is never too early, say the scholars, for young people to embrace a moral purpose, nor ever too late for an older adult. Joan of Arc was a teenager when she rallied her countrymen. Greta Thunberg and Malala Yousafzai were teenagers as well when they first stirred our social conscience. Nelson Mandela told his friends at a young age that he intended to be the first president of an independent South Africa. By contrast, Grandma Moses began painting at seventy-eight, when her scenes from farms and rural life brought widespread acclaim.

Every leader, as I hope our conversation has shown, must begin an inner journey. History repeatedly suggests that leadership starts from within—until you can master your inner self, you cannot serve others. Our focus here has been limited to three essentials for that inner journey: the development of character, the capacity to snap back and grow from a crucible moment, and the embrace of moral purpose. I have come to believe these traits are the essentials that allow a leader to exercise the moral courage to do what is right. Without them, the odds a leader will speak conscience to power and risk career and accolades for the sake of advancing the country's needs are significantly lower.

For moral purpose and moral courage to count, though, and to make an impact, leaders also need to face a different set of challenges that equip them with an ability to persuade and inspire. They must set off on an outer journey, where they learn how to build a following, how to execute, and, through patience and persistence, achieve the central purpose that motivates them.

PART TWO

YOUR OUTER JOURNEY

SEVEN

LEARNING TO LEAD UP

In our twenties and thirties, when most of us start our outer journeys, we might entertain visions that within a few years we will be running our own organization and telling others what to do. After all, we think, we have addressed our inner issues, studied hard, and our credentials are in order. Surely, we are the ones our new boss has been waiting for. Wrong!

Little do we appreciate when young that the path forward will possibly be a lot longer and more complicated than we think. That was certainly my own experience. For over twenty years after law school, I served primarily as a member of a staff reporting to someone higher up the chain. Thankfully, as I gained experience, my responsibilities grew so that I went from flunky to presidential counselor. But still, I was rarely running the show—I was serving the person who did. Looking back over the past half century, I can count over a dozen organizations and at least fifteen different bosses for whom I worked in the public, private, and nonprofit sectors. Over those years, I continued to learn about myself and my values, continuing my inner journey, while starting to understand what it might mean to take the reins at times.

This chapter and the next are devoted to those of you on promising leadership paths who are still learning how to manage—manage not only yourself but your boss, your colleagues, your team, and even your outside collaborators. There is an art to managing up, sideways, and down—especially when done at the same time. To lead is to effectively organize and interact with those with whom you work, to understand the priorities and goals of your colleagues, and see that those goals are put into action. I often say that every leader knows how to manage, but being a manager in itself does not make for a great leader. In other words, management skills are a foundation upon which leadership is imagined and built. As Warren Bennis frequently said, "The manager does things right; the leader does the right thing."

Over the years, most of my own bosses were wonderful. But occasionally I had a boss who was a real loser. In my first naval assignment, I was completely miscast as a junior engineer. I barely knew the difference between a nut and a bolt. My captain, a gruff, overbearing man, must have sensed what a klutz I was, and every day he showered me with notes demanding that I immediately fix this, repair that, stop that leaking faucet. But I also noticed that he rarely asked to see the results; he just enjoyed making people jump. That became tiresome. So when yet another note arrived, I would quietly squirrel it away in a drawer and wait to see if he ever asked again. If he did, I would hop on it; but if he didn't, the note would somehow find its way into a wastebasket. I am sure the navy was glad to see the back of me, but I survived. This would be my first of many lessons I would have in managing up—a skill I have tried to honed through countless trials and tribulations.

MANAGING YOUR BOSS

So what can I tell you that may add to your storehouse of knowledge about managing others? What are the key lessons I have learned over the years, serving in so many staff jobs? How can you best support your boss, making them as well as your team more successful?

Let me provide an overview of the best ways I have found to manage up. Most of the takeaways will apply to support jobs across the organizational landscape.

So let's dive in:

In the Early Days of a Job, Figure Out Your Boss and Play to Their Strengths

In previous chapters, we focused on your inner journey—developing your own self-awareness and self-mastery, learning to navigate on your own. In managing up, you embark on your outer journey—learning how to help your boss navigate and succeed as a leader of others. What do you see in your bosses? What are their strengths? Their weaknesses? How can you build up one and diminish the other?

In the early 1990s, four months into his presidency, Bill Clinton recognized that he was floundering and asked if I would join him as a counselor at his White House. It was a controversial appointment—both for him and for me, as I had worked previously for three Republican presidents. But he was a friend, and he was our president, so I said yes. And indeed, I was honored.

In my first days there, I discovered that the Clinton I knew, the man who had been one of the best, most innovative governors in the country, had lost more than his footing. In the hurly-burly of Washington, he had also lost his self-confidence. After a public event, he frequently asked me how he had done, anxious for advice. I wasn't sure what to do but decided that we shouldn't try to recast him as someone else. No, as I had seen with Reagan, we had to "let Clinton be Clinton." We had to encourage him to rediscover his old strengths and reassert his own authenticity. And that worked! The staff and I didn't get him out of the ditch; he gradually did it himself as we cheered him on. That's what a good staff does: It brings out the best in others, starting with the boss.

Keep One Eye on Today, the Other on Tomorrow

In addition to getting each day's work done well, a smart staff member also pays serious attention to what's coming down the pike. What is just over the horizon but will be hitting us sooner than we think? How can we get out in front? What should our strategy be? What preparations would help? One of Mike Deaver's successes in the Reagan administration was to assemble an inner circle of advisors off campus in periodic retreats to map out strategy and tactics for coming months; a White House that fails to think long term is a White House heading for trouble. Donald Trump would have been much more successful—and might have been reelected—had he directed his team early on to dig deeper into the possible effects of a pandemic. His chief of staff was just as responsible as the president himself for a massive failure of leadership.

Speak Conscience to Power

The traditional rule of thumb, of course, is that a good staff member should speak truth to power. We hear that so often that it almost goes without saying. But the more meaningful occasions have come when followers speak conscience to power. That often takes greater courage because you are challenging the judgment and even the ethics of your boss.

Perhaps the most famous exemplar is George Marshall. When Marshall was a young officer with a combat regiment in France, General John "Black Jack" Pershing, the commander of the American Expeditionary Forces, paid a visit to troops on the front lines. Finding them worn down and disheveled, Pershing lashed out at the soldiers and began to stomp off. Marshall pulled him aside and acidly defended his men, saying they would be battle ready if Pershing's headquarters had done its job.

Afterward, other young officers offered Marshall their condolences, certain that he would be cashiered. But Pershing remembered that moment and later reached out to Marshall, making him his top aide. The two enjoyed a long, productive relationship. A similar incident occurred when Marshall was deputy army chief of staff preparing for World War II and went toe to toe with his commander in chief, Franklin D. Roosevelt. Despite the fact that he was the lowest ranking member in the discussion and all other attendees agreed with the president's proposal to expand American air power, Marshall flatly rejected FDR's plan. Once again, colleagues thought Marshall was through. Instead, FDR promoted him, and Marshall eventually became the most respected public leader in the country, and deservedly so. Speaking conscience to power is not only the right thing to do—it can also build your reputation.

Argue Your Case, Then Get on Board

A good organization encourages dissenting voices, but once the boss makes a decision, a staff member salutes and gets to work. If you can't live with the decision, there's the exit door.

I well remember a vigorous argument in Gerald Ford's White House over the content of one of his State of the Union addresses. Approaching a presidential election, some wanted a laundry list of promises; others wanted a more thematic address. The president asked his longtime advisors from Capitol Hill to draw up the laundry speech and asked me to join Alan Greenspan (then his top economic advisor) in writing the thematic address. After we had drafts in hand, Ford summoned us all to the Oval Office to take a vote. As I recall, there were twelve votes, for the thematic and just two for the laundry list—but Ford was among those two. Guess what: Ford delivered the laundry list, and it didn't work well. But every single one of us locked ranks, cheering him on. That's the way it is supposed to work.

A No-Surprise Rule

Increasingly, good leaders now push responsibility deeper into the ranks. From cabinet officers to executives in the corner office, top leaders remain responsible for developing strategies, but they empower leaders one or two tiers below to execute. A typical directive: "Here's our destination. Now you figure it out how to get there." There's much to be said for that approach.

But it comes with one catch: It is essential that leaders up and down the ranks must be transparent and candid with one another. "No surprises!" Otherwise lack of trust will break down and metastasize. It's especially important to know bad news and act on it before it reaches the press.

Serve as Good Eyes and Ears—as Well as Chief Diplomat

One of the hardest challenges for a boss is to have a clear, honest reading of his or her own team members. Is their morale high? Do they feel respected? Do they see the work of the organization as meaningful? Someone has to have a finger on the pulse, quietly keeping the boss well informed. No surprises, remember. Usually the person who plays that role is the executive assistant to the boss or a deputy. Or it may be someone else close to the CEO.

Conversely, that same person ought to be the chief diplomat for the boss, reaching out to colleagues beyond the inner circle, keeping them informed about the morale, moods, anger swings, and perspectives of the leader in the front office. Absent a steady flow of reliable information, members of the team may begin to feel distant and distrustful. Rumors can spread and morale can deteriorate.

The range of responsibilities for any top assistant can be massive. For a decade and a half, Rosanne Badowski was the executive assistant to Jack Welch, and she went on to write a fine memoir, *Managing Up*. Here's how she summarized her experiences with Welch: "For more than fourteen years, I've been a human answering machine, auto-dialer, word processor, filtering system, and fact checker; been a sounding board, schlepper buddy, and bearer of good and bad tidings; served as a scold, diplomat, repair person, cheerleader, and naysayer; and performed dozens of other roles under the title of 'assistant' for a man dubbed by *Fortune* in 1984 as one of the ten toughest bosses in America." Welch summed up his view in two sentences: "Rosanne was—and any great assistant has to be—loyal, discreet, and forgiving. And not just a little of any of these, but a huge amount."

Be Emotionally Supportive

One of the most unlikely relationships in the modern presidency developed between President Harry Truman and his secretary of state, Dean Acheson. The former grew up on a farm in Missouri, never finished college, and worked as a haberdasher. By contrast, Acheson was born into an elite family in the Northeast, went to Yale and then Harvard Law, and became a prominent attorney and an advisor to the high and mighty. He and Truman were never close friends, but they had an exceedingly warm professional relationship.

In one of the best books about the Truman years, *Present at the Creation*, Acheson describes Truman's leadership in warm, glowing terms. Drawing from Shakespeare's Henry V at Agincourt, Acheson writes of how inspired he was time and again by "a little touch of Harry in the night." A moment in their relationship that stands out occurred after the midterm elections of 1946. Republican voters gave Truman's Democrats a shellacking, and his administration seemed destined for failure. Whenever Truman returned to Washington by train he would customarily be met at Union Station by his cabinet and many others. On this occasion, with rain pouring down, the platform was empty except for one man, Dean Acheson. He gave Truman the emotional support he needed. Truman was always grateful.

We often think of our presidents as rather distant figures who have climbed a slippery pole and are different from the rest of us. In truth, they are complex human beings who suffer the slings and arrows of life just like the rest of us. Like so many other leaders, they need emotional reinforcement.

In fact, looking back over American presidents, you will find that the most successful relied heavily upon one or two trusted confidants for help in getting big things done. George Washington called on Alexander Hamilton, headstrong but indispensable. Leaving Illinois, Abraham Lincoln brought two young men with him: twenty-three-year-old John Hay and twenty-nine-year-old John Nicolay; they helped to execute his policies, knew his every mood, and lightened his spirits in the darkest days of the Civil War. Hay went on to become a leading statesman and secretary of state in late century. In the mid-twentieth century, FDR had Louis Howe, Harry Hopkins, and Frances Perkins—not to mention his wife, Eleanor. Harry Truman had George Marshall and the "wise men" of national security. For John F. Kennedy, it was his brother Bobby, plus Ted Sorensen and others; for Richard Nixon, it was Henry Kissinger.

AN IRON FIST IN A VELVET GLOVE

In our own time, it seems too early to make final judgments about those who best served recent presidents. But if I was asked to choose one contemporary who should be singled out as the best, that strikes me as an easy call: James A. Baker III. I had the privilege of working with him during the 1976 Gerald Ford campaign and then in the early 1980s, serving as one of his chief lieutenants during the opening three years of the Reagan presidency. Through example, Baker taught me more about leadership—up, down, and sideways—than anyone else. And he made it both rewarding and fun.

Well into his adulthood, no one imagined that Jim Baker would leave a footprint in the sands of public life. His great-grandfather, grandfather, and father were highly successful corporate lawyers in

Houston and played leading roles in transforming that city into a thriving metropolis. From the start, it was assumed that Jim Baker would follow in their footsteps. His grandfather drilled into him, "Work hard, study . . . and keep out of politics." And for decade after decade, he did just that.

Baker's early years very much fit the mold for a man of southern privilege. His family sent him to the best boarding school, then to Princeton. While on a college rugby trip to Bermuda, he met the woman who would become his wife: a Finch College student named Mary Stuart McHenry. In the summer of 1950, war broke out in Korea. Baker, age twenty, signed up for the marines, married Mary Stuart, and began buckling down in life. Returning after two years in uniform, he earned a law degree at the University of Texas and joined one of the most prestigious corporate law firms in Houston. Over the next ten years, his successes in the field suggested his entire career would be in the law.

Life was good. He spent his free moments in the great outdoors of Texas and at a family ranch in Wyoming. He also joined a country club in Houston, where he and George H.W. Bush, both in their twenties, became tennis partners and for several years blew away their opposition. They also began an abiding, lifelong friendship.

Then tragedy struck. In 1968, Jim's wife, Mary Stuart, contracted cancer and was given little time to live. It was a devastating crucible for Baker. He and Mary Stuart each tried to protect the other from knowing until the very end. She left behind their four sons and a moving farewell letter to her husband. He wasn't sure he would ever fully recover.

As we have seen, crucibles can make you or break you. In Baker's case, his resilience gradually helped to make him anew, and he began thinking of leaving the legal practice. Two other figures also emerged whose support changed his life. One was Susan Winston, a family friend who was struggling with divorce at the time; the two eventually married in 1973. She helped him back on his feet and has been a constant source of strength since. The other figure was his friend George H.W. Bush. A Republican, Bush was in the hunt for a Senate seat in Washington and asked Baker to run his Harris County operation. Taken aback, Baker told him, "There are two problems here, George. First, I don't know anything about politics. Second, I am a Democrat!" Bush insisted they could cure both.

In his mid-forties, Baker began the second half of his life in a completely new field. He had taken on a higher calling. During the next quarter century, this political novice became the most successful chief of staff in White House history. He ran four presidential campaigns, winning two and losing two. As secretary of the treasury, he helped to avoid at least two international disasters. When he served as secretary of state to his pal George, the two of them were one of the most effective foreign policy teams in the twentieth century. It's a remarkable story, told best by Peter Baker (no relation to Jim) and Susan Glasser in their first-class biography of Baker, *The Man Who Ran Washington*.

How did Baker rise so quickly in Washington? And what made him so successful as Reagan's White House chief of staff? Quite simply, he had so much natural talent and applied it with so much discipline that his ascent seemed straightforward at the time. In retrospect, it was meteoric.

It started in 1976 when George H.W. Bush—by then a Republican member of Congress—persuaded him to explore a career in Washington. Baker soon accepted an offer to be number two at the Department of Commerce in the Ford administration. Typically, that is a low-profile post, but in this case, his number one was Rogers Morton, a GOP heavyweight. Morton, who was not well, often asked Baker to fill in for him at Ford White House meetings. The White House staff, led then by chief of staff Dick Cheney, was increasingly consumed by Ford's primary contest with Ronald Reagan, a former California governor. Within a few months, Cheney and others saw that Baker had "the right stuff" to go head-to-head with the Reagan forces. As chief delegate hunter, Baker persuaded the Mississippi delegation to switch sides at the GOP convention and ultimately put Ford over the top. Thus was born "the Miracle Man," as Baker was called. His pal George H.W. Bush rightly took note. So did Ronald Reagan.

Four years later, during the 1980 primary campaign, establishment Republicans led by George H.W. Bush were locked in another tight, rugged fight with Reagan. This time, Reagan swept the boards. But even in defeat, Baker had shown a striking capacity for organizing and advancing the Bush campaign. The day after the election, Reagan invited the man who had run two campaigns against him to serve as his chief of staff in the White House—then considered the second most powerful job in Washington.

One secret to their success together was how quickly they bonded. Reagan saw that Baker was not only talented but loyal; he also knew how to play the game in Washington. Baker realized that Republicans on the East Coast had totally underestimated Reagan: The Gipper had remarkably good instincts. Each man came to trust the other's judgment. It also helped that Baker developed strong alliances within Reagan's inner circle—Nancy, for starters, along with his deputy Mike Deaver, and Stu Spencer, the Louis Howe of Reagan's political advisors.

Of course, there were detractors, especially among conservatives who had worked hard for Reagan during his eight years as governor of California. Advisors like Ed Meese and Bill Clark regarded Baker as an East Coast liberal, not as a Texas conservative. They wanted to force him out, but Reagan had his back on more than one occasion.

In a White House where knives flashed in the night, Baker had to learn a new skill set—managing sideways. Carefully but persistently, he moved forward on three related fronts. First, he arranged that his would-be enemies enjoyed the perquisites of power. He ensured, for example, that Meese became a member of the cabinet but that he, Baker, remained staff and that Meese had a standing invitation to all key policy meetings. Baker skillfully gave Meese prestige even as he, Baker, retained power.

Initially, Baker, Meese, and Deaver served as a troika for Reagan. Baker had responsibility for congressional relations, communications, outreach, and the like—the operational side of the White House. Meese on paper had a bigger portfolio, responsible for both domestic and international policies. While Meese had a sweetness about him that I liked, he was no match for Baker organizationally. Power naturally gravitated toward Baker. Deaver, almost a son to the Reagans and a key player, gradually joined the Baker camp. By the end of year one, Baker was primus inter pares among the three—and had become known as "the velvet hammer."

Third, Baker assembled and then empowered one of the finest White House teams in recent memory. Richard Darman was his intellectual strongman, and in sorting out the implications of various policy proposals, he had an uncanny ability to look into the future, around corners and past potholes. He was arrogant and territorial, but he delivered. Margaret Tutwiler was close to both Baker and George H.W., was not afraid of telling Baker hard truths, and eventually became chief spokeswoman for Baker at the State Department. As we shall see, John F. W. Rogers became a key insider as well.

Together, Baker's three-pronged approach—gaining the trust of the Reagans, consolidating power in his own office, and surrounding himself with talented lieutenants—created a strong foundation from which he could work. Baker did not see himself as the chief decision maker; rather, he saw the president as the one who made the big calls and then looked to Baker to execute them.

In most organizations, the hard part isn't coming up with ideas but transforming those ideas into reality. Toward that end, Baker knew he also needed to cultivate two of the most powerful forces in Washington: Congress and the press. Once congressional leaders realized he was the man to see in the White House, they called him frequently with requests and complaints; he made it a practice not to go home at night until he had returned every call. He also realized that if he called past ten o'clock, he could leave a message—a blessing after a long day. Conservatives complained that Baker talked Reagan into compromising with Capitol Hill too easily. Baker saw that Reagan preferred to get half a loaf and then come back the next day for the rest.

Baker also built strong ties with the press, especially reporters from mainstream media. He recruited me—as well as Darman—to talk to reporters on background or off the record so that we could help shape the public narrative and pick up early warnings if big investigative stories were about to break. When internal intrigues were stirring in the West Wing, I found that reporters would tell me as much of the inside story as I could tell them.

Not long ago, Baker and I, along with his wife, Susan, got together in Houston to reminisce. We had lots of good laughs while also sorting out the lessons of those days together. We both agreed that the single most important operational change he introduced in the Reagan White House—one that would serve others well—was the creation of the Legislative Strategy Group (LSG). The LSG would meet at least once a day in Baker's office to compare notes and agree on plans of action, starting with Capitol Hill. Baker would chair; Darman would prepare the agenda (on the theory that he who controls the agenda usually controls the outcome); and I focused on communications and governance. Meese and his contingent would be there, along with Deaver and pertinent cabinet officers, lieutenants in charge of congressional relations, press, communications, and political outreach. We spent hours hashing out how to put a bill through Congress or change the public narrative. Most decisions sent up to a president are close calls. We would not go to Reagan seeking a decision until we had thoroughly thought through every option. It seemed unfair to him and to the process if we went flying in and out of his office without being prepared first at the staff level—as we have seen in other administrations. Baker has written many times how his family early in life instructed him in the Five Ps: "Prior Preparation Prevents Poor

Performances." That's the philosophy he followed throughout those White House years.

Baker has long struck me as a case study in how to manage up, down, and sideways. And how to make it work with the ultimate boss, President Reagan. Over the course of his first term, with Baker's help, Reagan passed economic legislation early on that unleashed a long period of robust growth. Moreover, alongside a commission led by Alan Greenspan, Baker guided the White House and Congress in overhauling Social Security—one of the most important bipartisan bills of the past forty years. Not only was Reagan reelected in a landslide, but his vice president, George H.W. Bush, went on to win the election after that (some called it "Reagan's third term"). As his grandfather had instructed him, Jim Baker studied and worked hard all of his life, but I sure am glad he didn't "keep out of politics."

EIGHT

LEADING YOUR TEAM

When you envision effective leaders of the past, you might recall an image of John F. Kennedy in the thick of his presidency. One of the most memorable photos of him captures Kennedy standing alone in the shadows of the Oval Office, slightly hunched over, the weight of the world on his back, *Camelot* perhaps playing softly in the background. For decades, Americans have considered him the perfect embodiment of a leader.

Leadership studies have historically focused on such lone, heroic individuals grappling with the forces of darkness. But much has changed over the years. In this new century, rather than battling alone, leaders are often embedded in teams, their success resting heavily upon how well they and all other parties collaborate with each other. "Creative collaboration" has become the new model of well-run organizations. The most memorable photo of President Obama in office, for example, is not in the loneliness of the Oval Office but in the Situation Room of the West Wing, where he and half a dozen members of his national security team are huddled together, electronically engaged with Navy SEALs halfway around the world, ridding

137

the world of Osama bin Laden. Working closely together—a tight, effective team.

Consider another recent example that illustrates an even more dramatic departure from the past. As discussed earlier, Black Lives Matter was a nonprofit start-up created in 2013 by three young Black women angered by the inhumane treatment of young Black Americans by police and white supremacists. The organization took off in 2017 when George Zimmerman, a white man, was acquitted in the fatal shooting of Trayvon Martin, an innocent young Black boy. The surprise acquittal touched off massive street demonstrations with BLM at the forefront. Soon some thirty communities had organized local chapters of BLM and formed alliances with other like-minded groups. But BLM resisted the notion of empowering a single, heroic figure to represent it publicly. It was to be decentralized. Its founders intentionally wanted power to flow from the bottom up instead of top down.

The rise of BLM and other bottom-up structures has clearly taught us that in this new century, teams have become as important as individuals in shaping our future. Reflecting on how leadership has changed, I am reminded of the advice the first CEO of the Gates Foundation, Patty Stonesifer, frequently gave to young social entrepreneurs. She recited an old African proverb: "If you want to go fast, go alone; but if you want to go far, go together." As Patty recognized, that doesn't mean we no longer need to develop individual leaders of character and courage. Far from it—we need them more. They remain indispensable in pulling together organizations, determining strategy, and inspiring others. But in today's world, a leader's principal job is also to recruit and empower members of a good team. Going forward together is now the way to get big things done.

BASICS IN BUILDING A GOOD TEAM

Since entering professional life, I have had the privilege to lead half a dozen teams—some good, some great—and my teammates have always taught me a lot along the way. The teams have been diverse both in structure and purpose—a group of fifty sailors aboard a navy ship home ported in Japan in the late 1960s; a small team of six or seven chosen by the Nixon White House to help in overhauling the military draft; the speechwriting and research team of about fifty at that same White House; a communications team of about a hundred at the Reagan White House; an editorial and administrative staff of about a hundred plus as top editor for *U.S. News & World Report*; and a team of several dozen in building the Center for Public Leadership (CPL) at the Harvard Kennedy School. I have also served on two dozen nonprofit boards and led several of them. And as noted earlier, I have learned a great deal about the promise of young, aspiring leaders by working closely with them—our two children on fast tracks, a series of talented college graduates who have formed my core team, and a stream of students in my classrooms eager to change the world. They have all been a blessing.

Drawing upon those experiences as well as a rapidly growing literature from other public policy schools and business schools plus outstanding biographers and historians, let me spend the rest of this chapter addressing three central questions for leaders of tomorrow:

- What are the basics you should know in creating a good team?
- How can you take a team from good to great?
- When is a team best served by less hierarchy and more collaboration?

Neither the academic nor the management gurus have yet found definitive answers to these questions, but they have begun conversations that are pointing the way, whether in business, government, or the social sector. The late J. Richard Hackman, a a former colleague of mine at Harvard, was highly influential in arguing that instead of focusing heavily upon the role of individuals in creating and running an organization, we should first determine what surrounding conditions enable teams to flourish. In his pathbreaking book *Leading Teams: Setting the Stage for Great Performances*, Hackman identified five conditions that help a team flourish: personal responsibilities on the team are well defined; its supporting structure is solid; the team has a compelling direction; the overall context is supportive; and the players have expert coaching. The leader's prime role, he says, is to ensure such conditions are in place. Let's take a quick look at the three most important enabling conditions Hackman identifies.

Well-Defined, Mutually Acceptable Responsibilities

In too many instances, Hackman points out, teams have suffered because individual responsibilities have overlapped, members have strayed outside their lanes, or because, frankly, the principals could hardly abide each other. In the Carter administration, for example, the secretary of state, Cyrus Vance, was a dove, but the national security advisor, Zbigniew Brzezinski, was a fierce hawk. They frequently clashed over policy and power. When President Carter was preparing for a commencement address at the Naval Academy, each advisor sent in a draft reflecting his own point of view. Asked what to do, Carter replied: "Weave them together." The speech was a mishmash, and so was the policy.

Clashes of that kind also plagued the early Reagan years because Al Haig, the secretary of state, believed he had been charged with overall leadership on national security while the secretary of defense, Caspar Weinberger, vehemently disagreed. Early in the administration, *Time* magazine ran a cover story featuring Haig and a headline calling him "The Vicar." That caused an internal uproar. Clashes soon became titanic until Reagan pulled the plug on Haig's tenure. Trump, of course, faced many of the same challenges, and as we are learning from many tell-all books, life in that White House was complete chaos.

Strong Enabling Structures

Another basic requirement for team building, identified by Hackman, is the importance of creating an efficient, effective process for making decisions and carrying them out. When the World Health Organization reported an Ebola outbreak in March 2014, President Obama and his team had not previously anticipated such an event, but they were well equipped to fashion a response in real time. As reported by *Vanity Fair*, the administration "had clear protocols and chains of command for these kinds of threats." They knew how to mobilize a federal response and, perhaps as important, had a leadership team that supported its mission and its research. Ron Klain was appointed the Ebola czar. Very smart and well organized, Klain corralled different arms of the federal government to work in sync, effectively and quickly doing all they could to combat the virus. In the end, Ebola barely left a mark on the country—thanks in large part to the rapid cooperation and organization of Obama's team.

Afterward, they realized just how vital structures had been in enabling their success in a pandemic, and they created a permanent unit within the National Security Council to prepare for future ones. They also wrote up a sixty-nine-page guidebook on future handling of emerging infectious disease threats, including novel coronaviruses. When the coronavirus pandemic struck in 2020, however, the new Trump administration rejected the Obama playbook—indeed, they threw it out. When storm clouds were gathering, President Trump averted his eyes. When crises hit, Trump did take one important step—reducing the flow of Chinese into the United States. But his overall approach was stumbling, uncertain, and focused more on his own political welfare than on the welfare of the country. His team was as discombobulated as he was. His national security advisor, John Bolton, actually closed the NSC unit designed to protect the country in a public health crisis. Neither Trump nor many on his team trusted science and federal institutions. Even more damning, they persuaded large sections of the country to refuse vaccinations, leaving us exposed to new outbreaks. As of the winter of 2022, over 900,000 Americans have died from the pandemic.

Obama's team had ultimately proved effective because they relied upon existing structures and a clear chain of command. Trump's team failed in large part because they had no such structure and thus no uniform response. As Hackman recognized, it is easy to credit the person at the top of the organization chart for leading a good team, but embedded structures are the supportive tissue that enables a team to succeed. Notably, when President Biden was inaugurated in 2021, Ron Klain came with him as his chief of staff. His experience in pushing back Ebola—putting a strong, supportive structure in place—proved invaluable in tackling the coronavirus.

A Compelling Direction

Finally, in thinking about what it takes to create a good team, let's consider the role of a leader in setting the course. In his popular book *Leadership Is an Art*, Max De Pree wrote: "The first responsibility of a leader is to define reality. The last is to say thank you. In between the two, the leader must become a servant and a debtor." Giving meaning to work and setting forth a compelling direction—that is the essence of the most successful teams. Throughout our history, Americans have banded together in informal groups or teams to pursue equal rights for all. Elizabeth Cady Stanton could not have partnered with Susan B. Anthony for over half a century in leading the women's rights and suffrage campaign had they not shared a clear set of goals. Nor would Thurgood Marshall have joined the leadership of the NAACP and transformed it into a powerful force for racial justice. One after another, important teams have found meaning in working for higher causes.

Emerging alive from Nazi concentration camps, the psychiatrist

Viktor Frankl poured himself into a book recounting his experiences. In only nine days, he wrote his 1946 bestseller, *Man's Search for Meaning*. In it, he concluded that the difference between those who had lived and those who had died in the camps turned on one thing: meaning. Those who found meaning in life were much more hopeful and resilient. He argued to other prisoners that they should stop asking what they could still expect from life; instead, they should ask what life expected from them.

Wise leaders understand that regardless of whether a team is formed in the public or the private sector, morale rests heavily upon the degree that its employees—its teammates, if you will—believe they are serving a larger purpose. In the Manhattan Project, for example, the army was so worried about the secrecy of its race to build an atomic bomb that the number who knew the actual purpose of the project was kept purposefully low. Soon a physicist who later won a Nobel, Richard Feynman, found that technicians on his team were performing at a discouragingly mediocre level. Feynman asked J. Robert Oppenheimer if he could disclose the mission of the project to his team on an extremely close-held basis. Oppenheimer agreed, and as soon as Feynman confided in the technicians that they were playing a central role in developing the bomb, he saw "a complete transformation" in their work. They began laboring into the night and increased their productivity tenfold. They were inspired by the thought of bringing the Allies to victory.

TURNING A GOOD TEAM INTO A GREAT ONE

So far we have focused on what it takes to build a good team. But what does it take to turn that good team into a great one? What's the magic behind the very few who become great ones? As the Hackman analysis suggests, I would argue that in order to build a *good* team, organizers must put into place management rules and structures that enable the team to excel. The emphasis must be on achieving a consistent, strong level of performance. But a *great* team requires not just an excellent management structure; it also requires women and men at the top who share high aspirations, keen imaginations, and ways of working with others that spark great performances. They are exceptional in word and deed.

In the 1990s, a former professor at Stanford, Jim Collins, became a guru on building great teams. He first achieved a following with a book on why some companies last and others fail. After that success, he assembled a team of some twenty researchers to undertake a five-year study of twenty-eight major companies, asking why good and even mediocre ones can break out of the pack and achieve lasting reputations. Collins once told me that in his initial investigations, he asked his researchers to fence off studies of individual leaders. "Forget about them for now," he said. He thought that leaders were already given too much credit for the performance of their organizations, and he wanted to focus more on general practices of a corporation—that is, on which teams worked best. What surprised him was how often his researchers found that quality individual leaders in a company—especially in top management—could not be ignored. Indeed, they were central to the success of a great organization. Equally surprising was the profile that emerged of the best leader: "an individual who blends personal humility with intense professional will." Intense will? Yes, said the research. But personal humility? For those who had come through the 1990s when CEOs like Jack Welch were celebrities, few would have expected that the 2000s would become the decade of the humble CEO.

As unlikely as it seemed, Collins won the argument about what it takes. In 2001, he and his researchers published their results in their book titled *Good to Great*. It sold 4 million copies and became a number one bestseller. To this day, it remains a "bible" of aspiring companies. Later on, Collins wrote a monograph asking why social enterprises can also become great. That too was a bestseller.

Getting the Right Team on the Bus

The most influential advice in Collins's *Good to Great*, still pertinent today, was not about management structure but about the connectivity of people on a team. As noted earlier, "Get the right people on the bus, the right people in the right seats, and the wrong people off the bus." That has become one of the most quoted refrains in the literature of leadership. As proof, the Collins team cited the fifteen-year success of Wells Fargo in the 1980s and 1990s. Its leadership realized that big changes were coming in the banking industry, but they couldn't be sure what changes. So they changed their focus: Instead of asking *what* they should do, they asked *who* should do it. They built a pipeline of talent into the firm, and over fifteen years, starting in 1983, they had a spectacular run as a company. Many of their hires went on to become CEOs of other big companies. As Collins found, every organization depends heavily upon the capacity of its leadership to spot, recruit, and empower topflight talent.

In the 1960s and 1970s, America's space program gained a similar reputation for the quality of men and women chosen. Tom Wolfe spent a couple of years interviewing astronauts and their families, marveling at the physical as well as psychological demands placed upon them. In his 1979 bestseller, he memorably said of those who had won out that they had the "Right Stuff." The Apollo program over the years employed a staggering 400,000 people. Recently, we have learned that a significant number in critical roles were women and people of color. Some three dozen Black women, for example, worked tirelessly as human computers, calculating the trajectory of space missions. Their calculations were so respected inside the organization that John Glenn would not depart for his first orbital mission until he knew that Katherine Johnson, a Black woman responsible for calculating his flight path, had given the all-clear signal.

Getting the Wrong People Off the Bus

As Jim Collins recognized, a great organization has to do more than get the right people on the bus in the right seats; it must also get the wrong people off. That is more challenging than it looks, as I discovered on my own journey. When Mort Zuckerman, the new owner of the weekly newsmagazine *U.S. News & World Report*, asked me to be his top editor in 1986, he made it clear he thought the magazine had grown sleepy and needed an overhaul. He directed that we fire a couple dozen reporters. They were the wrong people on the bus; we needed to build a new team, he said. I had never fired professional people en masse before. I was also new to the organization and didn't know who was good and who wasn't. I wanted to be fair and wanted to protect the reputation of those leaving as well as the reputation of the magazine as a good place to work. In short, I needed to proceed with great sensitivity.

Over the next several weeks, as I resolved who should go, I called them in one by one for a private talk. "I am afraid we have to end our relationship," I said, "but we also need to protect your reputation. It will not be helpful to you in finding a new job if word gets out that you were fired. So here's what I propose: We keep this secret between the two of us. You spend the next ninety days quietly looking for another job. When you find one, we will announce that you have decided to accept a new post at a different publication, and we will have a big, festive going-away party. If you need more than ninety days, let me know. But until then, mum's the word." I was proud that almost every one of them found another job and, with heads high, moved on with their lives. As for the magazine, Mort's investment of energy and money sure helped as we scored record gains in circulation and advertising. These days, *U.S. News* is making a tidy profit as an online publication.

A Roll Call of Great Groups

A quarter century ago, in a book titled *Organizing Genius*, Warren Bennis and Patricia Ward Biederman coauthored a glowing account of great groups and how they collaborate. Americans, they pointed out, are a people who love heroes, affording them more status than other individuals and groups. But almost without design, groups of people have successfully blended individual and collective efforts to produce something new and wonderful.

In addition to the Manhattan Project and Project Apollo, the Bennis-Biederman honor roll of great teams includes:

- Steve Jobs at Apple, who created the Macintosh computer, pursuing his dream of putting "a dent in the universe."
- Xerox's Palo Alto Research Center (PARC), which played a key role in tech innovations such as the modern personal computer, ethernet, and laser printing.
- Lockheed Martin's "Skunk Works," a team given a high degree of autonomy within the corporation and freedom from excessive bureaucracy, which achieved success in secretly designing U.S. aircraft at the height of the Cold War.
- The Bauhaus movement, which attracted to England and the United States pathbreaking architects and artists fleeing from Nazi Germany.
- Black Mountain College in North Carolina, a storied experimental institution of the 1930s and 1940s that attracted leading artists, composers, poets, architects, and designers. It served as an incubator and a refuge for modern artists who were under attack from Senator Joe McCarthy.

Since Bennis and Biederman published their book over twenty years ago, there has, of course, been a massive stream of other innovations, especially in science and technology. But what they wrote then remains true today: The twentieth and early twenty-first centuries, for all their flaws, have been "a golden age of collaborative achievement for America." Indeed, as Tocqueville argued almost two hundred years ago, Americans seem to have a genius for collective action—when we are united!

What Distinguishes Great Groups?

Most great groups have characteristics that separate them from average organizations. They tend to be motivated internally and like to be problem solvers. "If you can dream it, you can do it," Walt Disney believed; he was one of the original leaders of a great group and is still revered in Hollywood today. Participants in great groups see jobs as missions and don't mind living and working in challenging surroundings. At Black Mountain College, for example, students had to build their own living quarters with hammers, nails, and wood.

Recruiters for great groups want to know whether applicants have a passion for excellence, a talent for problem solving, and an ability to work and play well with others. Since the days of Thomas Edison, groups have often created their own sets of measurements. Edison would give job applicants tests with 150 demanding questions, and he timed them with a stopwatch. Examples from the Edison quiz: "How is leather tanned?" "What must you pay for 12 grains of gold?" In our own day, Google has become well known for its questioning. One sample: "Why is a manhole cover round?" When I and my accompanying students spent a day at their new quarters in Midtown Manhattan, the halls of Google were abuzz with activity, employees skating from one office to another. Similar to other tech companies, Google has had its struggles in recent years, but I have rarely seen such a playful, irrepressible work environment. They were having a blast.

One caution about great teams: They should not be confused with a team of great stars. A team of stars is made up of individuals looking out for themselves; players on a great team look out for each other. In many competitive organizations, however, there is still a tendency to believe that if you just assemble enough stars, they will naturally be a winning combination. Geoffrey Colvin, a respected columnist at *Fortune*, argues that you can't count on a bunch of hotshots jelling as a team. In 2004, for example, the U.S. Olympic basketball team filled its ranks with NBA stars who had little use for one another. It didn't work: they lost to Argentina in the semifinals and wound up taking home the bronze. In contrast, as Colvin writes, the U.S. Olympic hockey team of 1980 was built explicitly on anti-dream-team principles. "I'm not looking for the best players," their coach said. "I'm lookin' for the right players." The Americans he recruited were a bunch of college kids with an average age of twenty-one; the Soviets had stars who had been skating together for years. The U.S. team was seen as heavy underdogs at Lake Placid. But in a dramatic showdown—what some have called the biggest sports event of the twentieth century, the "Miracle on Ice"—the U.S. team upset the Soviets in the semifinals and went on to win the gold.

THE LEGACY OF GROUP-CENTERED LEADERSHIP

In our national memory, the civil rights movement evokes images of Martin Luther King Jr. addressing a sea of followers at the Lincoln Memorial. Perhaps, alternatively, we envision Rosa Parks sitting in the front of that bus in Montgomery, Alabama. We have been taught that leaders like John Lewis, Malcom X, and Thurgood Marshall paved the way forward as spokespeople for change. But there were others who stayed resolutely in the background.

One figure history seldom remembers is a woman by the name of Ella Baker. Baker did not deploy soaring rhetoric nor draw national attention in the way that heroes like MLK did. But through her dedication to a different theory of leadership and through her persistence, she brought empowerment to communities across the country. In the eyes of most Americans, the civil rights movement was largely run by the "Big Six"—it was very much top down. Ella Baker was a driving force in making it much more of a bottom-up, grassroots movement. We are seeing the reverberations in movements of today—just as her theory of leadership is being tested.

Baker's disciplined commitment to work at the grassroots level allowed her to bring real change to communities across the country. She began her activism early in life, starting as national director of the Young Negroes' Cooperative League during the Depression while working on labor issues in Harlem. Building a strong network of relationships, she then applied to work as an assistant field secretary of the NAACP—a job that would bring her back to her native South to recruit members and build new chapters. As she made her way up in the organization, she became increasingly critical of its focus on expanding membership numbers without actively engaging those members in programming; the NAACP's focus on legal battles meant that the potential of its hundreds of thousands of members went largely untapped. Baker eventually moved away from the organization, serving other civil rights groups, including a two-and-a-half-year stint as executive director of the Southern Christian Leadership Conference. Again, she felt her grassroots philosophy was underappreciated, as large groups of Black women and young people went ignored by the programs of the SCLC.

Baker's work at both the SCLC and the NAACP did not satisfy her goals of building the civil rights movement from the ground up; when students began staging sit-ins in the 1960s, however, Baker capitalized by leveraging the multitude of local connections she had built over the years, spreading word about the protests across the country. She saw that students everywhere were eager to act and invited them to convene at her alma mater, Shaw University; from that conference, the Student Nonviolent Coordinating Committee was born. Finally, she was able to create the organization she had always dreamed of, one in which women and young people were active participants, rural communities were engaged, and leadership was encouraged and developed at the local level. John Lewis, who was participating in the Nashville sit-ins at the time, was unable to join that meeting but soon after became heavily involved in SNCC—eventually becoming its chairman. Baker's belief that the movement should focus more on grassroots change very much resonated with Lewis, who believed that the student movement "was as much against this nation's traditional Black leadership structure as it was against racial segregation and discrimination." SNCC activists continued their sit-in campaign following that initial meeting, then extended actions through other campaigns, including significant involvement in the Freedom Rides. After the Freedom Rides, SNCC activists spread across the South, connecting with communities and going door to door in efforts to register voters. Their work was not always glamorous, but through hundreds of sustained conversations, they were able to build trust in the communities in which they worked and made real inroads in encouraging Black people to vote.

Though Baker was in many ways a leader of SNCC, she made sure to empower students to make decisions and lead on their own. In that sense, Baker fostered what has been referred to as "group-centered leadership" rather than creating a "leader-centered group." She said, "I have always thought what is needed is the development of people who are interested not in being leaders as much as in developing leadership among other people." She insisted on the importance of "organizing people to be self-sufficient rather than to be dependent upon the charismatic leader." Baker understood what so few of her time would acknowledge: Sometimes the slow, hard work of reform comes from the efforts of many, working together over weeks, months, and even years. They did not need a figurehead to direct them; each member of the SNCC felt they had their own stake in furthering the efforts of the organization.

Today, we are increasingly seeing organizations emerge that follow the group-centered leadership model of "Miss Baker," as her disciples affectionately called her. Pro-democracy protests spanning from the Middle East to Hong Kong have taken on this form, as they gain momentum and supporters through social media and organic organizing tactics. In many ways, global movements for climate action and gender equality have done the same. With the rise of social media and the democratization of exchanging ideas, local issues can draw national attention overnight. Some people refer to this new model of leadership as "nonhierarchical"; others call it "leaderless." Patrisse Cullors, a co-founder of BLM—perhaps the most prominent contemporary example of this mode of leadership—prefers the term "leader-full," suggesting that the "leaderless" designation discounts the multitude of leaders in the movement who propel its work forward. Whatever you call it, there is no doubt that organizations without a single spokesperson are on the rise—and they're leaving a mark on our national landscape.

In many ways, this model stems naturally from the collaboration we see in great teams. By entrusting individuals with leadership responsibilities and empowering them to advance a set of goals, leader-full organizations require a high level of group trust and cooperation. Deploying this model allows for those at the margins—women and people of color, as Baker experienced, but also other underrepresented individuals—to have a central voice and a seat at the table. Anyone can be involved in a movement like BLM or pro-democracy demonstrations; all it takes is showing up at a rally, volunteering for a nearby chapter, or answering a local call to action. As everyday people rise to build these movements, they have intentionally steered away from appointing charismatic figureheads and dealmakers. We have learned from Martin Luther King Jr.'s tragic assassination that the death of a leader can cause a movement to lose its force. Beyond protecting its leaders and interests, Erica Chenoweth, who studies nonviolent resistance at the Kennedy School, notes that decentralized organizations can also respond more quickly to changing dynamics, unburdened by the bureaucracy of leaders calling the shots. What is more, a wide range of goals can be advocated in a leader-full movement. There need not be singular focus on a specific policy, which allows for a high degree of intersectional collaboration.

With these benefits, of course, come shortcomings and logistical challenges. In a crisis, for example, a leader-full organization does not have one individual calling the shots. Additionally, the lack of central control can lead to ideological fragmentation and departure from the goals of the group. For instance, when a small number of white people took to vandalizing stores during the BLM protests in 2020, the conservative right capitalized upon the extremist behavior to further their own views and pointed to it as representative of the whole movement. Even though the vast majority of demonstrations were peaceful, Black Lives Matter gained a reputation in more conservative, and frequently bigoted, circles for violence and radicalism. The group unfortunately was the victim of racist slurs, leading some to believe any Black protest movement is inherently angry and violent. Last, and most crucial, when a leader-full organization becomes *too* full of leaders, disagreement is inevitable in trying to translate goals into policy changes. The jury is out on whether groups like the Sunrise Movement, March for Our Lives, and BLM will see their demands answered with government action. One thing, however, is sure: By empowering a diverse intersection of individuals—young and old, Black and white—to become leaders, these movements have caught the attention of the world. Public discourse has undoubtedly been swayed in response to their actions, and our political leaders are taking heed. On a series of issues from racial equity to climate change, gay rights to gun control, activists have already begun to sway public opinion in their direction, and political leaders are paying attention. If activist groups can inspire a new generation, they can transform the country.

CHAPTER 9

THE ART OF PUBLIC PERSUASION

One day in 1830, at a shipyard in Baltimore, a thirteen-year-old enslaved boy listened intently as a group of white boys whom he knew recited passages to each other from a reader assigned in school. Intrigued, the young boy saved up fifty cents polishing boots and went to a local bookstore to buy his own copy of *The Columbian Orator*.

As recalled by David Blight, editor of a recently republished version of the book, the young boy turned to the *Orator* for instruction and inspiration almost as much as he did to the Bible. He copied from both, studying and reciting lines to himself while also drawing from their moral suasion. "Every opportunity I got I used to read this book," he observed years later.

A year later, a twenty-two-year-old farm boy on the Illinois prairie also discovered *The Columbian Orator* and soon devoured it himself. He too had only dribs and drabs of formal schooling—a total of a year or so—and was hungry for self-education. He was drawn not only to the moral tales in the *Orator* but also to its collection of speeches from the British parliament emphasizing the importance of democracy and freedom.

Remarkably, the two would meet for the first time thirty-three years later at the most unlikely of places: the White House. Frederick Bailey had changed his name to Frederick Douglass and become the greatest Black leader and orator of his time. His host at the White House was Abraham Lincoln, arguably the greatest American leader and orator of all time.

The parallels in their two lives are striking, of course. To paraphrase David Blight, they both rose from below, mastered the English language, and spoke to America as no one else had about how the country might reinvent itself. Their lives also offer lessons about leadership that are as relevant now as they were in the nineteenth century. Today as then, developing your capacity for persuasion—finding your own voice, learning how to mobilize others—can be the most powerful force at your command. You do not need to be born with a silver spoon in your mouth; indeed, those who work most closely with their communities—or have proximity, as human rights lawyer and founder of the Equal Justice Initiative Bryan Stevenson would say—are often best at judging their needs. What matters most is that you learn a mastery of public persuasion through hard work and lots of practice—just as Douglass and Lincoln did. Brilliant speaking is not a gift; it must be earned.

Public discourse has changed in recent years, of course, for both good and bad. Lengthy expressions of thought have given way to tweets, the writing of letters has given way to emails. In many ways, today's technology has democratized communication; we are reaching people where they are, giving the world access to the tools once available only to a smaller group. But with progress has often come a degradation of our public discourse. We speak more today in political platitudes and sound bites than we once did. In the seven debates that Lincoln and Stephen A. Douglas had in their senatorial campaign of 1858, each spoke for ninety minutes and on a single subject: the expansion of slavery. Curious people walked as many as nine hours to hear them, then stood in a field for three hours to listen. During the presidential campaign of 2020, by contrast, in the first debate between Donald Trump and Joe Biden, the candidates spoke for only thirty-nine and thirty-eight minutes respectively and covered fifteen topics. Argument gave way to assertion. In 1985, educator Neil Postman captured the sentiments of his day with his bestselling *Amusing Ourselves to Death: Public Discourse in the Age of Show Business*. And that was thirty years before Trump. We are no longer amused.

The roots of public discourse were first planted some twenty-five hundred years ago in ancient Athens, when Greeks began to experiment with more democratic forms of governance. Practiced orators eked out a living by walking from one community to the next, offering lessons to men caught up in politics and governance. Eventually, orators opened schools in which Aristotle and Plato would teach. In the eyes of Cicero, Isocrates was the father of oratory. He got his start— no joke—as a speechwriter; over time he developed a reputation for his own speaking. Others regard Demosthenes as the most influential rhetorician of classical Greece. He was not a great speaker early on, having grown up with a weak voice and a stutter, but through arduous practice, he became more skillful and then rallied Athenians to resist the expansion of nearby Macedonia. A son of the Greek Revival of the 1830s to 1860s, when Athenian democracy was very popular in America, Lincoln liked to quote from Pericles, especially his funeral oration at the end of the first year of Athens's war with Sparta.

Over the centuries, the practice of persuasion has become so entwined with the practice of democracy that it seems likely they will survive together. Indeed, historians suggest that times of great stress and division within a society often prompt an outpouring of speeches and writings; these are moments when public intellectuals try to understand the realities of their day and to give them fresh meaning. Public persuasion, practiced as a high art, can thus become a source of unity. But we can't count on it for sure. That is why we must begin by cultivating a healthier civic environment, persuading obstructionists, as Ted Turner liked to say. "Do something. Either lead, follow or get out of the way."

Certainly, the American experience has been defined by the rhetorical leadership of men and women who have stepped forward during crucial moments and inspired others to take a high road: Patrick Henry, Thomas Jefferson, and Alexander Hamilton during the founding; Henry Clay and Daniel Webster in the early nineteenth century; Lincoln, Douglass, Sojourner Truth, and Dorothea Dix as the Civil War approached; Teddy Roosevelt during the Progressive Era; Anna Howard Shaw as women struggled for suffrage; FDR and Eleanor in the Great Depression and World War II; King, Kennedy, Reagan, Barbara Jordan, Ann Richards, and Hillary Clinton in more recent times. Studying their lives and their methods of public persuasion remains indispensable if you want to understand America's past. Surprisingly, the American who became one of our most gifted writers, Jefferson, hated public speaking. As president, he gave only two public addresses—at his first and second inaugurals; he relied on his pen to persuade others.

Fortunately, there are those among us now who keep the fires burning here and overseas, reminding us that words and ideas can still mobilize a public following. In 2004, out of nowhere, a young Black man burst onto the national stage with a single speech. He proclaimed there is no such thing as a red America or a blue America; there is only one America. More recently, X González's emotional call at the March for Our Lives awakened the nation to the gun violence epidemic. And after a well-spoken thirty-seven-year-old woman won the prime minister's office in New Zealand, her leadership quickly became a global antithesis to that of the American then in the Oval Office. For all our poisonous differences, leaders still have the power to persuade.

The question is how. How can you master the study and practice of public persuasion? How should you begin? How can you practice? How can you develop a public reputation so that others want to hear and read what you have to say? Let's turn now to those very practical questions.

FINDING YOUR PUBLIC VOICE

Among the many quotations President Kennedy liked to recite, one of his favorites was an exchange in Shakespeare:

> GLENDOWER: I can call spirits from the vasty deep.
>
> HOTSPUR: Why, so can I, or so can any man;
> But will they come, when you do call for them?
>
> Shakespeare, *King Henry IV, Part 1*

Kennedy was also a great fan of Churchill's and learned from him that one of the first orders of business for an aspiring orator is to develop your own public voice—one that will draw spirits from the vasty deep when you do call for them. Churchill was not a brilliant student; in middle school, he failed a course and was held back, and as a result he never studied Latin. As it turned out, that was a lucky break: In retaking his English course, he studied the English language so intently that he developed a mastery and put it to great use. He did more than memorize great speeches. Before graduation, he delivered without notes 1,200 lines of Macaulay's *Lays of Ancient Rome*. He didn't have the academic marks to be accepted at Oxford or Cambridge and wound up at Sandhurst only upon his third try. Again, a lucky break. He was posted overseas as a junior military officer and an ambitious journalist; his colorful tales of his exploits in Cuba, India, Sudan, and South Africa were so well written that he gained a following across Britain.

In his off hours, Churchill also became a voracious reader and had his mother send him trunkloads of books. Among them were verbatim accounts of debates in Parliament; Churchill read the debates and then carefully thought what he would say if he were on one side of the aisle or the other. He also began to read extensively among the English classics like Shakespeare and the King James Bible, along with the works of historians and poets. By the time he returned to Britain, he had developed enough public skills to enter politics. He was ready.

At twenty-six, he won his first seat in Parliament. And he remained in the public eye for nearly sixty years.

Over the decades, through speeches, writings, and parliamentary debates, he developed a singular public voice. "Churchill mobilized the English language and sent it into battle," said the journalist Edward R. Murrow. As noted, he would invest as much as an hour of preparation for each minute that he would hold on the floor of Parliament. "Of all the talents bestowed upon men," Churchill is quoted as saying, "none is so precious as the gift of oratory. He who enjoys it wields a power more durable than that of a great king. He is an independent voice in the world."

Developing your own voice is often seen as developing your own style or a distinctive philosophical view. For better or worse, Donald Trump has one style and perspective; Barack Obama has a completely different one. Everyone can spot the differences. Similarly, if someone blindfolded you and then read out loud editorials from *The New York Times* and *The Wall Street Journal*, you would instantly know which is which.

But voice also has a more significant meaning. It is your passion in life—what gives meaning to you deep inside. When you want to speak that voice, it comes surging out of you. In his famous essay "Self-Reliance," Ralph Waldo Emerson writes about listening to that inner voice and going with it: "Insist on yourself; never imitate."

Lincoln was just another politician from Illinois until southerners in Congress threatened to spread slavery into the new western states. That triggered deep passions in Lincoln, and he devoted himself thereafter to changing the nation's course. Early on, Martin Luther King Jr. saw himself as a preacher—and only a preacher. But in Montgomery, as he preached to his congregations about the evils of segregation, he felt he had to get into the streets with them, according to Garry Wills. That's when he began to find his voice. Time and again, I have found that the most effective communicators are those who speak to audiences from their inner voice.

William James notably wrote: "I have often thought that the best way to define a man's character would be to seek out the particular mental or moral attitude in which, when it came upon him, he felt himself deeply and intensely active and alive. At such moments, there is a voice inside which speaks and says, 'This is the real me.'"

When is your voice most effective? When your passion gives voice to the people themselves. When what you believe and what you say actually stir a resonant chord within them. When Gandhi was summoned to return home to India from South Africa in order to lead the fight against colonialism, he refused at first to attack in public. Instead, he traveled third class across his native land for a year, listening hard to the voices of his people. When he finally spoke up, it was apparent that he was giving voice to the people themselves.

Finding your voice is not an easy or quick process. It usually comes from living life for a while, sifting through your experiences, beginning to understand yourself. Sometimes, as we have seen, self-understanding comes early because of a crisis in your life or a crisis in the world beyond. In the 1960s and 1970s, many young Americans found their voices in the controversies raging over civil rights, women's rights, Vietnam, and the environmental movement. Many today find their voices over the systemic inequalities facing us. But for most, finding your voice comes with time—as you develop your interior life and reflect upon it. So many of us are wrapped up in our professional or external lives in our twenties and thirties—and even later—and there seems less time than we would like for self-examination. But over the years, we start to pay attention to that "inner voice" described by William James and Emerson. Begin by noticing those events and issues around you that strike a resonant chord. Speak up when you believe in something, or when you oppose what is going on in the world around you. Be conscious of what is true to you and your values. Then you will discover your true inner voice.

THE BASICS OF PUBLIC SPEAKING

Some years ago, a pollster reported on the three greatest fears of Americans. Their results: Number three were bugs, snakes, and other animals; second was heights; the greatest fear was speaking in front of an audience. Even the best have experienced difficulty. Winston Churchill spoke well in his maiden speech in Parliament, but in his second, he had incomplete notes, tried to cover too much, and fainted in the middle. The actress Rosalind Russell put it more pointedly: She compared public speaking to standing naked in front of an audience of strangers and turning around . . . very slowly. So please don't feel you are alone if you feel scared in your first few appearances. You are actually better when you have some butterflies because your anxiety injects you with energy.

In fact, the more experienced you are with speaking, the more exhilaration you may find. Over the past four decades, I have given well over a thousand speeches. Many were in universities or for nonprofits. Others came through the Washington Speakers Bureau (WSB). The latter brought honorariums that helped to put our two kids through school and allowed me to spend more time in the public arena. I also came to see that the opportunity to speak before different audiences can greatly broaden my understanding and appreciation of our complex country. It can be great fun, too.

Up front, you just need to learn some basics about public speaking. Let's start with explaining a few:

First, Know Your Purpose

Before you stand in front of an audience, you had better know what purpose you are trying to serve. Are you there to inform, to advocate, to spur into action, to commemorate, or to entertain? Each requires its own distinctive approach. It matters too what time you speak. A morning presentation typically is one that informs. Your audience is most receptive to a serious talk then. Over lunch, you can also inform, but you had better wind in a couple of funny stories. When I was scheduled to speak at a midsize lunch a few years ago, an older gent in the audience began snoring loudly while I was being introduced! As for the evening, try to speak before dinner; after dinner, when you get a microphone around nine-thirty, half the audience is eager to go home. In Florida, I was once told by my evening host, "Don't go late. Remember, we observe the HBT rule here." "HBT? What's that?" I asked. "Horizontal by ten!" he replied.

Second, Have a Clear Message

What does this audience want from you and how can you deliver? A speech is not an opportunity to say what's on your mind; it is an opportunity to address what's on their minds. Through my friends at WSB, I have learned to spend half an hour or so with sponsors a week or two before an upcoming event so they can brief me on audience concerns. Arriving at the site, I play cub reporter, seeking out the leaders of the group for their latest take on whatever might be of interest to them on that day. Again, learning about your host can be a hugely educational experience for you. One more point: Remember that in giving a speech, *you* are often the message—people evaluate what you have to say by whom you appear to be.

Third, Pay Attention to the Key Elements of a Speech

Aristotle and other ancient Greeks elevated the study of rhetoric so that for most of Western history, it became one of the seven basic liberal arts (the trivium of grammar, logic, and rhetoric; the quadrivium of geometry, arithmetic, astronomy, and music). Rhetoric had widespread appeal as a study of not only oratory but also ethics. The liberal arts themselves were at the heart of university educations until the twentieth century, when we started to abandon them.

Even so, much of the teaching by the ancients survives to this day where oratory is taught. If you want to excel at public speaking, I urge you to become acquainted with studies of the humanities. In his influential writings of the mid-twentieth century, Mortimer Adler argued that oratory is by definition the art of persuasion and that, as the ancients believed, there are three main elements of oratory: logos, pathos, and ethos. These formed the tripod dating back to Aristotle. A moment on each element and then we will see how they fit together:

- *Ethos* signifies a person's character. People will listen to you attentively only if they believe in your credibility, trust, and likability. Ethos stood for the identity of the speaker in the Greek mind. Sometimes one can best open minds through humor. The famous economist Joseph Schumpeter visited Harvard on his eightieh birthday. He reportedly said that he had always harbored three ambitions in life: to be the world's greatest economist, the greatest horseman, and the greatest lover. Now that he was older, he said, he felt he had to give up one of those ambitions. He no longer wanted to be the world's greatest horseman.
- *Logos* is the reasoning of a speaker in advancing an argument. A speaker resorts to logos not to produce conviction but to convince a listener to prefer one path over another. Logos is much more important than generally realized.
- *Pathos:* As opposed to an appeal to reason, pathos is an appeal to emotion. Most of us are moved by the heart as much as the head. As the philosopher George Campbell has argued, "When persuasion is the end, passion also must be engaged." A speech that is entirely rational stirs neither the imagination nor the soul of an audience. Poetry enters where prose does not.

A well-constructed speech often follows a pattern: Your introducer tells the audience why you deserve their attention (ethos), you perhaps open with a funny story (pathos) before moving into your key arguments (logos), and then you build to a stirring ending that leaves people buzzing about your call to action (pathos).

Fourth, the Importance of Stories

To paraphrase Mark Twain, every good speaker should have the calm confidence of a Christian with four aces up his sleeve. Deep into a speech with too much dryness, you need to be able to pluck those stories out of the air and entertain as well as persuade your audience. Kathleen Hall Jamieson, a specialist in communications in the electronic age, points out that Ronald Reagan never made a speech to rival FDR's first inaugural or Kennedy's speech in Berlin or LBJ's on civil rights, but Reagan was a very effective communicator. He loved to tell stories and, as Jamieson says, translated words into memorable television pictures. When you have a moment, please revisit his first inaugural as he recalled the heroes who gave their last full measure in order to protect American democracy.

Fifth, Master the Elements of Eloquence

Since the days of Shakespeare in the mid-1500s, poets, dramatists, and public leaders alike have turned to the English language for eloquence of expression. Figures of speech in particular have served as a source for many of the best speeches in history: King's "I have a dream," FDR's "We have nothing to fear but fear itself," Churchill's "We shall fight on the beaches," Lincoln's "house divided," to name a few. The Oxford dictionary defines a figure of speech as a word or phrase used in a nonliteral sense for rhetorical or vivid effect—a metaphor, alliteration, and simile among them.

No one can agree how many figures of speech there are; some say over a hundred, others say there are less than twenty. If you are an aspiring writer, I suggest that you first master the half dozen or so that are commonly used.

PERSUASION IN A DIGITAL WORLD

Lincoln, perhaps our finest orator, was one of the first presidents who seized upon new technology to govern successfully. In his case, he saw that the coming of the telegraph could be a powerful tool for him as commander in chief. He would no longer have to agonize for days, awaiting word from a battlefield. He heard results within hours so that he could quickly decide on next steps and also keep his wayward generals in check. The telegraph office became his second home. In Teddy Roosevelt's era, daily newspapers had acquired mass circulations. TR soon became the darling of the White House press corps, providing them with a steady stream of news. No one had ever seen anything like it before.

For Franklin Roosevelt, the coming of the radio made a huge difference; his fireside chats, while modest in number, held the country together during the Great Depression and World War II. It was said that on a summer night, with windows open, a man could walk the streets of Baltimore and hear FDR's every word. For John F. Kennedy, it was the coming of television. He once told his press secretary, Pierre Salinger, "We couldn't do it without TV." Soon Ronald Reagan made even better use of the medium, starting a realignment of our politics. We are now experiencing yet another massive evolution: the digital age.

As with previous tech breakthroughs, the internet and social media represent enormous possibilities for young, aspiring leaders to reimagine our politics. Just ten short years before the election of Donald Trump, Facebook became available to the public after its initial launch in a Harvard dorm room. That same year, Jack Dorsey launched Twitter. Social networks like LinkedIn and MySpace had already taken off, but few of us could have anticipated the impact online life would have on our life and politics.

Several months after the public launch of Facebook and Twitter, an emerging political star by the name of Barack Obama declared his campaign for the U.S. presidency. He seemed the clear underdog—but his team had an advantage. Obama's 2008 presidential bid was the first real political foray to exploit the potential of social media. Traditional wisdom says that politicians should meet voters where they are; Obama saw that his voters—particularly the young—were online, so that is where he met them. The campaign established a page for their candidate on every major social network, leaning into Obama's personal appeal.

Randi Zuckerberg, Mark's sister and a former marketing director at Facebook, has noted that Obama's authenticity on social media was his secret sauce. "You really felt like you were connecting to him and to his campaign," she said. "They were constantly updating their profile, telling people they were on the campaign trail or eating pizza or stuck in traffic. It was this kind of voice that made everyone feel like they were in one conversation together."

Beyond establishing a relatable presence for the candidate, social media and digital mechanisms enabled Obama's team to disseminate their message, recruit volunteers, and raise money in a way never seen before. His team built a grassroots network of supporters using their own social network, MyBO, which attracted 2 million users by the close of the campaign. They digitally persuaded volunteers to host their own events, empowering those who might not typically be involved in campaigning. And crucially, by meeting the voter online, Obama was able to bring in 6.5 million digital donations. Obama's use of digital tools broke the political playbook; he used it not only to connect with his voters but to inspire people from all backgrounds and corners of the country.

The Obama campaign seized upon social media as a way to expand the reach of a U.S. senator, soon to be the presidential nominee of his party. Today, however, social media can also catapult those who are traditionally left unheard to national stardom. Take the case of a twenty-eight-year-old Latina woman and part-time bartender from the Bronx. She had quietly become a social activist in her community—going door to door for Bernie Sanders in 2016—but had never considered entering the political spotlight. When she received a recruitment call in 2017, asking her to run for Congress, she was shocked but then decided to take the plunge. With a ragtag set of volunteers in her tiny Queens political office, she officially launched a challenge to the fourth-ranking Democrat in the House, Joe Crowley. It seemed a suicide mission. But by pairing the power of her personality, intellect, and ideological force with that of social media, she has now become the darling of the left and a villain of the right. Drawing upon the timeless tools of rhetoric and voice, she crafted a potent message—one that, using pathos, ethos, and logos, related to many and paved the way for her growing popularity. Through social media, she brought her vision to the world. Most politicians spend decades in the public arena before people identify them with their three initials, but not AOC.

You don't have to agree with her politics to acknowledge that Alexandria Ocasio-Cortez is both a testament to the power of social media and an exemplar for any rising leader trying to make themselves heard across digital channels. She is a digital native, well versed in what appeals to voters on each social media platform; she is authentic, passionate, pithy, and oftentimes quite funny. Interestingly, many of her staffers were former actors turning a new page in life, their rhetorical and dramatic training proving invaluable in telling her story.

Her personal narrative was one of her primary selling points. She highlighted her real self online and leaned into the scrappy nature of her campaign. By contrast, her Democratic opponent was a ten-term incumbent whose use of social media relied upon stale political jargon. AOC's online presence seemed fresh and true to the district she represented. As of this writing, she has not let her newfound government duties change her online persona. She has remained authentic to herself and to her beliefs as she navigates life as a Millennial daughter of the Bronx. She has become known online for her Instagram Live sessions, in which she answers questions that range from nuances of a stimulus package to how she prepares for committee hearings—all the while preparing mac and cheese for dinner that evening. One

moment she will deliver a witty retort on Twitter, the next she is playing online games on Twitch while encouraging the young to vote. Just
weeks into office, she told Democratic colleagues in a training session
on social media, "The way we grow our presence is by being there."

In the digital age, embodying authentic leadership goes a long way.
It allows leaders to relate to and inspire their followers without an air
of superiority. It also allows leaders to build continuous momentum
and maintain a constantly evolving conversation. Perhaps most important, digital platforms have become a great equalizer. Just look at what
young people have self-created: AOC, the Sunrise Movement founders,
Tarana Burke, high school and college students at the forefront of BLM
activism in their communities, the Parkland students, Little Miss Flint.
Each of them might have been among the powerless and the voiceless
ten years ago. Social media has given them a new microphone through
which they can amplify their ideas. Using these tools adeptly, they have
attracted mass followings. Their authentic voices have the potential to
mobilize millions of followers in coming decades.

But let's face it: Social media can also be exploited by the forces
of darkness and evil in our society. Social media is like most other
technologies: morally neutral but able to be used to serve negative as
well as positive purposes. In recent years, we have increasingly seen
how social media is being used to deepen the chasms between left and
right, Black and white, rich and poor, urban and rural, the hopeful and
the hopeless. For the left, it is not just the anger stirred up by Donald
Trump and Tucker Carlson but their disdain for democratic traditions.
Largely through social media, they are injecting poison into the body
politic that could take years to drain out. Unfortunately, the left doesn't
have a spotless record; they too have sometimes felt the power that
comes from misrepresenting the other side. Conservatives believe, with
some justification, that they are being treated like second-class citizens,
painted by the mainstream media as a lesser group. Trust in our leaders
and our institutions is plunging, along with confidence in the future.

We shouldn't be totally surprised that so many demagogues are rising in our midst, taking advantage of new technologies. We have seen similar patterns in the past. When radio became king, FDR was not the only one to seize upon its power. In the Midwest, a Catholic priest, Father Coughlin, had a Saturday afternoon radio show that spewed out anti-Semitism and fascism. It became must listening for huge segments of the population: *The New York Times* estimates that at Coughlin's peak, his fiery sermons "commanded a weekly radio audience of 90 million who hung on his every richly enunciated word." Hate sells. Or take a look at *Triumph of the Will*, a famous Nazi propaganda film made by Leni Riefenstahl; her film prowess dramatically deepened Hitler's hold on the German imagination.

The answer to demagoguery, today as in the past, is not simply to bemoan. Rather, we must work to keep alive the rhetorical traditions of the past. Despite their obvious differences, the formats of the digital world lend themselves to the tried and true practices of rhetoric. Understanding the purpose and message of a tweet or radio hit, for instance, is just as important as having a clear purpose and message in a public speech—and clearly defining these elements might be even more important given the constraints of media today. Logos, pathos, and ethos are challenging to establish in a tweet or a Facebook post, but you should think how to interweave those elements into any public appearance or published commentary. The public today is not as easily convinced by a television speech as in the past; now leaders should also learn to make their case for an idea or policy through well-written online opinions, social media posts, and pithy television hits.

My friend Jamie Humes wisely said some years ago, "The art of communication is the language of leadership." If he is correct—and I think he is—then these lessons are essential for any emerging young leader. Public persuasion cannot be learned overnight, but in practicing these tips on a frequent basis, you might well come closer to inspiring others to follow.

PART THREE

LEADERSHIP
IN ACTION

TEN

WHEN JOURNEYS CONVERGE

In Parts One and Two of this book, we have explored the inner and outer journeys that many take as they develop their leadership capacities. As we have seen, leadership is not for the faint of heart. It can be exasperating and even endangering. But we have seen that it can also be energizing and even ennobling.

Part Three now opens a conversation about the integration of one's inner and outer journeys—and how that integration can lead to the ultimate goal of leaders these days: getting big things done. We begin by telling the stories of three leaders in different fields: Senator Robert Kennedy in the days after his brother was assassinated; Susan Berresford, who became a high-performing president of the Ford Foundation; and Stacey Abrams, whose community organizing could turn our national politics upside down. Each has taken a different path, often arduous and frustrating, but each has had the internal fortitude and external social skills that make them role models for emerging leaders today.

In the final pages of this chapter, we will come inside recent White Houses where I have served to take a closer look at the early days of presidential administrations. Those days are the most precious and important of every new president; those are times when presidents and their staffs have translated vision into action. What has worked? What has failed? And what lessons do they offer rising leaders in other fields? A couple of the stories here will be lighthearted, as we need to see more clearly the human side of leadership.

THE CONVERGENCE OF INNER AND OUTER JOURNEYS

Robert Coles, a child psychiatrist and the author of over fifty-five books, once wrote about his experiences trying to awaken Americans to the suffering of hungry children, especially in the South. Try as he and his team might through their research, writings, and personal pilgrimages to poor areas and their advocacy in Washington, they could not stir the nation into action.

After many failed excursions elsewhere on Capitol Hill, they received an invitation from Senator Robert Kennedy to come by for coffee. To their surprise, Kennedy spent hours engaging with them, taking notes and coaching them on how to maneuver on the Hill. Slowly at first but then picking up steam, Kennedy became an ardent supporter. And he also had the social skills to make things happen in the halls of Congress.

After hearing their stories, Kennedy arranged for the team to testify before Congress and for one of the doctors to sit down with Walter Cronkite, the most trusted journalist in the country. When it became apparent that official Washington was still indifferent, the senator himself embarked on a tour of the poorest counties of Mississippi and West Virginia, meeting hungry children and their parents and persuading newscasters to cover his experiences. Eventually, their stories won public attention and legislative victories that once seemed out of reach.

Coles and his team concluded that as important as their original work was, what spelled the difference was tapping into Kennedy's leadership, which converted their thoughts and experiences into action. Their odyssey was a perfect example of how the inner and outer journeys of a leader can converge and create a meaningful change in our national life.

In his early years, Kennedy had been a ruthless, no-holds-barred political figure. That he had once worked for Senator Joe McCarthy only added to his reputation. But his brother's assassination and other unhappy events were devastating blows—crucibles, as we have seen with so many leaders. He retreated into himself and underwent a remarkable transformation. He became a tragic, almost saintly figure on the national stage as his tortuous inner journey converged with his outer. He was now the embodiment of a moral leader trying to make the world modestly better. In his final farewell with the Coles team, the senator told them, "You learn what's ahead through the living of it—and what to do, the same way." There are many examples of leaders over time who have integrated their inner and outer selves in ways that served others: Colin Powell, Robert Gates, and Oprah Winfrey, for starters. None knew what life would bring them, but they had a higher sense of what they would bring to life. Bobby Kennedy helped show the way.

One of the most unusual integrations of inner and outer journeys I have witnessed was also the most unexpected. In the late 1980s, I was asked to chair a nonpartisan selection committee to give annual prizes to the best innovations in American government of that year. The program was sponsored by the Ford Foundation, now the second largest foundation in the country. That's where I first met Susan Berresford, a ranking member of the foundation.

A few years later, the CEO of the foundation announced his retirement. Several board members thought that, as in the past, they should find a successor through a head-hunting firm. But one of the most respected board members, Henry Schacht, objected. No, he argued, they already had the best possible person in their own ranks. It was time for the foundation to name its first female president and CEO: Susan Berresford.

Schacht won the day (as he so admirably did in sponsoring other women who became corporate CEOs). But even he may not have anticipated what a great leader Berresford would be. Given that when appointed she had worked internally for the foundation for over twenty years, the board graciously granted her a three-month sabbatical away from the organization. Over a ninety-day period, she cut off contact with the foundation's leadership. Instead, she traveled the world to talk with clients and allies about what role Ford should play in coming years. She also rented a small apartment in New York where she could work alone, reflecting on what she had heard. There on the walls she put large sheets of paper so that she could compare notes and insights. Out in the world, she took time to reflect upon her own experiences and engage with others who were often overlooked as sources of inspiration.

On her first day back, Susan was armed with a plan for immediate action and was prepared to work with others in rethinking strategy for the long haul. Her transition from the outer world to the corner suite, from thought to action, paid off. The Berresford years continue to be fondly remembered at the foundation. During that sabbatical, she was able to integrate her past experiences with future opportunities and was prepared to work with others in shaping the foundation's future.

Not all of us will have the opportunity for time away before taking on a new role, as Berresford did. We have families to build, bills to pay, careers to consider. Your chances for leadership can seem far down an uncertain road. For many, leadership opportunity comes unexpectedly. Others can identify an opportunity and choose to seize the moment.

We saw that in November 2010, after the Democratic Party took a particularly brutal beating in the midterm elections. In Georgia, Republicans swept to victory in every statewide race and thought they had a lock on state politics for a decade or more. Democratic State House Representative Stacey Abrams, however, was determined to find a silver lining for her party. As her fellow Democrats struggled, the young representative had just been elected minority leader by her colleagues. Looking at the future of her party, she refused to dwell on recent failures. Instead, Abrams saw enormous potential. Demographics within the state were already beginning to shift toward a more diverse—and therefore more liberal—population. Now she just needed to ensure that new voters were engaged and able to vote.

Armed with the notion that Democrats could eventually flip Georgia blue, Abrams embarked on what would become a ten-year crusade across her state and the country. She crafted a twenty-one-page Power-Point examining how Democrats could win back the state and charting their path to victory by 2020. She brought the presentation with her to party meetings and to donors, urging them to not leave Georgia in the dust. While most people were skeptical that the solidly conservative state would ever turn, some bought in and joined her efforts.

What Abrams found in her meetings was that there were existing groups working toward her ultimate goal: organizing voters and communities in Georgia to commit to a progressive agenda. The sentiment and mission were there, she found, but these existing small organizations lacked funding, scale, and infrastructure to craft a common goal across the state.

Having identified both her problem and a potential solution, Abrams got to work. She and her colleagues trained hundreds of young people to engage in statewide policy and politics, creating a pipeline of talent that would continue to galvanize their party. Then, in 2013, she launched the New Georgia Project to organize South Georgians and advocate for increased health care; the next year, the organization began a voter registration drive with the goal of registering 800,000 unregistered people of color in ten years. In succeeding years, Abrams and her network of organizers laid the groundwork for statewide Democratic victory. They did not see instant results; instead, progress came slowly, often in the form of marginal gains or a few seats in the Georgia legislature. Frustrations abounded.

In 2018, building on her near decade of commitment, Abrams ran for governor and fell just short of her Republican opponent. Her effort was the most successful statewide campaign Democrats had run in recent years; rather than dwelling on her loss, however, Abrams saw her gains as proof that her PowerPoint plan was working. She doubled down on her efforts. Having catapulted to national stardom during her gubernatorial run, she now had the attention of not just her state but the entire country. No Black woman had ever come this far.

Finally, in 2020, Abrams's commitment paid off when Joe Biden flipped Georgia blue and, in the 2021 U.S. Senate runoff election, Jon Ossoff and Raphael Warnock defeated their Republican opponents to secure a Democratic majority. Today, Stacey Abrams is a household name, though her rise to leadership and fame was hardly instantaneous. She had a long-term vision, the realization of which many thought improbable, and she committed herself to it. Grassroots organizing and political fundraising can be slow, hard work—especially as a Democrat in a state as red as Georgia. Abrams was undeterred. As she told *Rolling Stone*'s Tessa Stuart, "I'm nothing special. I'm just— I'm kind of relentless."

I would say she is both. Ushering through reform, as Abrams did, takes patience, perseverance, and a fierce commitment to cause. She was unafraid of dreaming big and understood the dedication it would take to see those dreams become reality. She was also a case study in the development of leadership: first, as she became self-reflective and gained an inner calm; then as she cultivated her skills in politics and grassroots organizing. The combination dramatically increased her impact on her state and the country.

1600 PENNSYLVANIA AVENUE

What these stories suggest is that moving into leadership takes many shapes. Integrating your inner and outer journeys looks different for each leader, but taking the time to combine the two is essential for those stepping into power. These stories show that as individuals take the reins, a careful, consistent vision and an understanding of one's circumstances are also necessary precursors to effective leadership. You must become a student of your context before you can become its master.

The leadership of RFK, Berresford, and Abrams depart sharply from the exercise of power we often see in the White House. That said, the happenings of 1600 Pennsylvania Avenue also provide an illuminating lens through which to view leadership in any sector. Let's look now at a few key lessons from my time in four presidential administrations. Those years were formative in shaping my understanding of leadership. I hope these stories will provide a peek into that world and that you too can learn from these tales.

Hit the Ground Running

Since the first inauguration of Franklin Roosevelt in 1933, it has been an article of faith that an incoming president will be largely judged by how well he performs during his first hundred days in office. So it was with some trepidation that I accepted a directive from the Reagan team to join up with Richard Wirthlin, Reagan's pollster and confidant, to map out a proposed first hundred days of the Reagan presidency. We called it "An Early Action Plan." Dick did a first-rate job providing a political overview, while I decided to form a small team to see what we could learn from the history of five newly elected presidents stretching back to FDR. We thought it imperative to plot out precisely what each of the five presidents had done during his first hundred days: his legislative proposals, executive orders, symbolic gestures, meetings with Congress, an evening with the Supreme Court, et cetera.

I derived three key lessons from our study: First, it became apparent that in those opening hundred days, the public makes a fresh evaluation of a new leader. Before then, they have been able to judge him only as a candidate; now he is occupying the most powerful office in the world. Who is this person, anyway? How strong? How tough? How honest? Second, those first days provide an opportunity to put a firm, thematic narrative on the entire administration. As president, FDR became "Doctor New Deal"; Ike became the president in search of peace; Kennedy and Jackie became the world's most glamorous couple. Third, the hundred days is also a time of great peril for a new president, a time when he and his team are least informed and have to make the biggest decisions. Kennedy had his Bay of Pigs, Ford had his pardon of Nixon, Carter and Clinton both had their stumbles. So it was important to hit the road running but also to be supercautious about the exercise of great power. Those same lessons, I believe, apply to corporate as well as political leaders today.

Keep an Eye Out for Young Talent

One of the blessings of being in the halls of power is that you often run into talented young people who have great potential to make the world a better place. That was certainly my experience with one of my favorite college students. In 1975, when I accepted an invitation from President Ford's White House to return from exile at the Treasury Department ASAP, I immediately had a question: Where could I get the furniture to put into my empty office across the driveway from the West Wing at the Old Executive Office Building?

"Well," they replied, "you can call the General Services Administration and you can probably get your furniture in three months. Or you can call John Rogers, and you will get it tomorrow."

"Who is John Rogers?" I asked.

"Oh, he is a college intern who comes over here in the afternoons."

At my request, John F.W. Rogers came to see me the next day. Furniture would be there within twenty-four hours, he assured me. After we had talked for a while more, I could see John had a magic touch and urged him to come work with me. He did, and that began a marvelous partnership—then friendship—of some fifty years.

John, as I learned, had seen that in the wake of the Watergate scandal, people were coming and going in staff positions in the Ford administration. Whenever someone was about to leave, John would inquire whether he could commandeer the furniture. He had found empty space on the fifth floor in an attic of the Old EOB and he began building a clandestine warehouse of unused furniture.

John was both entrepreneurial and amusing. In those days, presidents kept presidential cuff links in their desk in the Oval Office. They were nice send-offs for visitors. As I recall, one day I saw John wearing cuff links I had never seen before. I said nothing, but a few days later, I saw him wearing yet a different set. "John," I inquired, "where did you find those cuff links?"

He was sheepish until I wrangled it out of him. Using special White House stationery, he sent letters in his name to the top jewelers across the country. The president, his letter said, wanted to develop a new line of cuff links and would be most appreciative if the recipient would design and send several different sets he could review. Boom! In flowed newly designed cuff links from all corners. I have no idea what happened to that jewelry, but John's caper remained a secret for years.

Not surprisingly, word spread of John's general prowess. Arthur Burns, former Fed chairman, hired him as a close aide. Then Jim Baker discovered him, and he joined Margaret Tutwiler and Richard Darman as part of Baker's tight inner circle. When Reagan's first inaugural was approaching, Baker, on Reagan's approval, assigned John to organize the planning and execution of the physical transition to the White House offices. At the split second of 12:00 noon on January 20, when Reagan officially became president, the gates opened to the White House and trucks stacked with furniture rolled in. By nightfall, the West Wing had been transformed, displaying photos of the new president and First Lady and ready for business the next morning.

John was on a roll. Later on, when Baker became secretary of the treasury and then secretary of state, he appointed John to top administrative jobs—among them, undersecretary of state for management. When his work in government ended, John was hired by Goldman Sachs to manage their offices. He also became a very good leader, especially effective in persuading donors to finance a refurbishing of the Old EOB. He remains devoted to the office of the presidency. He also remains a gem of a person—one of those people you try to spot early in life because they have so much potential to be great citizens.

Remember Common Sense

The Group of Twenty in today's world was launched a little more than half a century as the Group of Eight. Its goal was to forge strong bonds of friendship among leaders of the Western World. I was privileged to travel with President Reagan to a couple of their summits and watched in fascination as Margaret Thatcher treated Reagan almost as a son, very protective of him. Each year responsibility for hosting the summit passed to the next leader in line. In 1975, Reagan was to host, and he selected Colonial Williamsburg as a site. It didn't quite turn out the way anyone in the American delegation expected.

To be frank, most of our U.S. delegation was apprehensive. By tradition, the host leader was responsible for running plenary sessions, an arduous job all by itself. But as president of the most powerful country, Reagan also had to host each of the other leaders in one-on-one conversation—a bilateral, as it was called. That meant Reagan was carrying a heavy burden of sitting down for longish meetings with every other leader while also hosting the plenaries. In short, Reagan had to carry out an agenda that would have been challenging for a president half his age. And we knew that the international press corps would be covering him like hawks, eager to see whether he had the strength and intellect to carry it off.

Equally challenging was this stark reality: For each bilateral and plenary, our national security squad would crank out thorough briefing papers of ten or fifteen pages. Reagan was diligent in reading them, but since his Hollywood days, he read slowly, letting words and ideas sink in. If given a lot to read, he would be late to bed and tired the next day. Then the staff would suffer the worst of fates: The First Lady would explode the next morning, furious that his staff had imposed these intolerable burdens on her Ronnie. If you valued your life (or some precious part of your anatomy) you did not want to cross swords with Nancy Reagan.

As White House chief of staff, Jim Baker was responsible for keeping peace in the family. So when he received a big, thick notebook full of overnight briefing papers in Williamsburg, Baker approached Reagan gingerly. He was especially eager that Reagan scan the book quickly and get to bed on time. Mr. President, Jim would say in effect, you don't have to read all of these papers. Just skim them, sir, and please get to bed. Reagan reassured Jim that he would and sauntered off.

The next morning, when Reagan arrived for breakfast with our team, he looked like he had been hit by a Mack truck—his face was sallow, his eyes dry. *Oh my God,* the staff whispered under their breaths, *this is going to be a terrible, horrible, no good, very bad day.* Where was Nancy? And where were those vipers in the press corps?

Reagan sat down to eat, and about twenty minutes into the eggs, he said in effect, "Fellas, I have a confession to make. I sat down with your briefing book around nine o'clock last night and want to thank you for your diligence. But did you know that *The Sound of Music* was on last night? That's my favorite movie, and I stayed up to watch the whole thing. I am afraid I never read your briefing book."

But do you know what the real surprise was that day? Reagan was terrific in those bilateral sessions, as good as we had ever seen him. Why? Because he wasn't bogged down by all the facts and minutiae that we on his staff, in our arrogance, usually insisted that he read. How could he ever manage without us? In truth, most presidents are smarter than those of us on the staff give him credit for. What Reagan did that day was rise above all the details and spend time with each leader on the big picture: What are we trying to achieve? What is our strategy? What can we do together to realize our vision?

That day actually taught me an important lesson. If we can draw upon a nautical analogy, the place of the leader is not down in the engine room of the ship. That's where junior officers like me should be, keeping the engines running. As I have said, the leader's role is to be topside, at the helm, determining our destination and keeping us on course.

Have a Plan B

When I returned to the White House under President Clinton, I found out that while faces had changed, some problems hadn't. The Middle East was still a cauldron of troubles. In the early 1990s, after Iraq invaded Kuwait, President George H.W. Bush successfully rallied nations across Europe to chase Saddam Hussein's forces out. It was a crushing victory, and afterward, Bush took a victory lap. The United States was enraged when Iraqi forces—presumably those of Saddam Hussein—tried to assassinate Bush, who was by then a private citizen.

Enter Bill Clinton as H.W.'s successor. Clinton could hardly let the assassination attempt go without a tough response. So he publicly declared that if the United States ever had convincing evidence of who tried to kill Bush, we would retaliate militarily. By chance, I joined Clinton's staff just days before U.S. intelligence had found that convincing evidence that Saddam's Iraqi Intelligence Service (IIS) was indeed behind the treachery.

Knowing he had to strike back—and fast—Clinton assembled a small circle of advisors to talk over options; I was among them. President Clinton had never ordered troops into action before, nor had anyone died at his hand. So he wanted to act with great care. He decided to have U.S. missiles destroy IIS headquarters, located just south of Baghdad—an appropriate call, since that's where Saddam's attack was generated. But Clinton also insisted that we minimize the loss of life, especially of Iraqi civilians.

Here was the basic plan that he adopted with support of both military and civilian advisors. On a Saturday afternoon in Washington,

U.S. ships would fire missiles at the IIS headquarters; the missiles were expected to hit shortly before 6:00 p.m. East Coast time but in the middle of the night there. Clinton reasoned that the fewest number of Iraqi civilians were likely to be working then.

For reasons I never fully understood, U.S. satellites would not be in a position to send back instantaneous overheads. So the plan was—I kid you not—that shortly before six o'clock, some of us would be in the West Wing and at 6 p.m. would tune in to CNN for instant coverage. When CNN reported, as we assumed they would, that the missiles had struck their target, I was to call U.S. television networks to announce that President Clinton would make a brief announcement to the country at 7:00 p.m. EST. He wanted people to know what he had done and why.

As planned, the ships at sea successfully launched their missiles. Our confidence was growing as we turned on our TV sets. But when 6:00 arrived, there was no news out of Baghdad—on CNN or anywhere else. Then 6:15 came and went quietly. By 6:30, a frustrated president was calling me and asking for explanations. By 6:45 or so, he exploded, striding over from the residence and demanding answers. "I thought you guys had this all under control" was his basic message.

Scrambling for solutions, I said something to this effect: "Mr. President, Tom Johnson is running CNN these days, and he used to work in the White House for Lyndon Johnson. He is also a personal friend. Let me call him in Atlanta."

Wish granted, I called Tom, fishing him out of a restaurant. "Tom," I said, "have you heard from any of your correspondents in Baghdad?"

"Well, no," he responded. "We don't have any correspondents there right now. We do have a couple on the way, now in Lebanon, because we heard there might be something going down there soon."

"Tom, how soon can your correspondents make it to Iraq?"

"Tomorrow afternoon," he said.

I was dying. "Tom, are you sure you don't have any word from Baghdad? Especially to the south of the city?"

"Well, now that you mention it, we do have a couple of Iraqi nationals there who work for us. One called and said he had a relative who reported a big explosion south of the city."

Bingo! I thought.

Tony Lake, the national security advisor, then joined up and we strongly recommended to Clinton that he go ahead, get the airtime, adjust the speech a little bit, and talk to the country.

"Yes," Tony added with a wink, "you can also say we are relatively sure we have hit the targets."

Just as Clinton was about to go on the air, we learned that satellites had confirmed the hit. It had all worked out. The president was relieved that he had succeeded. And the rest of us still had our jobs. But I kept thinking: *In future, let's make sure we have a Plan B ahead of time.*

Those days at 1600 Penn taught me a great deal about leadership in action: As my good friend Warren Bennis said, it can be an art and, more often, an adventure. The men and women I worked alongside in the White House showed me that wielding power can be difficult, exhilarating, and sometimes quite a good deal of fun. It also comes with twists and turns, as I saw time and time again in each of the administrations I was fortunate enough to work for.

In those times, when presidents faced challenging decisions and great responsibility, I saw that those who were most successful were not just those who had a clear set of goals and a supportive team, but also those who have an ability to roll with the punches. As Eisenhower once said, "In preparing for battle, I have always found that plans are useless, but planning is indispensable." The same applies to leadership in times of peace. Obstacles are bound to crop up; the best among us navigate them with grace. Others, however, are not so lucky. We have much to learn from those who have fallen off the track and can only hope that in examining their lives, we will be fortunate enough to not repeat their mistakes.

ELEVEN

HOW LEADERS
LOSE THEIR WAY

While it may seem dated now, the best political novel of the past century was *All the King's Men*, written by Robert Penn Warren. Published in 1946, it was twice turned into a film. It is a tale from the Depression about a charismatic populist governor in Louisiana named Willie Stark (a lightly disguised Huey Long).

Power hungry, Stark pushes his right-hand man, Jack Burden, to dig up dirt on a local judge. Burden resists, arguing that the judge has lived a blameless life. Stark growls back, "There is always something." "Maybe not on the judge," says Burden. And Stark replies with a line that has become a classic: "Man is conceived in sin and born in corruption and he passeth from the stink of the didie to the stench of the shroud. There is always something." Not long after, Jack Burden does find dirt on the judge: his engagement in bribes and other financial woes. Too often, there is indeed something out there—something that endangers a leader.

Leadership in the public arena can be one of the noblest and most fulfilling experiences that you can undertake. But it comes with temptations that have time and again been the undoing of men and women who lose their way. In the pages ahead we will first explore how leaders often veer off course, abandoning their True North and often self-destructing. Then we will consider the "low arts" of leadership, as Hamilton called them, and a paradox of American politics: how we want our leaders to be caring and compassionate when they should be but also tough, deceitful, and cunning when they need to be. When—if ever—should principled leaders resort to the low arts, and how should they defend themselves from others seeking to drag them down?

THE DANGERS OF SELF-DERAILMENT

A decade ago, in an epic fall from grace, Rajat Gupta created one of the great leadership puzzles of our time. From birth onward, he seemed a golden boy. Born and raised in India, Gupta was a top student at one of the most competitive educational institutions on the planet, the Indian Institute of Technology. Upon graduation, he won a job at another prestigious institution: the consulting firm of McKinsey & Company.

Gupta excelled at McKinsey, where his talent, drive, and urbane sophistication won friends and admirers throughout the corporate world. In 1994, the firm elected him as its managing director (CEO) and then reelected him in 1997 and 2000; he became the first CEO of the firm born outside the United States. While there were periodic internal controversies during Gupta's tenure, McKinsey grew into a huge international corporation, opening offices in twenty countries, doubling the number of partners, and increasing revenues by 230 percent.

When he stepped down as CEO and then as partner in 2008, Rajat was showered with praise and invitations. He had his pick of corporate boards, joined up with an array of philanthropic causes, and served in advisory capacities at numerous business schools. His bank account continued to grow, and he had properties around the world. I first became acquainted with him through the Harvard Business

School, where as a graduate, he chaired an outside advisory board. He was seen on campus as a role model for business leadership, and from our early conversations, I could see why: Alongside a glowing record of success, he was global in outlook, thoughtful, and charming.

Then his world collapsed.

In 2010, the U.S. attorney's office in Manhattan filed criminal charges against him, and the FBI arrested him in New York. He pleaded not guilty, but bail was set at $10 million. The gravamen of the charges was that in 2008, in the midst of the sharp recession, Gupta engaged in serious insider trading. While he emphatically denied this, the evidence was damning.

Gupta was serving on the board of Goldman Sachs at the time and also had ties with a financier named Raj Rajaratnam. At a top-secret meeting, Goldman's board learned that Warren Buffett planned to invest $5 billion in the firm, greatly boosting its financial standing. Within seconds of the board's adjournment, the government charged, Gupta had rushed down the hall and secretly called Rajaratnam to tip him off him to the news. Immediately, just five minutes before the final bell at the New York Stock Exchange, Rajaratnam placed a large investment in Goldman—an investment that allegedly reaped gains and loss avoidance totaling $23 million.

At trial, Gupta was found guilty of three federal felonies, all linked to insider trading and all creating a major scandal. He spent nineteen months in jail, eight of them in solitary confinement, where his only daily exercise was pacing around his thirty-by-ten-foot cage.

The puzzle arises because Rajat Gupta was plenty wealthy at the time. His net worth seemed well over $100 million. Why in the world would he allow himself to become tangled up in insider trading? Even if he believed he was playing inside the chalk lines, why would he expose himself to such risk?

Several McKinsey alumni have been students in my classrooms and have tried to sort out his possible motivations. Some have argued that McKinsey had strong ethical boundaries, and as long as Gupta was CEO, he knew he had to stick within them. But when he left the firm, he slid away. That may be true. But a more credible theory—to the alumni and to friends I have had at Goldman—is that during much of his career, he worked closely with CEOs as their equals. When they retired, they had billions, whereas when he retired, he merely had tens of millions. He groused about the unfairness of it all and was drawn to men like Rajaratnam, who also went to prison.

Gupta's story raises one of the most important questions about successful, highly paid leaders of today: When is enough enough? Why persist in a chase for money and prestige when you already have more toys and properties than you can possibly enjoy? Why this excessive hubris, narcissism, and greed? Why not spend your twilight years putting your money to work in providing opportunities for the next generation? Sometime in life—well before you leave the stage and usually during your inner journey—you need to get your values straight. If you don't find your True North and commit yourself to a high moral purpose in life, you can easily descend into darkness.

COMMON FAILURES AND THEIR ANTIDOTES

Stretching back to the early days of Christianity, Catholic popes and their followers have wrestled with questions about which sins are the most deadly. Over time, they have identified seven and have drawn upon them to instruct their flock in virtuous living: pride, greed, lust, anger, gluttony, envy, and sloth.

Of these, pride has often been seen as the most serious and one that is often the source of one's downfall. The immortal Dante saw pride as the love of self perverted to contempt and hatred of one's neighbor. Does that sound familiar in today's world? In his *Divine Comedy*, Dante wrote of penitents required to carry slabs of stone on their backs to induce humility. These penitents also show up in *The Canterbury Tales* and in *The Faerie Queene*. What we see in leadership is a close alliance—indeed, an overlap—between the seven deadly sins and what trips people up at the top of their careers.

As Catholics have learned, the best way to counter these sins is not to hate sin but to love virtue more. Embracing the virtues diminishes the possibility of personal derailment. In that spirit, let me suggest what I would call the Seven Deadly Sins of Leadership and an offsetting virtue for each. Here are my top choices:

Hubris vs. Humility

In leadership, the number one danger is that success will go to your head—that you will begin to believe your very success means that you are different, that you are above mere mortals, and that, in fact, the rules don't apply to you. Ambition leads to self-confidence, which leads to arrogance, which leads to self-destruction. Witness Rajat Gupta.

Such cases cover the landscape. Elizabeth Holmes drops out of Stanford at age seventeen and creates a drug-testing company whose valuation balloons to $9 billion. As this is written, she has been found guilty of fraud and could face a twenty-year sentence. As CEO for some twenty years, William Aramony built United Way into the country's largest charitable organization. He was then charged with fraud and went to prison. Jerry Falwell Jr., son of a respected evangelical leader, served as president of Liberty University, a school with strict sexual codes. He was forced to resign when accused of being at the center of a sex scandal.

There is but one clear answer to hubris: HUMILITY! In ancient Rome, a victorious general would return to the city for a celebratory parade. On his chariot, standing right behind him, a slave boy would continuously whisper into the general's ear, "Remember, you are mortal." We need more celebrations like that.

Narcissism vs. Empathy

Closely related to hubris, of course, is an excessive love of self that we see in narcissists. Some can succeed despite themselves. It was said of Teddy Roosevelt that he wanted to be the child at every christening, the groom at every wedding, and the deceased at every funeral. But he was still an excellent president because he also loved others and had enormous empathy for those who lived life on the margins. He famously said, "The rock of democracy will founder when people in different parties, regions, and religions and races think of each other as 'the other' rather than the common American citizen." What he lacked in self-awareness, he more than made up for with common understanding.

In contrast, President Reagan appointed Don Regan, a retired CEO of Merrill Lynch, to be his chief of staff in his second term, not appreciating the extent of Regan's narcissism. Soon Nancy Reagan realized that Regan was inserting himself into every photograph of the president in the Oval Office, frequently taking personal credit for the administration's accomplishments. He seemed to have no redeeming qualities. Regan had a CEO mentality, as Nancy saw it, and she had him fired. Regan should have paid more attention to a sign the president kept on his desk: "There is no limit to what one can accomplish as long as you don't care who gets the credit." As a leader, you must keep your ego under control and remember, it is not about you.

Greed vs. Modesty

Among leaders who grew up with modest means and then rose to power, there is a natural tendency to want a more secure financial base. Many become greedy, as we saw with Raj Gupta, but many others are driven by their hardscrabble lives to make the world a more supportive place. Some become billionaires who care; as of this writing, over two hundred signatories from over twenty-four countries have now signed the Giving Pledge established by Warren Buffett and Bill Gates, publicly promising to give away at least half their assets to philanthropic causes. And many billionaires are inspired by their own impoverished backgrounds. Former Starbucks CEO Howard Schultz, for example, grew up with a deliveryman father who broke his ankle in an accident. He soon lost his job, and with it his access to health care and his dignity. Memories of those days inspired Schultz to ensure that baristas at his Starbucks, even though part time, have health insurance and an array of other benefits. The point is that yes, our economic system has created inequities that demand correction, but billionaires can actually be part of the solution.

Obstinacy vs. Resolution

We praise leaders who are strong and decisive. Since 1880, every American president—save three—has chosen to sit in the Oval Office at the Resolute desk. The desk was a gift from Queen Victoria made from the timbers of a British warship, the HMS *Resolute*. President Obama chose to sit at the same desk, as did President Trump.

Yet we have also learned that if a leader carries a strength too far, it can turn into a weakness. Certainly we have learned that resolution—carried on too long in the face of growing arguments to the contrary—can turn into obstinacy and become the undoing of leaders. In her 1984 book *The March of Folly*, the historian Barbara Tuchman studied how leaders from Troy to Vietnam lost their way. She called them "wooden headed" for their obstinacy. We could add several chapters to her book since its first edition.

Imprudence vs. Wise Judgment

Our culture celebrates leaders who are bold, decisive, and willing to take risks. The pioneers who opened up the West were people like that. So were the leaders who built Silicon Valley. But there is a fine line between smart versus rash, prudent versus reckless. That is especially important in the leadership of public institutions.

In 1972, a correspondent for *The New York Times*, David Halberstam, published one of the best books on the origins of the Vietnam War. It was a foundation for Tuchman's book a dozen years later. Halberstam titled his account *The Best and the Brightest*; students today assume that he intended it as a book of praise. In reality, he was highly critical of the academics and intellectuals who encouraged Kennedy to intervene in Vietnam—the Ivy League "whiz kids," as they were called. In his view, they insisted on "brilliant policies that defied common sense" and often overrode analysts at the State Department. In short, he accused them of rash, even reckless imprudence. Some fifty-six thousand Americans perished in that war.

The ancients would have instantly recognized what went wrong. In Greek mythology, Daedalus and his son Icarus were trying to escape from Crete. Daedalus built wings from feathers and wax and instructed Icarus not to fly too high or the sun would melt them. He warned Icarus of hubris. But Icarus ignored his father's advice, flew too close to the sun, and after his wings melted, plunged into and drowned in the sea. His judgment failed him.

As we have stressed, good judgment is indispensable to good leadership. And that judgment must be found through a blend of experience, mistakes, study, and reflection. You aren't born with it. Like so much else in life, you must earn it.

Basic Dishonesty vs. Straight Shooting

The Trump years should dispel all doubts whether honesty still matters in public life. Chronic lying hardly started with Trump, but he took it to levels we have never before witnessed in the White House. *The Washington Post* kept a record of President Trump's lies and deceptions; over four years in office, he had been untruthful on 30,573 occasions.

By contrast, I remember growing up when Dwight Eisenhower was president and how immensely popular he was. Over his eight years in the White House, his approval rating averaged 64 percent; among recent presidents from Bush 43 to Biden, approval ratings have hovered in the 40s. Ike was not only a war hero but a straight shooter, too. He understood as well as any that honesty and transparency are some of your best tools in building trust and a connection with the public. History suggests that the number of public lies Ike told over his eight years in the White House could be counted on the fingers of one hand. And the biggest one was rooted in national security, when he told the public a U-2 spy plane shot down by the Russians was simply a civilian weather research aircraft. The Russians had found the plane and its pilot, Francis Gary Powers. They cleverly concealed their catch until Ike publicly lied; then they pounced, to Ike's enormous chagrin. A single lie was a humiliation for Eisenhower. By contrast, on average Trump told more than nineteen lies a day and they were rarely justified.

There are times when a leader must lie for the sake of national security. Witness how we fooled the Nazis about our troop placements on the eve of D-Day. But when lies become chronic, as they did with Nixon and Trump, nothing that a leader says can be accepted at face value. Everything needs to be double-checked, especially in an age of vast disinformation. Trump was smart enough to keep his base loyal to him. But he lost his power to persuade others, derailed by his own hand. Fortunately, our democracy remains stronger than any single leader—especially one who reminds us of Willie Stark.

Distrust vs. Openness

Trust must run in both directions in a democracy: Followers must trust their leaders to tell them hard truths, while, similarly, leaders must trust followers will believe in them. There was once a time in the mid-twentieth century when leaders like Eisenhower and Kennedy enjoyed such relationships. I can remember in the 1950s how Ike could take to the airwaves on a national security problem and over half the people would automatically agree with him because he was Eisenhower. When Kennedy early in his administration bravely and openly told the public that he was the one to be held accountable for botching the invasion of Cuba's Bay of Pigs, Gallup polling found his popularity had gone up 10 percent. But today, public trust in our national leaders and our national institutions has plunged to dangerous levels.

THE LOW ARTS OF PUBLIC LEADERSHIP

As you can tell by now, I am a big fan of the Roosevelts—Franklin, Eleanor, and Teddy. It was Teddy who best expressed the high ideals of leadership a century ago—ideals we have tried to extol in these pages. In a presidential visit to his prep school, Groton, Teddy urged students to embrace "a strenuous life."

"We need leaders of inspired idealism," he told them, "leaders to whom are granted great visions, who dream greatly and strive to make their dreams come true, who can kindle the people with the fire from their own burning souls." Eleanor would have endorsed every word.

Franklin, however, had a harder-nosed point of view. He agreed with Machiavelli, who argued that we would all love to have leaders who are virtuous and pure, but the nature of men around them is darker. So be on your guard. "A prince," Machiavelli famously wrote, "must imitate the fox and the lion, for the lion cannot protect himself from traps, and the fox cannot defend himself from wolves. One must therefore be a fox to recognize traps, and a lion to frighten wolves . . . If men were all good, this precept would not be a good one; but as they are bad and would not observe their faith with you, so you are not bound to keep faith with them." A prince must be feared or loved, Machiavelli continued, but if one has to choose, it is better to be feared. Tough stuff! Notably, a leading political scientist of the twentieth century, James MacGregor Burns, subtitled a positive biographical work on FDR: *The Lion and the Fox*.

In a more recent analysis, political scientists Thomas Cronin and Michael Genovese argue that the public actually wants it both ways from our leaders, certainly our presidents: "We want a decent, just, caring, and compassionate president, yet we admire a cunning, guileful, and on occasions that warrant it, even a ruthless, manipulative president . . . The public demands the quality of toughness."

There is plenty of evidence to support the proposition that in evaluating leaders, Americans demand the sinister as well as the sincere, the cunning as well as the compassionate, Clint Eastwood and Mister Rogers. Carter, Ford, Clinton, and Obama were all faulted for occasional indecision and timidity. But Ike, Kennedy, Reagan, and George H.W. Bush were celebrated for standing up to Soviet leaders, taking a hard line against North Korea, and chasing down Saddam Hussein and Osama bin Laden.

The central question is not whether others around you will resort to the "low arts" to get their way. They will. And some of them will run over you if need be. It is naive to think otherwise. The questions are these: When is it appropriate—even necessary—for you as a principled leader to resort to the low arts yourself? And as a leader, how can you best protect yourself from enemies trying to take you down?

In difficult storms, I believe, your first recourse as a leader is always to values and principles. When I worked in the Clinton White House, I was impressed that whenever the president had to make a hard call, Vice President Gore would ask: "What is the right thing to do here?" One reads that in leadership books, but I have rarely seen it happen in practice, where the main question is usually: How will this affect my power? My image of Gore rose instantly.

But it is also important to recognize that the world is a tough neighborhood in which other nations and people will exploit any sign of weakness. If they perceive that the U.S. government is in disarray or that it is weak, they will find ways to advance their interests, often at the expense of the United States. If people were angels, as James Madison wrote in the Federalist Papers, we wouldn't need government. But government needs to be strong in order to be effective. During my time in the White House, the one clear lesson that both parties shared is that the United Sates should never fear to negotiate with adversarial nations but we should always have a club in the closet. Using the club should always be a last resort, but it shouldn't be tossed away. One of the worst mistakes of the Obama presidency was to draw a red line in the sand with Syria, only to back down when the Syrians crossed it.

Similarly, when citizens believe their leader is weak or vacillating, the leader may have a hard time building coalitions and getting big things done. Adlai Stevenson was one of the most honest and articulate presidential candidates in my lifetime, but he was dismissed by voters because he seemed to lack inner confidence and was indecisive. Gerald Ford and George McGovern were fine men, but voters thought both were a little squishy.

At the White House, I also learned that I was overly naive about life. When Alexander Butterfield disclosed that President Nixon had secretly installed a taping system, I joined others who had gone to elite schools in celebrating—we finally had a way to prove his innocence! In contrast, those who had come up in tougher circumstances got drunk because they knew (correctly, of course) that it was all over. They were the realists.

So be cautious about assuming everything you see on the surface is the full reality. During Watergate, I worked three doors down the hall from John Dean, but until he testified and wrote a memoir, I never knew that on presidential orders he was running a mafia-like operation. During the Reagan years, I worked next door to Mike Deaver in the West Wing but never knew that under lots of stress, he became an alcoholic. Even as you should be caring about others nearby, you should be careful among the powerful in high places, keep your antennae up, learn whom you can trust, and figure out who would be a good companion in a foxhole. And when you become a leader yourself, build an organization and a culture in which people trust and are honest with each other. Trust but verify, as Reagan liked to say.

As much as leaders should pledge themselves to run open, transparent organizations, it is also worth remembering that there will be moments when they must give up transparency for a cone of secrecy. The very founding of the country was accomplished with stealth: When delegates to the Constitutional Convention gathered in Philadelphia in 1787, the publicly stated reason was to modify the Articles of Confederation. The real reason was to throw out the Articles and replace them with a new written constitution. The founders met behind closed doors—away from the press and other prying eyes—so they could draft the constitution in secret. Had they met in the open, it is likely they would have failed.

Lincoln decided to hide the Emancipation Proclamation from public view until Union forces had won a major battle. Only when victory was secured at Antietam did he reveal the Proclamation. In 1937, FDR gave a speech in Chicago suggesting the United States might be dragged into a second European conflict. The public response was so furious that FDR quickly backed down, but in secrecy, he continued preparations for war—a wise decision, as it turned out.

In his memoir *Edge of the Sword*, Charles de Gaulle wrote that a leader "must know when to dissemble, when to be frank. He must pose as a servant of the public in order to become its master . . . and only after a thousand intrigues and solemn understandings will he find himself with full power." The man who introduced me to de Gaulle's memoir was Richard Nixon.

How should you decide whether use of guile, dissembling, and the like is justifiable? There is no easy answer, and much depends on context. But as a rule of thumb, the use of the low arts should be rare and should be employed only when they serve the legitimate needs of an organization—not the aggrandizement of the leader.

As mentioned earlier, when Francis Gary Powers was shot down flying a spy plane over the Soviet Union, for example, President Eisenhower publicly lied, insisting that Powers was flying a weather plane. Justifiable? Yes, I think so. Ike was trying to prevent sensitive arms talks from collapsing; he also hated to deceive the public. When his lie about Powers was exposed and the talks crumbled, he was mortified and thought of quitting. He told a friend that if a president has lost his credibility, "he has lost his greatest strength." Ike seems in a whole different moral universe than ours today, when we are drowning in political lies and misrepresentations. We should recognize that when leadership has no worthy purpose, it becomes manipulation and deception; leadership in a good cause is much more justifiable.

We should also recognize, however, that leadership today requires a hard head along with a soft heart. Almost every leader I have known has at one time or another had to be tough. After serving as president of Duke University and Wellesley College, Nan Keohane told an audience at the Kennedy School how she occasionally needed to be "ruthless." Young leaders could learn a great deal from Nancy Pelosi about combining realism with idealism. She has always remembered what her father taught her: "No one's going to give you power. You have to seize it." Richard Nixon liked to quote William Gladstone, thrice British prime minister, who argued that in organizing the team around him, "Every prime minister must be a good butcher."

We live in an age of cacophony, surrounded by cries of despair and a hunger for power. The leaders who serve us best will be those who are steadfast in pursuing their True North—and also keep a club in the closet.

TWELVE

LEADING THROUGH
A CRISIS

In 1962, the apartheid government of South Africa clapped Nelson Mandela into jail on false charges of sedition. He spent the next two years behind bars and was then sentenced to life imprisonment on Robben Island, just off Cape Town. There he remained for eighteen of an eventual twenty-seven years in prison, living in an eight-by-seven-foot cell with a tiny window and three blankets. Only by making a pilgrimage to Robben Island can you fully understand the cruelty inflicted upon him. Conditions were harsh: He toiled under the blazing sun of a quarry day in and day out, cycled through solitary confinement, and could write and receive only one censored letter, initially just from family, every six months. "You have no idea of the cruelty of man against man," Mandela said later, "until you have been in a South African prison with white wardens and Black prisoners." For him, as for some thirty other imprisoned members of the African National Congress (ANC), life became an unending crisis.

But Mandela reached deep inside and, miraculously, left stronger than he had entered. As his biographer Anthony Sampson has written, when he was stripped of all political trappings—newspapers, crowds, well-tailored suits—Mandela was "compelled to think more deeply about his principles and ideas." He stood back to see himself as others did; he learned to control his temper and strong will and to empathize and gain influence and authority over his wardens. He had been an ANC leader while underground, and upon his release, he emerged as their leader again. After his imprisonment, Mandela and his team ended apartheid and won the right to free elections; in 1994, he won that first fully representative election, becoming South Africa's first Black president.

When other prisoners at Robben Island became despondent, Mandela comforted and inspired them. As encouragement, he loved to recite to them the final stanza of "Invictus," a poem by the popular Victorian writer William E. Henley:

> *It matters not how strait the gate,*
> *How charged with punishments the scroll,*
> *I am the master of my fate,*
> *I am the captain of my soul.*

Invictus is Latin for "invincible." The poem tells us that life can bring great crises and suffering, but no matter how hard it is to get to heaven, others cannot determine your fate or steal your soul. You make yourself. For years, British schoolchildren learned the poem by heart, and that last stanza remains a staple of civic life today. Churchill paraphrased the last two lines in a speech bucking up Parliament during the war. After his impeachment in 1995, a dejected and angry President Clinton said that Mandela consoled him through conversations about its message. President Obama quoted the poem in a memorial service in South Africa in 2013. John Lewis liked to repeat the poem as a teenager and in Congress.

We have seen in earlier chapters how leaders must frequently struggle with crises in their individual lives—crucibles, as we called them. The Mandela story takes us up to a whole different level: how leaders and their allies must overcome crises that threaten a whole society. Had it not been for the leadership of Mandela and allies like Archbishop Desmond Tutu, Walter Sisulu, Oliver Tambo, Winnie Mandela, and—let us be frank—F. W. de Klerk, South Africa might have plunged into a bloody civil war; instead, it avoided catastrophe—at least for a while. "There is no easy walk to freedom anywhere," Mandela warned, "and many of us will have to pass through the valley of the shadow of death again and again before we reach the mountaintop of our desires." He learned when young how to lead by watching and admiring the skills of negotiation and persuasion by tribal chieftains. He noticed that the leader was "like a shepherd . . . He stays behind the flock, letting the most nimble go out ahead, whereupon the others follow, not realizing that all along they are being directed from behind." For most of his life, he embraced the role of shepherd, leading from behind. But when the South Africans wanted a negotiated peace, Mandela immediately moved to the front where he could work things out.

ADAPTING TO A VUCA WORLD

Crises have come and gone over time, but we have now entered an age when they are striking the world with a force, frequency, and intensity most of us have never experienced before. Massive deaths from a virus, plunging economies, gun violence, inequities in race, class, and gender, climate changes that are becoming irreversible, democracies threatened, a loss of trust in our leaders and institutions—the litany has become distressingly familiar. And if past is prologue, even nastier crises lay ahead.

In the 1990s, the U.S. Military Academy at West Point tried to pull together a memorable way to focus cadets on the world they would be entering after graduation. What kind of characteristics would it have? They settled upon an acronym, VUCA, which stands for:

Volatility

Uncertainty

Complexity

Ambiguity

The acronym stuck and is used today to train not only young army officers but officers of numerous corporations as well. We now live in a VUCA world.

The question becomes: How can we prepare a generation of rising leaders to prepare for challenges just over the horizon? What are the values that will be most essential in their leadership? What steps must they take in their institutions to deal effectively with future crises? It is obvious that we must act—and act with urgency—to confront these ever-growing challenges. In the pages ahead, we will explore the personal qualities that seem most essential for leaders coping with crises today, and then we will look at a four-step approach that institutions can use in like situations.

THE RIGHT STUFF TODAY

We have emphasized in earlier pages qualities leaders should have regardless of circumstance or sector: character, courage, integrity, moral purpose, vision, adaptability, grit, and persuasion foremost among them. Those same qualities remain essential in times of crisis. But crises also make other demands on leaders, and they must find qualities inside themselves that they may not even realize are there.

The historian David McCullough, for example, tells the story of a young Harry Truman in World War I. Truman was then running a small haberdashery in his hometown of Independence, Missouri. When America entered the war, he tried to enlist but was refused because his eyesight was too poor. So he memorized the eye chart and made it on a second try. He and his artillery battery then shipped out to France and were soon trapped in the terrifying Battle of the Argonne.

While they were camping in the mountains at night in the rain, the Germans unleashed a frightening barrage of artillery on them. Inexperienced, his troops thought it might be a deadly gas attack, threw on their masks, tried to mask their horses, and then ran in all directions. Truman's horse threw him off, nearly crushing him. But Truman lifted himself up and shouted for his men to return, "using every form of profanity he'd ever heard. And back they came."

He eventually brought his men home alive, and they were his devout followers for years after. Truman, concluded McCullough, "learned two vitally important things about himself. First, that he had courage, plain physical courage. Until then he had never been in a fight in his life . . . Second, that he was good at leading people. He liked it and he had learned that courage is contagious. If the leader shows courage, others get the idea." The war had become his proving ground.

Drawing from the past and my own experiences, I would suggest that there are four other qualities essential for effective leadership in a crisis:

"A Great Carelessness of Self"

In his delightful 2007 memoir, *This Time, This Place: My Life in War, the White House, and Hollywood,* the late Jack Valenti wrote about his visit to graveyards of soldiers lost at Normandy. A Frenchwoman, then mayor of Deauville, urged him to visit one particular tombstone to understand the bravery of those who had died in battle. There at the bottom of a grave marker, he found this inscription: LEADERSHIP IS WISDOM AND COURAGE AND A GREAT CARELESSNESS OF SELF.

Among the leaders we most admire, we so often find that sentiment today. Think of the firefighters and policemen on 9/11, knowing they would likely die, climbing up the stairs of the World Trade Center while civilians were climbing down. Or Rachel Carson racing against time to finish her pathbreaking book about the environment

even as cancer was exacting its deadly toll. Or John Lewis crossing
the Edmund Pettus Bridge, knowing that he would be clubbed and
might die. Or Lenny Skutnick, a federal employee, jumping into the
icy Potomac River to save a young woman who had gone down in
a commercial aircraft. Or Dietrich Bonhoeffer insisting he return to
Nazi Germany to save his country, knowing Hitler would make him
a marked man. All of them put the lives of others first, showing great
carelessness of self.

Prudent Judgment

As we have seen, the need for prudent judgment is one of the most
important qualities a leader must have, especially in a crisis. But how
does one acquire something as elusive as keen judgment? Ted Sorensen, a JFK confidant, liked to tell the story of a junior associate
asking a senior partner in a New York law firm, "Why do you have
this reputation for judgment?" "Well, I guess I've made the right decision enough times." "But what was the basis on which you made the
right decisions?" "Oh, that comes from experience." "One last question: What's the experience based on?" "Wrong decisions."

Students of decision-making tend to agree on the main qualities
needed for judgment. A prudent leader, it is often said, must be informed by experience and have a curiosity about the world, a grasp of
relevant data and information, a sense of responsibility for their team,
and the patience and perseverance to see it through hard times.

There is one other asset that is little discussed but that historically has proven to be critical: the strength that comes from years in
the wilderness. We have seen it repeatedly among great statesmen:
From Charles de Gaulle to Konrad Adenauer, Mandela to Churchill,
all experienced years when they were sidelined or imprisoned, during
which they had time to reflect and write. Even Nixon made serious
use of his wilderness years in the 1960s.

Fingerspitzengefühl

This is a German word that means "fingertips feel"—an elusive concept describing how a person might have an instinctive feeling or intuitive flair. In English, it might be thought of as situational awareness. Those who possess it often have a feel for how events are likely to unfold and can prepare themselves early. Some leaders are born with it, but more often it builds up through extensive experience in the public arena, refining one's sense of social dynamics and the capacity to anticipate. Over the years, I have learned that those who can look around corners and into the future often have an advantage in shaping outcomes. They can anticipate, think through possible scenarios, and know how to react when the landscape shifts beneath their feet. Before battle, Napoleon would work through half a dozen scenarios of how the fight might evolve, so that if it changed direction, he had already anticipated and could stay ahead of the enemy. A leader always needs a capacity for swift response.

Similarly, smart leaders see that the best way to reach an objective is not always a straight line. A young Abraham Lincoln, for example, made a couple of trips down the Mississippi River to New Orleans to trade in goods. One might assume that he would put his raft in the middle of the river and float it straight down. But he learned from experience that if you pursued that strategy, your raft would likely capsize. Instead, he was instructed to first steer his raft toward a farmhouse downriver on the right side, then turn and aim toward a big tree downriver on the left side, and so forth. It might take longer but he would eventually make it—without drowning. I call that "point-to-point leadership," and I urge students to keep that metaphor in mind as they plan out their lives.

Coolness under Fire

On my dream sheet for my first billet in the navy, I had two requests: to serve in Asia and to avoid service as an engineer. Of course, they assigned me to be the assistant engineer and damage control officer for a large ship home ported in Sasebo, Japan. First, they said, I needed to go to damage control school on Treasure Island, where they trained us in fighting fires, combating flooding, and the like.

I thought I was well prepared for duty—until trouble actually hit. While our repair ship was providing service for four destroyers in Japan, an admiral came on board for an inspection. Shortly after his arrival, one of our four engines went down. Keeping it going was my responsibility, so I rushed to the scene. As we were trying to get the first engine up and running again, a second engine went down. Within an hour, all four engines were down and some mates were looking daggers at me. It took over two days of intensive effort to get any power. Even if I had wanted to extend my time in the navy, I was sure that the navy no longer wanted to extend its time with me. But I did get credit for one thing: My sailors thanked me for keeping my cool. Cool and steady—that is a prime requirement for leadership. In the years since, I have come across an observation by Herman Melville in 1850 that says it all:

In time of peril, like the needle to the lodestone,
obedience, irrespective of rank, generally flies
to him who is best fitted to command.

Later in life, a bigger incident occurred that drove home to me just how important it is for leaders to remain cool in a crisis. Just eight weeks into the presidency of Ronald Reagan, John Hinckley Jr. shot him at close range and his bullet ripped to within an inch of Reagan's heart.

As soon as word spread in Washington, leaders of our government rushed to the West Wing and then downstairs into the Situation Room. Several key players were scattered. Vice President George Bush was in an airplane heading toward Texas, and Chief of Staff Jim Baker had gone to the hospital along with Ed Meese and Mike

Deaver. Secretary of State Al Haig, Defense Secretary Caspar Wein-
berger, NSC Director Richard Allen, White House heavyweight
Richard Darman, and I gathered in the Situation Room. (I was White
House staff director at the time.)

It wasn't clear who was in charge of our government. Al Haig, former chief of staff to Nixon and now secretary of state, proclaimed that
he was. "The helm is right here in this chair," he announced. No one
was in a mood to protest, but tensions between Haig and Weinberger,
always high, soon boiled over. Weinberger had unilaterally raised the
country's defenses to high alert, and Haig was furious at him, worried
that our adversaries would think us in disarray and vulnerable.

Unexpectedly, our deputy press secretary, Larry Speakes, returned
from the hospital through a side door and, unaware of heated conversations in the Situation Room, innocently went to the podium to take
questions. On about the third question, reporters began asking Larry
about DEFCON (the level of military alert). Larry had no idea and
began stumbling over answers.

"We have to get him off the podium!" shouted Haig as he jumped
up, ran out of the Situation Room, and lurched up the stairs toward the
press room. Dick Allen and I went scooting after him. As he reached
the top of the stairs, Haig was red-faced and perspiring heavily. But he
refused to stop, catch his breath, and compose himself. He didn't look
cool; he looked crazed.

In he burst, seizing the podium in front of clamoring reporters
and whirring TV cameras. After a couple of softball questions, a
reporter demanded, "Who is in charge here?" Haig couldn't resist:
"Constitutionally, gentlemen, you have the president, the vice president, and the secretary of state in that order, and should the president
decide he wants to transfer the helm, he will do so. He has not done
that. As of now, I am in control here, in the White House, pending the
return of the vice president."

With that assertion, all hell broke loose. Al had meant to calm
things down; instead, he set off alarm bells across the country and

perhaps the world. He had created a jarring impression that the White House itself was out of control. It didn't help that he had also mangled the legal line of succession.

Later on, Al ran for president, but his candidacy quickly went down in flames. What voters remembered was his intemperate, red-faced, perspiring performance in a moment of high stress. He never recovered. It was a lasting lesson that a leader who loses his cool during a crisis won't be a leader very long. Crises are make-or-break moments for institutions as well as their leaders.

One of my favorite Reagan stories came fifteen months into his presidency when he decided to make a prime-time speech to the country, urging passage of his budget. Budget talks can be real snoozers; my job as his communications director was to spice it up.

White House technology in those days was primitive, so I suggested to Reagan that he use an easel and a chart. In the middle of the speech, he was to get up from his desk, walk over to the easel, and then use a red felt-tip pen to draw a thick line on the chart, showing how high deficits would rise if Congress failed to act. He agreed, and we set the speech for 9:00 P.M. East Coast time.

Even an experienced speaker like Reagan likes a warm-up, so I also recommended that he come over to the Oval Office early, to give him time to rehearse. The rehearsal went flawlessly, as Reagan—while continuing to read from the teleprompter—drew the line with a red felt-tip pen and returned to his desk. We were in great shape—or so I thought.

As the speech opened, Reagan sailed along until he got up and walked over to the easel. With horror, we realized that we had not put the cap back on that red felt-tip pen. Under the hot klieg lights of the television cameras, that damn pen had gone bone dry. When the president tried to draw the line, the only thing that came out of that pen was a long *screeech*. No line. An awful silence.

I was standing on the other side of the Oval Office, behind the cameras . . . mentally updating my résumé.

Thank goodness, our TV producer at the White House, Mark Goode, had more foresight than I had. He had brought a second pen! Mark immediately went down on his hands and knees, crawling toward Reagan. The Secret Service was perplexed—their rule book does not say what to do if a staff member crawls toward the president. Reagan himself was cool but seemed to be wondering, *Why is this jackass crawling across my floor?*

Mark quickly crawled around the back of Reagan's desk, got to the president's feet, and, off camera, held up the second pen. A little twinkle came into Reagan's eye. He scooped up the new pen and, without missing a beat, said something to the effect, "I think I will try my pen again." Magically, the line appeared and the night—and probably my job—was saved.

In the many times I have retold that story, I still imagine that if Nixon had been giving that speech, he would have thrown us into the Rose Garden, called off the speech, and had bombers flying over Hanoi the next morning. But Reagan was a natural at television. It was his friend. Like the Wallenda brother who said the tightrope was what mattered in life and all else was waiting, Reagan lived for the moments when he could move huge audiences.

AN OSTRICH NATION?

The United States has an enviable record of addressing national and international crises when we are fully engaged, especially in fighting threats to our way of life. One tale tells the story: As World War II approached, the United States was building five thousand planes a year. FDR asked experts how many we could build if fully mobilized. "Some twenty-five thousand," they replied. "Good," said FDR, "but not good enough." He then shocked Congress when he proposed building no less than fifty thousand aircraft a year by war's end. The critics scoffed that it couldn't be done. "You don't know Americans the way I do," he shot back. "Just you wait and see."

Well, it is true that by the end of the war, we weren't building fifty thousand planes a year—we were building some seventy-five thousand! That's who we are when we fully mobilize as a people. As Theodore Roosevelt once put it, "The American people are slow to wrath, but when their wrath is once kindled, it burns like a consuming flame."

Our problem is that in recent years, we have developed a bad habit of ignoring crises when they are just starting to bubble up and we aren't yet convinced the threat is serious, much less mortal. Our political leaders these days prefer to kick the can down the road, borrowing from the future and leaving the bills to the next generation. We have repeatedly paid no notice to the warning signs of trouble and stuck our heads in the sand. We have become an ostrich nation.

We no longer have that luxury. We are now hit by new crises on a continuous basis—they are rapidly becoming our new normal.

There is only one thing worse than the mayhem of these past twenty years: the tragic fact that so much of this death and destruction could have been avoided if we had paid attention and acted on early signs of trouble. A bipartisan national commission investigating 9/11 concluded that despite warning signs, federal intelligence agencies had failed to imagine the magnitude of the threat and thus never stopped it. Experts at Louisiana State University knew that New Orleans wasn't prepared for a Hurricane Katrina, warning government officials to no avail. Another federal inquiry concluded that the financial crisis of 2008–9 was foreseeable: "The captains of finance and the public stewards of our financial system ignored warnings and failed to question, understand, and manage evolving risks within a system essential to the well-being of the American public."

For years, climatologists around the world have issued dire warnings about rising temperatures, saying that a temperature rise of 1.5 degrees Celsius or more and its irreversible impacts on the environment within the next two decades are all but inevitable, and yet the international community still fails to take decisive action. Experts at the Lancet Commission on Public Policy and Health say that almost 200,000 American lives were lost to COVID in the Trump era because of an "inept and insufficient" response coupled with trends of poor management of American health. There is also nothing secret about the inequities that Black Americans suffer in the United States; the average white household has almost eight times the amount of wealth of the average Black household, the life expectancy gap between Black and white Americans grew to five years in 2020, and police brutality, imprisonment inequalities, and daily discrimination continually disadvantage Black Americans. We are beginning to acknowledge the depths of systemic oppression, yet we lack the will to make real change. We know as well that despite signs to the contrary, neither police nor members of Congress anticipated how massive and deadly a mob assault would be on the Capitol—and how close we came to an absolute catastrophe.

We could go on by probing other smaller but no less jarring crises—the Boston Marathon bombing, Sandy Hook, Parkland, and more—but the point is clear: The darkness that has descended upon our lives with one crisis after another, especially COVID, could well become a way of life unless we change course.

A growing number of scholars, journalists, and thought leaders have begun focusing on what must be done. The federal government is stepping up its investment in protection. Masters of industry have begun moving from shareholder to stakeholder capitalism. And young social entrepreneurs are trying to double and redouble their impact on society. Through their work, it has become apparent that when trouble approaches, a four-step approach is in order.

First, Head Off the Crises That Are Preventable

In their important 2004 book *Predictable Surprises: The Disasters You Should Have Seen Coming and How to Prevent Them*, Max Bazerman, a professor at the Harvard Business School, and Michael Watkins point to 9/11 and the Enron scandal as classic failures in anticipating crises. Too often those at the top of organizations have biases in favor of the status quo; they ignore the signs of impending trouble or underestimate the costs of inaction. "One of the main responsibilities of leadership," Bazerman and Watkins conclude, "must be to identify and avoid predictable surprises. Most leaders recognize growing system weaknesses in their organizations that have the potential to flash into major crises over time." It can't be repeated enough: Forewarned is forearmed.

Second, Prepare for the Worst

When confronted with evidence that a crisis may strike soon, organizations must pull together their teams to prepare for it and conduct repeated practices. New York City was much better prepared for 9/11 because a previous failed attack on the World Trade Center in 1993 had alerted leaders to its vulnerabilities. The city developed elaborate plans and practiced them carefully. When the planes struck, Mayor Rudy Giuliani didn't have to assemble firefighters and police around a table to figure out what to do. They already knew and were able to save countless lives—while sacrificing many of their own. Similarly, medical teams and law enforcement in Boston had practiced repeatedly in advance to prepare for an emergency. When terrorists struck at the Boston Marathon in 2013, ambulances began delivering victims to local hospitals within nine minutes of the first explosions; every single victim who made it to a hospital survived.

Following 9/11, the Centers for Disease Control reached out to faculty at Harvard's Chan School of Public Health and the Kennedy School to develop an executive education program for first responders nationwide. Dr. Leonard Marcus and associates at Chan took the lead, and I served as an early copilot. They have built a first-class platform to study and train first responders, the National Preparedness Leadership Initiative (NPLI). Now eighteen years old, it has trained thousands of leaders from government, humanitarian organizations, and businesses large and small. They have also developed a theory of how to weave together leadership across multiple organizations. They call it "meta-leadership," the concept that in complex systems, a big part of leadership is the capacity to work well with organizations beyond one's immediate circle, creating connectivity and collaboration. To repeat: In this field, as in so many others, collaboration has become the key to leadership success.

Third, When a Crisis Hits, Reassure the Public and Then Solve the Problem

Trouble can come in a thousand ways. The key to dealing with it is whether the response team is strong and prepared. If it is, a leader should unleash the team members to do their jobs without interference while the leader becomes the public face of the emergency response. For years, leadership studies have focused on the way Rudy Giuliani stepped up on 9/11, giving meaning to the event and reassuring a frightened public. He had been reading a biography of Churchill in the evenings before, and it showed. By contrast, leadership studies of tomorrow will focus on how a White House administration—led by the president himself—massively bungled their response to the coronavirus, losing lives, jobs, and a sense of mental well-being for a whole generation.

Fourth, When the Crisis Subsides, Write What the Army Calls an After-Action Report

What actually happened? Why did it unfold that way? What lessons have we learned? How can we be better prepared the next time? The report by the 9/11 Commission is a worthy template for others: The commission was bipartisan, had an excellent staff, delved deeply, and issued a wide array of recommendations. From it came a sweeping

effort to strengthen homeland security and intelligence. The road has
sometimes been bumpy, but we are far better prepared to combat terrorism than we once were.

As Jordan Tama of American University pointed out in *The Washington Post*, "The track record of U.S. commissions is decidedly mixed
but includes some striking achievements." A commission appointed
by Teddy Roosevelt led to formation of the Federal Reserve, one of
the best reforms of the twentieth century. A commission created by
Harry Truman was influential in shaping the Marshall Plan. And an
all-volunteer military grew out of a Nixon-appointed commission.
Keys to success here are a high degree of public interest; the quality of
the commissioners; the strength of the staff; and a commitment by a
White House or Congress to action.

As you can imagine, the literature on leadership in times of crisis is
vast and growing rapidly. If you have a deeper interest, I recommend
you start by reading recent books by two historians who are among
the nation's best storytellers: *Leadership in Turbulent Times*, by Doris
Kearns Goodwin; and *Forged in Crisis: The Power of Courageous Leadership in Turbulent Times*, by Nancy Koehn. Both are highly instruc-
tive and splendid reads.

In the meantime, let's return to the heart of what it means to lead
during a crisis: the capacity of men and women in the most dire of
circumstances to endure—even triumph—together over forces allied
against them. Their courage and their camaraderie are continuing
sources of awe. In his previously mentioned account from his days
as a prisoner of war, Jim Stockdale writes of the torture and solitary
confinement he regularly endured. On one occasion, dragged back
to his cell after months of torture, he passed by the tiny window of
Dave Hatcher, a fellow prisoner. Hatcher could not peek out, but he
could recognize Stockdale from his limping gait. Soon Stockdale noticed that a rusty wire in the washroom was pointed north. That was
a signal for any POW to look in a bottle under the sink for a message.

Stockdale scooped up the note and, back in his cell, unfolded it. There, Hatcher had used rat droppings to print out a verse for his comrade in arms:

> *It matters not how strait the gate,*
> *How charged with punishments the scroll,*
> *I am the master of my fate,*
> *I am the captain of my soul.*

THIRTEEN

BOOSTER ROCKETS

We have explored the qualities and skills that are universally acknowledged to be important for leaders—character, courage, moral purpose, self-mastery, and the like. But there are other qualities that receive too little attention in the literature—qualities that often spell the difference between a good leader and a first-class leader. In my experience, for example, those who have a keen curiosity and a love of history often have better judgment. Witness John F. Kennedy during the Cuban Missile Crisis. Similarly, I have found that leaders who have an abiding sense of humor, often laughing at themselves, can create a warmth that connects to others. Witness Ronald Reagan the day he was shot. I have learned as well that leaders who seek an integrated life, aligning their values and aspirations for both work and family, can achieve an inner calm that serves them well during storms. Witness Barack Obama, aka No Drama Obama.

In this chapter, we will take a deeper look at all three of these propositions: a reading of history, humor, and an integrated life. I would argue that each serves as a booster rocket for a leader.

LEARNING FROM HISTORY

Not often does a historian of the past shape our way into the future, but some six decades ago, Barbara Tuchman did just that.

In the spring of 1962, Tuchman published a book titled *The Guns of August*. It argued that through a series of miscalculations and misjudgments, Europe and eventually the United States blundered into World War I, one of the bloodiest and longest conflicts known to man.

President John F. Kennedy, a devoted follower of Tuchman, devoured the book and ordered every member of his cabinet as well as his military chieftains to read it. His army chief of staff in turn sent copies to every military installation, ordering the officers there to read it. It quickly rose on the bestseller list and remained there for forty-two weeks.

Then in October of 1962, the CIA discovered that the Soviet Union was installing missile sites in Cuba, ninety miles from the American shore and within striking distance of Washington, D.C. As I mentioned in our discussion of crises, the next thirteen days became the most perilous in American history.

Early on, John F. Kennedy brought in his brother Bobby, then attorney general and his closest confidant. According to Bobby, his brother warned, "I am not going to follow a course which will allow anyone to write a comparable book about this time, *The Missiles of October*. If anybody is around to write after this, they are going to understand that we made every effort to find peace and every effort to give our adversary room to move." Soviet leader Nikita Khrushchev was impulsive and could be erratic; Kennedy was determined that the United States play a steady, sure hand.

A moment of truth arrived when Kennedy's team of advisors reached a consensus decision: Just as the Soviets were installing missiles in secret, the United States should launch a secret attack against the weapon sites, wiping them out. There would be no forewarning, no alert to allies, and little advance notice to Congress.

But Bobby and a couple of others began having second thoughts. Gradually, the advisors moved away from their first consensus, embracing a less aggressive idea: a quarantine. Persuaded by Llewellyn Thompson, the former ambassador to the Soviet Union who knew Khrushchev well, President Kennedy also wanted to avoid pushing the Soviet leader into a corner where, like a snake, he would feel he had no choice but to strike back. No miscalculations this time.

Fortunately, the Soviets seized upon the American willingness to negotiate, and they backed down. Years later, the United States learned for the first time that the Soviets had tipped the missiles with nuclear weapons. Had the United States struck the Soviet missiles out of the blue, as first planned by the Kennedy team, some missiles would have survived and Khrushchev would almost certainly have fired them into Washington, D.C., triggering a nuclear holocaust. "We went eyeball to eyeball, and the other guy blinked," said Dean Rusk, the secretary of state. Had it not been for a willingness to negotiate, the world may have been incinerated. (One wonders if China and the United States would be equally eager to negotiate if we were on the edge of a precipice.)

Over the next several years, the Cuban Missile Crisis stirred strong academic interest in lessons learned for decision makers in the federal government. Ted Sorensen, as I have mentioned earlier, delivered a speech analyzing the judgment of Kennedy in a crisis. Professor Graham Allison organized a series of study groups and papers at the Kennedy School and six years later published a highly influential study of different models of decision-making.

Two other professors at the Kennedy School, Richard Neustadt and Ernest R. May, wrote a well-received book, *Thinking in Time: The Uses of History for Decision Makers*, that became the basis of one of the school's most popular courses. They argued that during the deliberations, Kennedy "shifted from the simple question of what to do *now* to the harder question: How will today's choices appear when they are history—when people look back a decade or a century more?" Kennedy came to see his decisions in a stream of time, his judgment well informed by his reading of history.

In leadership studies these days, we often overlook how important it is for leaders to have an abiding curiosity about the past and an eagerness to learn from historians how these lessons might apply to the future. The days ahead are full of uncertainty, but we can find solace in understanding how we have overcome challenges of the past; as Mark Twain is credited with saying, "History does not repeat itself, but it often rhymes." The ancients understood: Remember that Philip II of Macedon hired Aristotle to tutor his son Alexander. And when Alexander became a warrior, traveling the known world, it was said he kept under his pillow a copy of the *Iliad* as well as a dagger. Alexander was not only bold but also had a strong mind.

Most of our own founders—Jefferson, Adams, Hamilton, Madison, and Franklin—were extremely bright and attached to their books. Jefferson kept his first collection at his home in Albemarle County, Virginia; when it burned down along with his collection, he said he most regretted the loss of his books. Later on, after the British burned the original Library of Congress collection in 1814, he gave his new collection to the library and let them set the price. The 6,487 volumes became the foundation of the library Congress has today—one of the best in the world. John Adams gave his collection—some three thousand volumes—to his community in Quincy, Massachusetts, and they were eventually moved to the Boston Public Library. Adams often engaged in fierce colloquies with authors, penning notes in the margins. On my first visit to the Adams collection, the librarians showed me one Adams book in which he had written more words in the margin than were in the book itself!

America prided itself in the nineteenth century as the most literate country in the world. Lincoln, as we know, was not well schooled, but he'd taught himself to read, and when he had a book in hand, he would study its contents for hours, mastering its lessons. At the turn of the century, Teddy Roosevelt was a voracious reader, often tearing through a book a day in the White House. The novelist seen as the father of Western fiction, Owen Wister, wrote that he once visited his college friend TR in the White House and at dinner gave him a copy of his new novel. The next morning at breakfast, TR led a spirited discussion of the book, which he had read overnight. On the other side of the ocean in those same years, Winston Churchill was not only reading but writing at a furious pace.

Some years ago, I had an opportunity to speak at the Truman Presidential Library in Independence, Missouri. I fell in love with the place because it was modest—like Truman himself—and the docents would let you hold his letters and speeches. There I found a talk he made to visiting students, in which he told them: "Not every reader is a leader, but every leader is a reader."

No one provided better evidence than Truman himself. When he was a teenager, his mother gave him a multivolume book titled *Great Men and Famous Women.* His copy is there in his library, and in perusing it, you can see how many times he must have read or turned to it—it was clearly read and reread by the only president in the twentieth century who never went to college. When Truman graduated from high school, his parents could not afford further education, and he spent seven years behind a mule on his small family farm.

But he seized upon the moments to read, read, and read some more. Along the way, he became a model of a self-educated person. In 1948, President Truman faced an excruciatingly hard choice on whether to recognize the independence of Israel as a nation. Secretary of State George Marshall was against it (he worried that it would lead to a devastating war); Truman's White House counsel Clark Clifford was in favor (he argued it was a moral choice). Truman also knew that if he recognized Israel, there was a danger that Marshall would quit, costing Truman the presidential election in 1948. It was a very tough call.

Truman didn't duck. Instead, without notes, he proceeded to

trace for his advisors the history of the Middle East, the role of Israelis vs. Arabs, and the equities among the parties. He reportedly spoke nonstop for nearly two hours, reciting from memory. In the end, he accepted the risks and recognized Israel. To his credit, Marshall stuck by his president. Truman's love affair with history had paid off.

In our own time, General Jim Mattis captured the public imagination when he accepted an invitation from President Trump to serve as secretary of defense. Mattis was an intellectual, ramrod straight and deadly on the battlefield—a warrior monk, as he was called. As a boy, he wrote, he didn't really enjoy sitting in classrooms, and there was no TV at home, so he devoured books, from Hemingway to Faulkner to Fitzgerald. As a four-star general, he became one of the best-read figures since the founding of the corps.

The Marine Corps makes it a practice that with each promotion, a marine is given a new list of books to read relevant to his new responsibilities. Mattis pored over them and well beyond. He was partial to studying Roman writers, from Marcus Aurelius to Tacitus. As he wrote in his memoir, *Call Sign Chaos: Learning to Lead*, he followed Caesar across Gaul; marveled at the plain prose of Grant and Sherman, which revealed the value of steely determination; and studied strategy through Sun Tzu and Colin Gray. Before entering a new battle, he delved back into the history of the nations and the cultures where his marines would fight. By the time he retired, Mattis had a personal library filled with seven thousand books!

Mattis had stern counsel for rising leaders in the military: "If you haven't read hundreds of books, you are functionally illiterate, and you will be incompetent because your personal experiences alone aren't broad enough to sustain you. Any commander who claims he is 'too busy to read' is going to fill body bags with his troops as he learns the hard way."

Strikingly, I have also discovered that a number of our most successful CEOs are voracious readers. David Rubenstein, Bill Gates, Warren Buffett, Mort Zuckerman, Oprah Winfrey, and Sheryl

Sandberg, among others, have all made it a habit to read constantly. In every case I have encountered, across a number of disciplines, those who study the lessons of history make better leaders—more thoughtful, more aware of the vicissitudes of life, more hopeful about America's resilience.

In her leadership of the Children's Defense Fund, Marian Wright Edelman introduced me to an old Breton fisherman's prayer that can be used when thinking about service to others: "O God, thy sea is so great and my boat is so small." I feel the same way about books: Torrents of good books have been published in recent years, and I have managed to read so few of them.

My preferences have run consistently since college, when I switched out of political science studies midway through and pursued a degree in history. Political science is a good snapshot of where we are; history tells us how we got here. As Churchill said, a capacity to look farther back can also help you look farther ahead.

So I am mostly hooked on biographies and history. My favorite historians are great storytellers—like Doris Kearns Goodwin, Jon Meacham, David McCullough, Nancy Koehn, Fred Logevall, and others. David Rubenstein's conversations with historians have been a delightful surprise. And I still like to read a second or third time the writings of Barbara Tuchman and Stephen Ambrose.

Since I also have developed a deep interest in leadership, I have focused not only on American icons like Washington, Jefferson, Lincoln, and the three Roosevelts but also on international figures as well. Churchill and Mandela are my favorites; Plutarch helps me fill in other gaps. Warren Bennis got me started on leadership, and as you can tell from the pages here, he, John Gardner, Bill George, and others in their generation have had an enormous influence on my views.

For decades, I have tried to read every day *The New York Times, The Wall Street Journal, The Boston Globe, Financial Times*, and *The Washington Post*. And of course, I zone in on daily television news, starting with my friends at CNN.

For those of you who do not readily pick up a book, there are other ways to absorb the past. Video courses have become widely accessible to the public in the age of the internet, as have podcasts and audiobooks. Many schools and colleges these days are experimenting with ways to teach outside a classroom—"experiential learning," as it is called. Students welcome it. At Princeton, for example, students have flocked to a Civil War course long taught by Professor James McPherson, a renowned scholar of the war. One of their favorite classes each year is a trip to Gettysburg, where they walk the battlefields, seeing where Joshua Chamberlain and his men held off Confederates at Little Round Top and where Pickett's Charge failed, effectively ending Lee's campaign. Lessons from the trip are indelible.

One more point is in order: A habit of writing can be as important to leadership as a habit of reading. The discipline of writing things down on a blank page forces you to figure out what you really think. Whenever you can, you should take the opportunity to articulate your thoughts by jotting down early stage ideas, documenting phrases and questions as they come to mind, or perhaps keeping a daily journal. Sidney Harman, another highly successful CEO who was largely self-educated (he co-founded Harman Kardon), expressed the point well in his memoir, *Mind Your Own Business*: "Writing is not the simple transfer of fully formed intellectual inventory from brain to paper . . . Writing is discovery. It is, as Dylan Thomas said, 'the blank page on which I read my mind.'"

Churchill thought that one of the blunders of the British government in World War I was its reticence to write down for the record exactly what had been agreed upon in a meeting with military leaders. When instructions were orally sent down the line, they invariably lost clarity and mistakes were repeatedly made. During World War II, he insisted that only when an order was written down was it to be obeyed.

ON HUMOR AND LEADERSHIP

Years ago, I used to pal around on the lecture circuit with President Kennedy's press secretary, Pierre Salinger. He liked to tell the story of sitting in his West Wing office one morning when Kennedy summoned him to the Oval Office for a private talk.

"Pierre," said Kennedy, "I know you like a good cigar, as I do."

"Yes, sir, Mr. President!"

"Well, Pierre, I need a favor: I need you to get me some of Havana's finest by eleven tomorrow morning."

"Yes, sir, Mr. President. How many do you need?"

"A thousand."

"A thousand? Mr. President, that's going to be tough."

"You're a good man, Pierre. See you later."

The next morning at eleven, Kennedy called again. "Come see me, Pierre."

As soon as Pierre walked in, Kennedy asked: "Did you get those cigars?"

"Yes, sir, Mr. President. A thousand of Havana's finest."

"I knew you were a good man, Pierre. See you later."

An hour later, at noon sharp, the president of the United States announced to the world that he had just imposed a trade embargo against Cuba!

Now, that's a man with a sense of humor.

I retell this story because it underscores how important a sense of humor can be to effective public leadership. Certainly, that was true of the World War II generation, but a love of wit and humor began long before and, if we get our act together, will reappear as new generations come to power.

The most famous of storytellers in American history was Abraham Lincoln, of course. In 1862, with war raging and the Union Army stumbling, Lincoln called an emergency meeting of his top cabinet officers. He opened the session by reading a story from a humor book.

His cabinet was not amused. He read a second; still, no laughter. "Gentlemen," he has been quoted as saying, "why don't you laugh? With the fearful strain . . . if I did not laugh, I should die, and you need this medicine as much as I do." With that he turned to the business at hand: reading to them the first draft of one of the most important documents in the nation's history, the Emancipation Proclamation.

Lincoln found that at the most solemn and difficult moments in life, humor could ease his pain and lighten his spirits, and he often engaged in self-mockery. On one occasion, he acknowledged that he had "features the ladies could not call handsome." He then told a tale of walking through the woods when he met a woman on horseback. He stood aside to let her pass, but she looked him up and down. "Well, for land sake, you are the homeliest man I ever saw," she proclaimed. "Yes, madam . . . but I can't help it," he said. Said she, "No, I suppose not, but you might stay at home."

In Britain, wit often seems more prized than storytelling. Winston Churchill was a wonderful raconteur and an excellent dramatist, but he is better remembered for his repartee. Whole books have been written about Churchill's sharp tongue. I have long thought that among modern British leaders, Margaret Thatcher was second to Churchill in her witticisms. "If you want someone to deliver a speech," she once said, "ask a man. But if you want someone to get the job done, ask a woman." Hear, hear!

In America, we tend to prize humorous one-liners and storytelling more than repartee. No modern president has exceeded Ronald Reagan in those departments. A turning point in his presidency came two months after he took office, when an assassin nearly killed him, the bullet lodging an inch from his heart. On a gurney rushing toward surgery, Reagan looked up at surrounding doctors and said, "I hope you're all Republicans." That night from his isolated bed, he sent out notes to Nancy. "Gee, honey, I forgot to duck," he wrote, mimicking an old Jack Dempsey line. "All things considered, I would rather be in Philadelphia," he added, playing off a W. C. Fields line. Before the shooting, many Americans liked Reagan's warmth but weren't sure about his strength; after the shooting, they admired him as a man who could walk away from a bullet with a smile.

Reagan also understood the importance of self-deprecation. As the oldest president in history at the time, he often poked fun at his age. He famously transformed his campaign for reelection with a surprise one-liner. In his first presidential debate with Walter Mondale, Reagan was sluggish and seemed to lose his way. Stories appeared the next day asking if he had turned senile. His campaign was suddenly in peril. At their second debate, a journalist asked him directly about the age issue. Reagan's retort: "I want you to know that also I will not make age an issue of this campaign. I am not going to exploit, for political purposes, my opponent's youth and inexperience." Mondale knew in an instant that Reagan had just won the debate and the presidency.

What good leaders understand is that a capacity to laugh at the anxieties and absurdities of modern life won't solve your problems but will help you get through them. And if you are able to poke fun at yourself, especially your foibles, you will also be better at connecting with others and retaining your humility. To be sure, you must be careful with your humor, respectful and sensitive of those with different perspectives. But it is also true that we need more laughter in our public life today. Just as a Will Rogers could help us get through the Depression, we need humorists like Kate McKinnon and Stephen Colbert to get us through today.

CEOs should also appreciate that a light touch and a deft sense of humor can make the workplace a more enjoyable place. That was certainly true of the Reagan White House, where we enjoyed playing occasional pranks. White House ethics rules said that as staff, for example, you had to quickly give any gift you received to a special office in the old EOB. Our chief, Jim Baker, was fastidious about getting rid of any gift on the same day he received it.

One day, a large oil portrait of Baker himself arrived in his office. Before he had a chance to see it, Mike Deaver and I snuck it out of his office and into a closet, awaiting an appropriate moment. Not long after, the moment arrived: Reagan's birthday. As he and Nancy prepared to leave the White House for a weekend at Camp David, three of us—Baker, Deaver, and I—gathered in the Diplomatic Reception Room to talk with them, as we sometimes did. Deaver and I brought that portrait of Baker, all wrapped up in splendid paper. Baker wondered what the heck was going on.

"Mr. President," we intoned, "Jim has a very special gift for you and asked us to get it wrapped and present it to you here." Now Baker was really curious. "Oh, thank you, Jim," the president said. "Should we open it here?" "Yes, yes, of course," we said. So the president of the United States ripped away the wrappings and there he found— ta-da!—a portrait of his chief of staff! Baker went nuts. The president guffawed. And Deaver and I had our special moment.

AN INTEGRATED LIFE

Late one night in 1994, flying on Air Force One, President Clinton and I fell into a long conversation while traveling back from Morocco. I couldn't resist telling him the story of another president on a trip to Morocco years before. It was January 1943, and Franklin Roosevelt had flown to Casablanca for an important summit meeting with Winston Churchill, then British prime minister, and Allied chiefs of staff to plot military strategy against the Nazis. Charles de Gaulle also visited. Roosevelt and Churchill had met once before, but this was their first summit since the war started, so much was on the line.

FDR, absorbed by his day-to-day leadership of the war effort, was eager to complete their two-day summit and go home. Churchill, however, had other ideas: "You cannot come all the way to North Africa without seeing Marrakesh," he told the president. FDR was skeptical but Churchill persisted. "Let us spend two days there. I must be with you when you see the sun set on the Atlas Mountains."

So the two set off on the five-hour drive from Casablanca to

Marrakesh, stopping for a picnic break. Upon arrival, Churchill insisted that FDR accompany him to the top of a tower; two of his staff carried FDR up the winding stairs. There at the top, they could hear evening prayers while watching the sun capture the snowy peaks of the Atlas Mountains and then slip magically behind them. As FDR reclined on a couch, elated, he said to Churchill, "I feel like a sultan. You may kiss my hand, my dear."

FDR stayed a couple of days and was reenergized by his visit. Churchill stayed on a day longer to paint a watercolor. He sent it to FDR as a gift, the only such gift he gave during the war. Privately, Churchill exulted that he had achieved his underlying purpose: to bond with Franklin Roosevelt.

Talking with President Clinton that night, I mused with him how different his own trip to Morocco had just been. He had traveled to the Middle East for a series of conversations with leaders there. On the way home, he scheduled a quickie visit to Rabat to meet King Hassan; it was so brief that I am not sure if it counted as a foreign trip. To the best of my memory, we arrived at Rabat around two in the morning, roared into the city in a motorcade, had coffee with the king, and were back on Air Force One two hours later.

"Doesn't it seem strange to you," I asked Clinton, "that in a time of massive war, persuaded by Churchill, FDR could take a couple of days off to see the sun set in Morocco, while in a time of peace, you can't even take off a single day there? Are there too many time pressures on all of us these days?" He agreed—but only up to a point. "We have an important vote coming up back home. I have to be there."

I have often recalled that moment because it speaks so clearly to the rising demands on people's time these days. Whether you are a nurse in a hospital battling COVID, a young lawyer hanging out a shingle, or a farmer tilling the land, you must put in longer hours than a generation ago. The pressure of time, I have found, is even greater for most leaders. If you have climbed the ladder of success—a woman in Congress or a tech big shot—you are now expected to be connected

24/7. And the higher you climb, as Ronald Heifetz has observed, the greater your stress. Perhaps the pandemic will persuade people to cut back on travel and step up on Zoom. But it will not change one fundamental: Time has become the most precious asset in the lives of most leaders. To succeed in public life, you must learn how to discipline your time and focus your energies.

In earlier years, when the women's movement was getting underway with the leadership of Gloria Steinem and Betty Friedan, there was debate about how both women and men can create balance in their lives. If you work nine to five and try to sleep seven or eight hours a night, how can you also keep your marriage going, your children happy, and yourself mentally and physically fit? Or how can you join the local school board, take an active role in your church or synagogue, and get to your daughter's swim meet?

Over time, it became apparent that seeking balance was less and less successful as a strategy. As Warren Bennis argued, it is an engineering concept—a search for equilibrium—that has proven impossible with most professional lives. Especially since the pandemic hit, life has become too unpredictable to pledge how you will achieve balance from one month to the next or even one week to the next. Jobs are no longer nine to five. You must be prepared to change plans in an instant, going in early or coming home late. For centuries, Americans kept a Bible by the side of their bed; now we keep an iPhone.

Over time, the national conversation about work-life balance has evolved. Increasingly, the emphasis has changed to discussion of "an integrated life." Advocates essentially argue that you must be disciplined in how you spend your time but fluid in how you allocate it. There will be occasions when a big job comes along for a woman and her partner must adjust his own schedule to support her. Or a young child suffers an illness and a parent has to adjust. Careers can no longer be planned with certainty. Brad Stulberg, in *The Passion Paradox*, suggests thinking of balance in "seasons": One season might be heavily devoted to work projects and thus your hours are allocated toward those efforts, and another season might be more focused on building a family or personal life. Today, increasingly, young people are beginning to understand the benefits that come with viewing balance not as a dichotomy but as a continuum. Work and life often seamlessly merge into one another; flexibility options and the ability to be online from different locations can mean that work and life flow together. Gone are the days when "work" meant going to the office for a set number of hours. Of course, navigating this balance is a continuous struggle. The pandemic has, in many cases, further blurred boundaries between professional and personal life. Burnout and exhaustion continue to plague the workforce. But with increasing intentionality about how we consider our work and life, we might be able to strike an integration with which we can be satisfied.

In the literature about integration, authors usually divide one's time into four parts or buckets:

- Work
- Family and Loved Ones
- Community and Friends
- Personal Growth

The point is to prioritize how much you want each to fit into your life and then be quite intentional, even relentless, about integrating them into your day-to-day choices. In most surveys, people list work as their first priority. That is an age-old proposition for getting ahead. "Always bear in mind that your own resolution to succeed is more important than any other," Lincoln advised the young. "Work, work, work is the main thing." But if family and loved ones are also precious—as they are for most of us—you can't be obsessed with your work over months at a time. Instead, let your job dominate for a month or so before shifting back to serious family time—again, in "seasons." One of my biggest mistakes in life was to put work first month after month in the White House. As a result, I wasn't there much for our kids when they were young. Fortunately, my wife, Anne, was a superb mother who deserves the credit for how well they turned out. But I learned the hard way how important it is to achieve integration.

An integrated life demands an alignment of values and aspirations. Why are you here? What kind of person do you want to become? How do you want to serve others? What do you want in your relationships? What imprint do you hope to leave? Anne is a family therapist, working with hundreds on their family relationships. She has concluded that perhaps the best time to seek relational therapy is *before* marriage: What are you seeking in this relationship? Are your values and aspirations aligned? What kind of family might you wish to build? When people are on the same page, they are much more likely to be good partners. In that same spirit, I increasingly believe that you shouldn't take a job unless you find out in advance that it fits your values.

One of the reasons I became a huge personal fan of George H.W. Bush goes back to 1980 when he ran for president. After his team had initial talks with me about my joining the campaign, he invited me to spend a weekend with him and Barbara at their summer home in Kennebunkport, Maine. Arriving at the airport, I found to my great surprise that they had driven over twenty miles to pick me up. That same weekend they were entertaining an old friend, a Democratic congressman. We had a grand time talking, boating, and enjoying the beauty. I had an early plane out on Monday. At five-thirty that morning, a future president of the United States knocked at my door with a cup of coffee. And then he drove me to the airport, where he said, "I like to get to know someone before I work with them. I want to know who they are and what they are like." I had never met a political leader as gracious before or since. He had a well-integrated life, and we were in excellent alignment. I signed up!

As a leader, it is especially important that you also refresh and renew yourself on a regular basis. Followers take their cues from their leaders, a frequent theme of this book. If you exercise regularly, meditate, or find a related way to find an inner calm, have a reverence for a spiritual being, and are moderate in your habits, you will soon find that others on your team follow your inspiration as well as your instructions. Finding meaning and purpose outside the confines of work, of course, can also bring solace and contentment; make time for those practices as well. One of the reasons Bill George has become an authority on finding True North is that he is a seeker himself. Lamar Alexander is another public leader who has demonstrated an integrated life: After eight years as governor of Tennessee, he and his wife took their four children (ages eight to seventeen) for a six-month adventure together in Australia, to teach his kids about life outside a bubble. In my own case, after leaving the Reagan White House, I spent a semester at the Kennedy School (my introduction to it); most people thought I was on a fitness fellowship, as I worked off twenty pounds. If you can, take off for a sabbatical; it can be renewing.

Executive Summary: 20 Key Takeaways

When I wrote a book two decades ago, I was privileged to work with an extraordinary editor at Simon & Schuster, the late Alice Mayhew. Shortly before going to press, she called to say that we ought to tack on a series of leadership tips arising from the book—in effect, takeaways. I dashed off ten, sent them to Alice, and thought little more about them. What I discovered, however, is that readers said they got more nourishment out of them than anything else. Years later, audiences still recite them to me.

In that spirit, I herewith offer up to you twenty key takeaways from this book that I would suggest for your consideration. Hopefully, they will serve as an invitation to explore the full text.

OUR COUNTRY NEEDS A SERIOUS COURSE CORRECTION

A scant thirty years ago, the World War II generation left behind an America that was the strongest since ancient Rome in political, economic, military, and cultural affairs. Today we are tenth or twentieth in the world in terms of our well-being. We are on an unsustainable path, racing along the side of a cliff in the middle of the night with no headlights. The Biden presidency is trying to guide us to safety, but our path remains highly dangerous and will take years to secure. Our very democracy is threatened.

PREPARE NOW TO PASS THE TORCH TO NEW GENERATIONS

Fortunately, millions of talented young people are impatiently wait-ing in the wings to work for a better America. Our best hope in the years ahead is to identify, recruit, and help prepare them for lives of service and leadership. With the help of older generations, they must reach out across current divides to people of different backgrounds, races, and genders but who share basic values and common dreams. Whatever you may think of their politics, the MeToo movement, BLM, the Sunrise movement, the LGBTQ+ rights movement, and the Parkland students all prove it can be done.

LEADERSHIP, ALWAYS HARD, HAS BECOME HARDER

The long-term erosion of public trust and the complexity of our big-gest problems make leadership a much tougher terrain today than in years past. Yes, you can climb quickly through social media, but the pole is slippery and those who rise fast often descend even faster. Still, the younger generations of today have come through hell during their growing-up years and, from experience, have toughened up. They can do it. As an old saying goes, the strongest steel comes from the hottest fire.

LEADERSHIP STARTS FROM WITHIN

Those who aspire to lead others must first learn to lead themselves. As historian Nancy Koehn writes, leadership today must be exercised "inside out." Your path will have moments of exhilaration and moments of demoralization. Expect both. But never give up the fight. While it sure helps to have supportive friends, mentors, and sponsors along the way, you must ultimately make this journey on your own.

HAVE THREE OBJECTIVES EARLY

First, by your mid-twenties or a little later, figure out who you are inside. That self-knowledge is foundational. "An unexamined life is not worth living," as Aristotle said. Second, you need to build inner confidence in yourself. In her insightful book *Lead from the Outside* Stacey Abrams points out that women and people of color who are marginalized early on must overcome higher degrees of inner fear. Abrams spent much of her early journey coping with her anxieties. Third, become the master of your emotions. I was working in the White House when Richard Nixon's presidency collapsed. It was obvious that he had inner demons he had never learned to control. Eventually they brought him down.

FIND YOUR TRUE NORTH

Much of leadership literature has now embraced the idea that, over time, emerging leaders must settle upon the values and beliefs that will guide them through life. Through the centuries, leaders have been judged by their character, courage, and capacity. Those remain core values and should be your North Star in navigating through today's rough waters. In speaking about the American president, Henry Adams put it well: "He must have a helm to grasp, a course to steer, a port to seek."

FOCUS ON YOUR STRENGTHS

Ultimately, you must become the author of your own life. It may sound counterintuitive, but it's a waste of time working hard to go from mediocre to just plain average. Instead, as Peter Drucker and Jim Collins have argued, work on those areas of your life where you can go from good to great. Of course, you must overcome weaknesses that are disabling, but don't beat yourself up because you are not number one in every facet of leadership. That's why team building has become so central to corporate and social enterprises—pulling together people whose different strengths complement each other.

EXTEND YOUR LEADERSHIP JOURNEY OUTSIDE YOURSELF

You will discover that it is easier to decide what you don't want to do with your life than to decide what you really want to do. In my early years, I decided against half a dozen job paths—thankfully. In her book *When the Nightingale Sings*, Joyce Carol Thomas observes that a nightingale first sings when it hears another nightingale. And so it is with humans: We often come to life when we hear a voice that moves us. Two of the biggest figures in the leadership world, Warren Bennis and Bill George, each found themselves in powerful positions—one in academia, the other in corporate life—but their jobs didn't sing to them. Each left, accepting a less prestigious job that did appeal—and soon flourished. Each listened to his inner voice.

TRY HARD THINGS, FAIL, MOVE ON

President Kennedy liked to remind people of the Greek definition of happiness: "the full use of your powers along lines of excellence in a life affording scope." That was good advice then and it remains so now, especially as people today are aggressively searching for more happiness. Happiness comes, the Greeks believed, by seeking excellence in all that one does, no matter how trivial. And it comes from continually stretching yourself beyond your normal limits, whether at work or school. There is a temptation in all of us to live pleasantly, doing the easy thing. Spencer Johnson, who wrote *Who Moved My Cheese?*, urged me to not write a book that had leadership in the title because in their hearts, most people don't want the responsibilities of leadership. Instead, he said, I should title my book *Making a Difference*. Spencer knows a thing or two about book sales—*Cheese* sold 29 million copies. But I like to believe he was wrong and the Greeks were right about the true source of happiness.

YOU ARE NEVER TOO YOUNG TO LEAD

Just as you are never too old to serve others, you are never too young, either. One of the most persistent themes in this book is how often young people are now asserting themselves and attracting massive followings. After her reading at Biden's inaugural, the poet Amanda Gorman brought her voice to the nation; young athletes like Naomi Osaka and Simone Biles are bringing attention to social issues plaguing their communities and the nation; a wave of young, diverse voices made themselves heard in both 2018 and 2020, winning offices once held by those who traditionally wield power; we have also seen young people get to work protecting our democracy. They avoided what Tolstoy called "the snare of preparation"—spending so many years in a classroom preparing for life instead of living your life. By the time you hit your mid-twenties to early thirties, you should have begun your journey to service.

DEVOTE A YEAR TO NATIONAL SERVICE

Wherever you are in your journey, I urge you at some point to take real time out to serve others. Volunteer to work with an organization like City Year. Join with other young people of diverse backgrounds, helping other kids finish high school. City Year has had such a record of success that President Clinton modeled AmeriCorps after it. Go into classrooms as a volunteer in Teach For America. Sign up with the U.S. military for a couple of years; you will never find better training for leadership. Chrissy Houlahan served three years of active duty in the air force; later in life, after some time in the private sector, she signed up to teach science for Teach For America. Today, she is a representative in the U.S. Congress. In his first year as president, Franklin Roosevelt created the Civilian Conservation Corps (CCC), which, over time, invited unemployed men from around the country to refurbish our national forests and parks. No less than 2.5 million young men, many of them Black, served in the CCC; it was one of FDR's crowning achievements. It's time to create a robust AmeriCorps—one that can engage the energies of millions of our young.

SECURE YOUR FINANCES

Shoring up your personal resources has become an urgent priority for young, emerging leaders. We speak often about pursuing one's passions early in life, but we often forget to address the realities of financial security. For those of you who have the chance to save money early, do—it will provide you with freedom and independence down the line. For women and people of color, this becomes of particular importance in overcoming one of the many inherent systemic inequalities present in our society. In the workforce, women still make only 82 cents on the dollar compared to men, and women of color make even less. At upper levels, forty-one women—only 8 percent—are now CEOs of Fortune 500 companies. Building generational wealth begins with savings at a young age. Our society is ultimately responsible for bridging the gap, but until then, building personal financial security at a young age opens doors to opportunity down the line.

EMBRACE CRUCIBLE MOMENTS

Fate can deliver an unexpected and devastating blow in life. In his studies, Martin Seligman, the father of positive psychology, found that in a minority of cases, the victim never fully recovers. Others gradually regain their footing through strong, inner resilience. The good news is that some actually grow stronger inside; indeed, they come to embrace a moral purpose in life.

In 1881, nineteen-month-old Helen Keller lost her sight and hearing after an illness. She did not let that deter her from becoming an advocate and political activist. Several decades later, polio slammed into the life of Franklin Roosevelt; despite years of trying, he could never walk again. But through his struggle he became a deeper, more dedicated, more empathic leader. I believe that Joe Biden is a better and stronger president because of his crucible experiences, losing his wife and a child in a horrible accident and then losing a beloved son to cancer.

LEARN TO MANAGE YOUR BOSS

Many of us assume that leadership is about mobilizing people below you in a pecking order. In truth, most of us spend big chunks of our careers reporting to someone higher up. If you want more responsibility—and more pay—you need to figure out how to bring out the best in your boss. Take a leaf from major figures in the past: how Frances Perkins opened the eyes of FDR to poverty, how George Marshall took a big risk in speaking truth to his bosses, how James A. Baker III was masterful in working upward with President Reagan.

MOBILIZE OTHERS THROUGH PERSUASION

From the days of Demosthenes, who practiced speaking with stones in his mouth, to the days of Oprah, who can create magical moments with her guests, leaders have relied upon their capacity to persuade. As Churchill is believed to have said, "Of all the talents bestowed upon men, none is so precious as a gift of oratory." As in so many areas of leadership, there is only one way to master it: practice, practice, practice. Accept every offer to speak; prepare carefully (Churchill would spend an hour of prep for each minute he had in a parliamentary speech); and solicit feedback.

YOUR GREATEST ENEMY MIGHT BE YOU

One reason the public so distrusts politicians is that they often seem splendid at first but then we discover they have feet of clay. Controversy erupts, enemies reach for their knives, and soon there is blood in the water. When I first worked for Richard Nixon, he struck me as smart, well-read, and misunderstood. Indeed, he was one of the best international strategists of his generation. The closer I got to his inner circle, however, the more I saw he also had a dark side—a very dark one. Asked later by David Frost what happened in Watergate, Nixon replied, "I gave my enemies a sword, and then they ran me through." Bottom line: The single greatest danger for most leaders is self-derailment. Power goes to their heads, they think that the rules don't apply to them, and they overplay their hands. "Power tends to corrupt," as Lord Acton famously said in the late nineteenth century, "and absolute power corrupts absolutely." For this reason, it is all the more important to recognize your motivations for leading early in life and remember those values as you go along. You should foster a sense of commitment not only to your own ambitions but to the greater good. It is only through this commitment that we can become servant leaders.

LEARN FROM NEW MODELS OF LEADERSHIP

In her study of Millennials, Charlotte Alter points out a significant change in the strategy and tactics of social protestors. First through the Occupy movement against Wall Street and then through Black Lives Matter, Millennials are beginning to seek change through large, collective movements from the bottom up rather than individual leaders from the top down. They are throwing out the playbook of an earlier generation, which rely on individual, charismatic figures like Martin Luther King for individual, charismatic leadership. They are instead pursuing a "leader-full" approach. A BLM founder, Alicia Garza, told Charlotte Alter: "If there are many leaders, you can't compromise a movement and you can't kill it. If there's one leader, it's very easy to neutralize." Resisters are also rejecting the old view that activists should have seats at the table; they don't even think there should be a table. While the jury is still out, there are growing signs that the new approach is beginning to work: The murders of Black Americans have triggered the largest street protests in American history and are giving voice to millions of young people. BLM has also brought about a national reckoning on the deep-seated racism in our country. Their innovative leadership models are paving the way for a change not only in public opinion but in the way we combat systemic inequities.

SEEK GUIDANCE FROM THE PAST AND PRESENT

As young leaders prepare for their time in the arena, knowing and mastering yourselves becomes crucial, but that does not mean you should only look inward. For centuries, our greatest leaders have also recognized the value and wisdom that can be found in studying the world around us. Harry Truman was the only president of the 20th century who never went to college. Yet through his questioning mind, he became one of the best educated and wisest of our presidents. The most effective leaders of tomorrow are usually those who are students of today. Maintain an abiding curiosity, engage in the passions of your time, and immerse yourself in history and biography. Yes, steer by your True North, but seek knowledge, too.

FRIENDS, AND NETWORKS, STILL MATTER

Even as they create new ways to bring about social change, Millennials and Gen Zers are old-fashioned about friends. They want plenty of them and they want them to join up in networks that will be there for them the rest of their lives. In top business schools, it is said, half the reason for attending is to develop professional networks. As of mid-2021, LinkedIn reported that it had 740 million registered members from 200 countries. Moreover, it reported that 64 percent of job seekers are hired through referrals. In a turbulent world, young people are searching for ways to stay anchored and pursue meaningful lives.

MAINTAIN A CELESTIAL SPARK

A person who invests a lifetime giving back to others needs a serious dose of idealism to stay the course. In his copybook from his younger years, George Washington wrote a final instruction to himself: "Labor to keep alive in your breast that little spark of celestial fire called conscience." Good advice!

Epilogue: Answering the Call

On Inauguration Day 1961, President John F. Kennedy stepped confidently to the microphone, looked out upon a gathering throng, and opened a new chapter in the American story:

> Let the word go forth from this time and place, to friend and foe alike, that the torch has been passed to a new generation of Americans—born in this century, tempered by war, disciplined by a hard and bitter peace, proud of our ancient heritage . . . In the long history of the world, only a few generations have been granted the role of defending freedom in its hour of maximum danger . . . And so, my fellow Americans: ask not what your country can do for you. Ask what you can do for your country.

And so began the saga of the World War II generation. In the three decades that followed, America had seven presidents—from Kennedy through George H.W. Bush. Each answered a call to service, volunteered for action, and was forever changed. All seven served their nation in uniform. Six served during the war itself; one, Jimmy Carter, was still studying at the Naval Academy when the war ended, and he went on to serve honorably as a submariner.

It was a generation of enormous relevance to us today. Those who signed up for battle entered young and callow; many emerged as heroes. Returning home, they didn't much like to talk about their experiences, but they were immensely proud. In his inaugural parade, Kennedy included a replica of the PT boat that he skippered when a Japanese destroyer sliced that craft in two in the middle of the night. When one of his men started to drown, Kennedy took a strap from the man's life jacket, stuck it between his teeth, and swam three and a half hours to shore. His seaman survived.

Years later, George H.W. Bush included in his inaugural parade a replica of the Avenger aircraft he was flying when the Japanese knocked his plane out of the skies. At twenty, he was one of the youngest U.S. pilots shot down over the South Pacific. Like Kennedy, he was lucky to be alive. These two men, like so many of their generation, had faced death squarely in the eye. They were willing to sacrifice their all in defense of their nation and its ideals.

The war became the defining experience of that generation. Some 16 million Americans served in uniform, nearly 40 percent of whom were volunteers. Throughout the conflict, countless women also served, working in factories and shipyards to make America "the arsenal of democracy." The women were often called "Rosie," after "Rosie the Riveter," a popular symbol of American feminism at the time. Meanwhile, Black Americans and Latinos also volunteered for hazardous duty and fought valiantly on the front lines. The war brought citizens together like no other experience in my lifetime. They were united in duty to their fellow countrymen, bound by ideals greater than themselves, and determined to win.

In the 1990s, television anchor Tom Brokaw traced down a number of veterans of the war to find out how their lives had evolved. One discovery was how successful they were. Hardened by experience, more humble about life, many had become distinguished leaders in their fields, ranging from business to nonprofits to public service. A surprising number had become CEOs or had been elected to public office, once again in pursuit of a better America. It was a generation that, with fits and starts, also advanced the rights of women and people of color. Having fought under the same flag overseas, they now worked together for a better America at home. Brokaw concluded that they were "the greatest generation"—a nickname that stuck.

Repeatedly, through word and deed, it was older people from the greatest generation who taught me about the arts and adventures of leadership—the character, courage, and moral purpose that are required. Those men—mostly male and white in those days, I regret— also inspired me to begin my own journey toward leadership and service.

I loved their stories. Tales of how Senators Bob Dole and Daniel Inouye were wounded in the Italian campaign and wound up in the same hospital. While they belonged to different parties, they became lifelong friends, happily working together in the Senate. Or how Senator Terry Sanford, who parachuted into the Battle of the Bulge, proudly told me shortly before his death that his years as a teenage Boy Scout in North Carolina taught him how to outfox Germans in the woods. Or the stories of Richard Nixon, who told me shortly before he died that one of his proudest moments came just after World War II when the Marshall Plan, then controversial, was put up for a vote in a Republican-controlled House of Representatives. A Republican himself, he stood up in support and on the other side of the aisle saw another freshman congressman standing up in support, John F. Kennedy. "When the chips are down in this country," Nixon told me, "we stand up together." Even Nixon, for all his flaws, understood that.

Another who comes to mind is Mike Mansfield. He lied about his age to enlist in the navy in World War I and joined the marines during the 1920s. He then went on to become the longest serving majority leader in Senate history and was a first-class human being. If you want to see his grave at Arlington Cemetery, you won't find it on Kennedy

Hill. At his request, Mansfield is buried with a small marker among the enlisted men.

I would not pretend that the leaders of the World War II generation were perfect. They weren't. After all, they gave us Vietnam and were responsible for Watergate, two terrible blunders that eroded much of the trust earlier leaders had built up. On many measures, they missed the mark or did not push hard enough in knocking down systemic barriers; unfortunately, too many knowingly reinforced, held up, and perpetuated such inequities. But on the whole, that generation raised our sights about what is possible when our civic culture is strong and our leaders work together across divides. On their watch, the country went to the moon, created the Peace Corps, passed major legislation advancing the causes of women and communities of color, reformed Social Security, created world-class universities, and invested heavily in science and technology. And by the way, they won the Cold War without firing a shot directly at the Russians. Not bad. Not bad at all.

We judge leaders by their legacies. The America that the World War II generation left behind was the strongest country in the world economically, militarily, scientifically, and culturally. No nation on earth had been in so envious a position since the days of ancient Rome. While racism, sexism, and other forces were eating away at our undergirding, most Americans were still proud and confident about our democracy. United and well led, the World War II generation proved that, when inspired, we are a can-do people.

Those lessons from another generation are of growing significance today. Once again, we are facing an existential threat to the republic. Once again, we hear a clarion call for unity and action. Once again, we face the question: Will our citizenry answer the call? We know the urgency. But do we still have what it takes to preserve the union? Can the next greatest generation rise up to lead us to brighter days ahead?

The honest answer is that we don't yet know whether the republic will survive as we have known it. Among public intellectuals, pessimism runs high. Books forecasting the demise of our democracy and the rise of an authoritarian state or, in some cases, a breakup of the union have now become a cottage industry. Certainly, the accelerating rise of global temperatures and the insanity we encounter when millions of our fellow citizens refuse to accept vaccinations, putting their own children at risk, are depressing.

Even so, the rising generations of today still have the potential and, indeed, the promise that we saw in the World War II generation. Politicians still pay attention to the public pulse, and it has not been lost on them that in recent years, resistance movements led by the young have mobilized the largest crowds in history in favor of the environment, women's rights, and gun control. Donald Trump not only lost the White House, House, and Senate on his watch; as of this writing, it is an open question whether he could lose his grip on his party. So it is way too early to give up on democracy. Rather, we should be looking for ways to encourage the young and indeed, their elders, to embrace lives of service and leadership. And we should do so with much greater urgency. This epilogue is designed as a special call to action by rising generations—ways they can walk in the footsteps of the World War II "greatest generation."

On the face of it, one might expect Millennials and Gen Zers to be reluctant warriors in the struggle to revive our civic life. Over the course of their lives, they have been repeatedly battered by external events and crises. Fortunately, there are growing signs that many Millennials and Gen Zers are starting to do just the opposite: They are answering the call with a vengeance, just as we have seen with Greta Thunberg and the Parkland kids. They have channeled hard times into hope, living their lives with a sense of idealism that can propel us to better days.

FIVE PATHS INTO THE FUTURE

How can one explain why so many young people today appear to be seeking a life of service over a life of grievances? Given their hardships, why do they see today's world as an opportunity for action? Why are they still so passionate and idealistic? At the moment, I am not sure anyone knows for certain. But it does appear that as a generation, they are responding to their setbacks in much the same way we saw earlier that individuals respond to crucibles: they momentarily fall flat, but through their own resilience, many bounce back. And in the best cases, they emerge stronger than ever, embracing a life of fresh moral purpose. Clearly, in one continent after another, the emerging leaders of tomorrow—especially those of talent—are fed up with the status quo and are eager to change the world.

Much of their impact is yet to be seen. But in observing many of these rising stars in recent years, I have found that they are influencing almost every cross section of society, tackling problems at the heart of every field. They aren't just challenging existing traditions; they want to reimagine the world. From my observation, I have found that in choosing their personal journeys, they tend to migrate into five different forms of servant leadership. In each, to borrow a phrase from Steve Jobs, they are starting to make "a dent in the universe."

Social Movements

For centuries, protests and activism have been a central feature of our democracy. The discontented have self-organized, taken to the streets, and demanded their leaders do better—from the Boston Tea Party (1763) to the Women's Suffrage Parade (1913), from the March on Washington for Jobs and Freedom (1963) to the Women's March (2017), from the Strike for Climate (2019) to the marches sparked by the murder of young Black Americans like Trayvon Martin, Michael Brown, Tamir Rice, and George Floyd. To this day, public intellectuals like Marshall Ganz are teaching about Cesar Chavez. Many past organizers live on in memory as some of our greatest leaders in the search for social justice.

For all his faults, Donald Trump paradoxically ushered in at least one change in current social movements: He spurred the resistance. His inauguration sparked a historic day of protests, as somewhere between 3 and 5 million protestors participated in the Women's March in communities across the country. After that, young people poured into the resistance. Not since Vietnam and the turbulent 1960s have so many of the young have stepped up and spoken out. As we have seen in earlier pages, Millennials and Gen Zers of all backgrounds have been at the forefront of these demonstrations.

These more recent demonstrations have several striking features. The first is the most important: Like them or not, these movements and their leaders are increasingly changing the direction of the country. Progress is painfully slow and frequently disappointing, but it is gathering force. Racial justice and income equity are now higher on the national agenda. A backlash is building on the right that could yet reverse our direction, but for now, the social swing is the most pronounced since the Progressive Era a century ago. Second, the protestors—and in particular, the activists—have discovered that the internet can often do as much to arouse and align followers as the streets. That gives resisters far more leverage. Third, the resistance is bringing a diverse cross section of people into action. The civil rights protests of the 1960s drew far more Black Americans than whites; that is no longer true.

Finally, the social movements of today are encouraging a different form of leadership, one we learned was inspired by the grassroots work of leaders like Ella Baker and transformed by the landscape of today. "Leader-full" movements—like BLM—do not have one person speaking for them, nor one person negotiating. They speak with a collective voice and are elevating the leadership of both young and old.

Elected Officials

Young people are also reinvigorating our city halls, legislatures, and Congress itself, institutions that have often seemed sleepy and stale.

Pete Buttigieg may be the best-known example: a Harvard under-grad, Rhodes Scholar, elected mayor of South Bend at twenty-nine, an improbable candidate for president whose talent turned him into people's favorite underdog; and now, at thirty-nine, he has become the first openly gay person to serve in an American presidential cabinet. Michael Tubbs is one of America's best kept secrets: Born to a teen-age mother and incarcerated father, he was elected mayor of Stock-ton, California, at twenty-six—the youngest and first Black mayor in a city of 300,000. Another example: Aja Brown, youngest mayor of Compton, California, when she was thirty-one. And another: Svante Myrick, youngest ever mayor of Ithaca at twenty-four, a person of color who rebuilt the center of his city. Michelle Wu, at thirty-six, be-came the first woman and person of color elected mayor of Boston. These may seem like a smattering, but if you consider what it took to convince a city that its future should be in the hands of a twenty-some-year-old, you can appreciate that victory was no small feat.

Coming off the elections of 2020, Millennials now occupy thirty-one seats in the House and one in the Senate. One stream of new, young faces comes from the left wing of the Democratic Party—most prominently, AOC and the Squad, a progressive cohort of House rep-resentatives with an increasing voice in the national agenda. A second stream is composed of military veterans and former intelligence of-ficers who, like the World War II leaders, are trying to build biparti-san coalitions. They are the backbone among newly elected moderates on both sides of the aisle. Once seated in the House, some twenty-five veterans now belong to a For Country Caucus, working together across the aisle on national security issues such as bringing allies of the United States out of Afghanistan. (Disclosure: I am a co-founder of With Honor, a start-up to identify, recruit, and help win seats for the veterans' group. Our hope is to help restore our civic life by rebuilding the center of American politics.)

Agree or disagree with their politics, I am a firm believer that a combination of new progressives and mainstream moderates will serve the country well. Alexandria Ocasio-Cortez, Ilhan Omar, Conor Lamb, Seth Moulton, and Joe Neguse have become stars of the left, while Mike Gallagher, Peter Meijer, and Adam Kinzinger have been some of the most outspoken on the center-right—albeit on different levels of conservatism. Along the way, many of them have used emerging technologies and modes of outreach to bring a new coalition of young voters and constituents into the fray. Notably, each of them belongs to the Millennial or Z generation.

Social Entrepreneurs

A few decades ago, many of the young people who wanted to put the world aright became social entrepreneurs. Most were idealistic, passionate, white, and graduates from top colleges who thought the government was failing to meet social needs here and overseas. By applying the principles of business, they believed their organizations could find new solutions. Since then, their thinking has evolved: They now tend to believe that to achieve systemic change, they need to partner more with government, become more engaged in politics, and seek much greater diversity in their ranks. They are right on all counts.

Many of the early pioneers remain legends in the field. Bill Drayton is the godfather of social entrepreneurship, graduating from Harvard College and Yale Law, winning a master's from Balliol, and working at McKinsey before launching Ashoka four decades ago. His central vision has held steady: "Everyone a Change Maker." Today Ashoka partners up with some three hundred nonprofits around the world. Wendy Kopp was an undergraduate at Princeton when she wrote a senior thesis proposing Teach For America; it now has 64,000 alumni serving fifty regions across the country and has expanded abroad. She met her husband, Richard Barth, when he came in for a job interview. Barth is now CEO of the KIPP Foundation, which has some 270 charter schools and 160,000 students and alumni. (Together, they also have four children.)

After completing dual graduate degrees at Harvard, Cheryl Dorsey joined up with Echoing Green and became its CEO. Under her leadership, Echoing Green has provided early funding for almost a thousand social innovators, many of them successful. Michael Brown and Alan Khazei, roommates in college, started City Year together at law school; it was so successful in providing a year or two of urban service that President Clinton modeled AmeriCorps after it. Khazei's wife, Vanessa Kirsch, started Public Allies in Chicago (where a young Michelle Obama worked for her) and went on to create New Profit, which provides mezzanine funding for dozens of promising new ventures. Most recently, a young woman named Emily Cherniack has created a smash hit called New Politics, which recruits servant leaders—military veterans and social entrepreneurs—to run for public office; she is an informal partner in arms with Rye Barcott, the founder in 2018 of With Honor, and Emily and Rye have become two of our most successful emerging leaders. Across the board, the quality of the young leaders who have signed up continues to be a great strength.

To their credit, all of these organizations are now aggressively seeking more diversity: From CEOs down through the ranks, demand is now high for more women and people of color and for graduates of a wider array of colleges to serve in leadership positions. (Disclosure: I have been so impressed with the efforts of these young social entrepreneurs that I have served with enthusiasm on a number of their advisory boards.)

National Service

One way in which some of these social entrepreneurs have left their mark is by ushering in the movement for national service. In recent years, a growing collection of American leaders have pushed for the creation of a modern corps of young volunteers who commit themselves to giving back a year or two to our country. Supporters have ranged from conservative William Buckley to Presidents Clinton, George W. Bush, Obama, and Biden, along with John McCain, Hillary Clinton, Elizabeth Warren, Pete Buttigieg, Bob Gates, Senator Chris Coons (a confidant of President Biden), and General Stanley McChrystal. McCain started out as a skeptic but swung around, building a large following in his calls to the young to embrace a life "greater than one's own self-interest." Today, national service provides to young people a foray into public life and servant leadership.

These past few years have highlighted ways in which young people can spur themselves into a life of leadership through service to community—either their local community or an underserved area in need of help. During the pandemic, AmeriCorps—the organization at the center of national service opportunities—enlisted volunteers to help communities across the country with efforts including contact tracing, food delivery service, and supplementing for gaps in education caused by remote learning environments. All told, AmeriCorps affiliates volunteered millions of hours to keep communities afloat in the wake of COVID.

However the pandemic may end, it has become clear that our communities would benefit from the service of young volunteers, rolling their sleeves up for a year or two of service. Projects ranging from environmental conservation to disaster response efforts to supporting underserved schools all fall under the purview of these programs. And, in return, young volunteers gain valuable skills from their experiences. They learn to work toward a common goal with volunteers from all walks of life, understand the value of service, and emerge with a greater sense of commitment to country and cause. Employers have found time and again that alumni of national service emerge as leaders in their next phase of life.

For those of you just starting on your path, please know that this is just a launching point. As the columnist E. J. Dionne has recognized, national service cannot become some form of "cheap grace," telling citizens to be kind and empathic to one another but asking little more.

Instead, it should become a bridge between volunteers and community. It must be a form of duty to create moral bonds across race, gender, and class lines, elevating the civic life of the country.

Voices of Change

The fifth group is harder to categorize but is equally influential in shaping the national narrative. We might call them "voices of change." They come from journalism, literature, sports, and nonprofit organizations and command national platforms on television, podcasts, YouTube, newsletters, social media, and elsewhere online. One thinks of Amanda Gorman, who brought the nation to tears with her poetry at Biden's inauguration. Or Abby Phillip and Kaitlan Collins, who have served as CNN anchor and chief White House correspondent, respectively. Or Natasha Bertrand at CNN and Astead Herndon at *The New York Times*. All are Millennials, barely breaking thirty.

Even those you would not expect have taken it upon themselves to speak up for social good. Megan Rapinoe led her soccer team to victory in the World Cup and then used her platform to promote equitable pay. Colin Kaepernick put his career on the line when he bravely took a knee to demand racial justice. Hundreds of young professional athletes followed him, supporting the Black Lives Matter movement. This year, gymnast Simone Biles and tennis star Naomi Osaka made themselves heard not just for their athletic dominance but for their advocacy. Both were courageous enough to bring international attention to mental health, an issue long overlooked in the athletic community and beyond. This account is not meant to be anywhere near exhaustive but instead should be inspirational. Young people who have been knocked down have scrambled back up, their voices now heard across the nation.

START NOW

When he was in his retirement, I visited with Warren Christopher, a major player on the national stage and a friend. Chris had enjoyed an incredible journey in life: Raised in California, educated at Stanford, clerk to Justice William O. Douglas, partner at a world-class law firm, deeply engaged in the civic life of Los Angeles, then the state of California, then on to Washington, where he wound up as secretary of state. "Chris," I asked, "what advice would you give today to a young, aspiring person like you who is just starting out on a career path? How would you make this work?" "Well," he replied, "it all depends on where you want to wind up. If you are starting out with a law firm and want to become managing partner, you should give your firm 150 percent of your time. But if you ultimately want to be in the public arena, you should give your law firm 100 percent of your time and give the other 50 percent to developing your public life."

That has always struck me as sound advice. If you are harboring ambitions to make a difference in the world, you should start your leadership journey early. You may indeed need to devote a big chunk of your energy toward your job and family, but begin volunteering small pieces of it to your public life. Show an interest, begin networking, pay your dues, and start serving your local community. As Teddy Roosevelt said, "No one cares how much you know until they know how much you care."

Remember too that those who have made the most difference in America have often risen up and answered a call to duty early in their lives. George Washington was a mere twenty-three when he gained command of Virginia's colonial militia. Alexander Hamilton became Washington's aide-de-camp at twenty. Thomas Jefferson was thirty-three when he drafted the Declaration. (And over a dozen signers were under thirty-five; two were twenty-six.)

In the Civil War era and beyond, Harriet Tubman was in her thirties when she guided three hundred slaves up the Freedom Trail;

Frederick Douglass was about twenty-seven when he wrote the first edition of his memoir and started his abolitionist newspaper. Martin Luther King Jr. moved the country from the steps of the Lincoln Memorial when he was thirty-three; by his side was a twenty-three-year-old John Lewis. Just a few years later, Bob Woodward and Carl Bernstein uncovered the Watergate scandal, at twenty-nine and twenty-eight respectively. Farther afield, Joan of Arc was just seventeen when she cross-dressed and led the French to victory in 1429. Jane Addams founded Hull House at twenty-nine, inspired by a moving trip to Toynbee Hall in London a few years earlier. Mother Teresa became a nun at eighteen. Our vision of leaders as seasoned old white men has been challenged time and again by the young. Thank goodness for it.

IN THE ARENA

When Theodore Roosevelt stepped down from the presidency in 1909, neither he nor anyone else could foresee what lay ahead for him. But they knew one thing for certain: He wasn't leaving the national arena. He had been the best-known figure in America for over a dozen years, and he rejoiced in the respect and power he still commanded. He was an electrifying leader, one headed for Mount Rushmore.

After giving up the presidency, he spent the next year hunting in central Africa, where he pursued big game and devoured great books. In 1910, he toured North Africa and Europe, restlessly visiting the powerful and delivering lengthy speeches. That April, he stopped at the Sorbonne to give a speech that still excites today. He titled it "Citizenship in a Republic," but it soon became known as "The Man in the Arena." (Were he alive now, he would certainly have included women.) The full passage goes as follows:

> It is not the critic who counts; not the man who points out how the strong man stumbles, or where the doer of deeds could have

done them better. The credit belongs to the man who is actually in the arena, whose face is marred by dust and sweat and blood; who strives valiantly; who errs, who comes short again and again, because there is no effort without error and shortcoming; but who does actually strive to do the deeds; who knows great enthusiasms, the great devotions; who spends himself in a worthy cause; who at the best knows in the end the triumph of high achievement, and who at the worst, if he fails, at least fails while daring greatly, so that his place shall never be with those cold and timid souls who neither know victory nor defeat.

Leaders of all sorts have continued to pause and recite chunks of it to each other for over ninety years. In modern times, Nelson Mandela read this most memorable passage to the captain of the South African rugby team just before they played the heavily favored All Blacks of New Zealand in the 1995 World Cup; the South Africans won. President Nixon read the same passage in his resignation speech; at the Democratic Convention in 2016, President Obama invoked it in support of Hillary Clinton. Leadership scholar Brené Brown used it as a book title. Summer plebes memorize it as incoming freshmen at the Naval Academy. LeBron James puts "Man in the Arena" on his shoes before a game; Miley Cyrus has a passage tattooed on her forearm. Hard to believe, but all true.

What these episodes suggest is that people who have been in the arena have found that the practice of leadership is not for the faint of heart. It is hard, grueling, and often thankless work as critics fire their poisonous arrows at you. And the higher up you climb, the tougher it gets. As Machiavelli said five hundred years ago, change is extremely difficult—those who have money or privilege want to keep it and those who would benefit from change will be hesitant or fearful of what might happen.

But the fact that leadership is hard should not make you retreat. Rather, it should encourage you to toughen up. To listen to the Teddy

Roosevelts of the world. You will need an inner compass—a True North—by which to steer and an outer strength that will help you overcome obstacles. But at the end of the day, you will find that the harder your journey, the greater the satisfaction you will enjoy upon completing it. So was the case of Mother Teresa. In the days before her death, someone asked her, "Why did you choose to give up family and money and security to go and live among the destitute and hopeless?" She responded, "I wanted a very hard life."

More than a hundred years ago, the New York City Public Library placed marble lions on either side of the front door that have become favorite landmarks. Why? Because they were soon nicknamed Patience and Fortitude—and that's what it takes to be a true New Yorker, people said. Well, that's also what it takes to become an effective leader.

So take to heart the message of the Man in the Arena. The nation needs you; indeed, the world needs you. We must have new, forceful leaders who have found their True North and can navigate past the crises that are coming their way. We need passionate idealists who will stand up to those blocking our way toward a more giving and just society. We need men and women of character and honor. We need you to step into the arena, your hearts touched with fire.

Notes

INTRODUCTION

1   *She began skipping school:* "Greta Thunberg Is TIME's 2019 Person of the Year," *Time,* accessed August 14, 2021, https://time.com/person-of-the-year-2019-greta-thunberg/.

2   *killing seventeen and wounding seventeen more:* "17 Killed in Mass Shooting at High School in Parkland, Florida," accessed August 14, 2021, https://www.nbcnews.com/news/us-news/police-respond-shooting-parkland-florida-high-school-n848101.

2   *some 1.2 million marchers in 880 events across America:* "More Than 2 Million in 90 Percent of Voting Districts Joined March for Our Lives Protests," accessed August 14, 2021, https://www.newsweek.com/march-our-lives-how-many-2-million-90-voting-district-860841.

3   *Greta was amazed by their successes:* Jonathan Watts, "Interview: Greta Thunberg, schoolgirl climate change warrior: 'Some people can let things go. I can't'" *Guardian,* March 11, 2019, https://www.theguardian.com/world/2019/mar/11/greta-thunberg-schoolgirl-climate-change-warrior-some-people-can-let-things-go-i-cant.

3   *"Skolstrejk för klimatet":* Kate Aronoff and Kate Aronoff, "How Greta Thunberg's Lone Strike Against Climate Change Became a Global Movement," Rolling Stone (blog), March 5, 2019, https://www.rollingstone.com/politics/politics-features/greta-thunberg-fridays-for-future-climate-change-800675/.

3 *[Greta Thunberg] was fifteen:* "Greta Thunberg Is TIME's 2019 Person of the Year," *Time*, accessed August 14, 2021, https://time.com/person-of-the-year-2019-greta-thunberg/.

3 *"You are failing us . . . your betrayal":* NPR Staff, "Transcript: Greta Thunberg's Speech at the U.N. Climate Action Summit," NPR, September 23, 2019, sec. Environment, https://www.npr.org/2019/09/23/763452863/transcript-greta-thunbergs-speech-at-the-u-n-climate-action-summit.

3 *"Blah, blah, blah":* Jennifer Hassan, "Greta Thunberg says world leaders' talk on climate change is 'blah blah blah,'" *Washington Post*, September 29, 2021, https://www.washingtonpost.com/climate-environment/2021/09/29/great-thunberg-leaders-blah-blah-blah/.

4 *[Tarana Burke] wanted a safe platform:* "Tarana Burke Biography," National Women's History Museum, accessed August 24, 2021, https://www.womenshistory.org/education-resources/biographies/tarana-burke.

4 *In 2017,* Time *magazine proclaimed her one of its People of the Year:* Ibid.

4 *created the social movement that came to be called Black Lives Matter:* "Herstory," Black Lives Matter, accessed August 24, 2021, https://blacklivesmatter.com/herstory/.

6 *"Courage is rightly esteemed":* "Excerpts from the Sixth Churchill Lecture 'Winston Churchill: Leadership in Times of Crisis,'" International Churchill Society, April 4, 2015, https://winstonchurchill.org/publications/finest-hour/finest-hour-133/excerpts-from-the-sixth-churchill-lecture-winston-churchill-leadership-in-times-of-crisis/.

6 *"a concern for establishing and guiding the next generation":* Erik H. Erikson, *Childhood and Society* (W.W. Norton, 1993), 267.

6 *"Aware of the controlling power of ambition, corruption and emotions":* Barbara Tuchman, The March of Folly: From Troy to Vietnam, (Alfred A. Knopf, 1984), 2014 Random House Trade Paperback Edition p. 410.

7 *"as educating the electorate to recognize":* Ibid., p. 411.

8 *"Let personal quarrels":* Winston Churchill, House of Commons, May 8, 1940.

8 *some 80 percent between the ages of eighteen and twenty-nine feel:* "Poll: Young People Believe They Can Lead Change in Unprecedented Election Cycle," accessed August 14, 2021, https://circle.tufts.edu/latest-research/poll-young-people-believe-they-can-lead-change-unprecedented-election-cycle.

8 *Some 60 percent "feel like they're part of a movement that will vote to express its views":* Ibid.

8 *in 2016, just 5 percent of those between eighteen and twenty-nine had participated in a protest demonstration; by 2020, that figure had shot up to 27 percent:* Ibid.

8   *jumped a whopping 266 percent:* "Number of Millennials Running for Congress Increased 266 Percent in Two Years: Survey-Millennial Action Project," accessed August 24, 2021, https://www.millennialaction.org/press-archives/number-of-millennials-running-for-congress-increased-266-percent-in-two-years-survey.

11   *"Our life evokes . . . rather than your lower":* Joseph Campbell, *The Power of Myth* (Anchor Books, 1991), 159.

ONE: HEARTS TOUCHED WITH FIRE

17   *his biographer Mark DeWolfe Howe has written, those years of combat did not diminish his life:* Mark DeWolfe Howe, *Justice Oliver Wendell Holmes, Volume 1: The Shaping Years, 1841–1870* (1957), https://doi.org/10.4159/harvard.9780674865860.

20   *Schlesinger made the counterargument that determinism at its core denies human agency:* Arthur M. Schlesinger Jr., "Democracy and Leadership," in *The Cycles of American History* (Boston: Houghton Mifflin Company, 1986), 419–36.

20   *"I do not understand why I was not broken like an eggshell":* Michael Pollak, "Not His Finest Hour," *New York Times*, accessed August 24, 2021, https://www.nytimes.com/2006/05/07/nyregion/thecity/07fyi.html.

23   *"one who mobilizes others toward a goal shared by leader and followers":* Garry Wills, *Certain Trumpets: The Nature of Leadership* (Simon & Schuster, 2013), 17.

25   *"He was as important to the founding of a modern . . . eighteenth century":* Jon Meacham, *His Truth Is Marching On: John Lewis and the Power of Hope* (Random House, 2020), 5.

26   *"Working for somebody else all your days":* Ibid., 25.

26   *"I literally started preaching to the chickens":* Ibid., 26.

27   *WHITES ONLY:* Ibid., 29.

28   *"I was not eager to die":* Ibid., 78.

28   *"This is the most important decision of my life":* Ibid., 86.

29   *"John would not just follow you into the lions' den":* Ibid., 220.

29   *Celia had encouraged her daughter to "love learning, care about people, and work hard":* Jane Sherron De Hart, *Ruth Bader Ginsburg: A Life* (Vintage Books, 2020), 8.

30   *her peers at the* Law Review *noticed no change in her work:* Ibid., 72.

31   *"stayed late sometimes when it was necessary":* Ibid., 82.

31   *"Ruth is basically a reserved person":* Ibid., 86.

32   *"The decision whether or not to bear a child is central to a woman's life":* "The Supreme Court: Excerpts from Senate Hearing on the Ginsburg Nomination," *New York Times*, July 22, 1993, https://www.nytimes.com/1993/07/22

/us/the-supreme-court-excerpts-from-senate-hearing-on-the-ginsburg
-nomination.html.

32   *Labeled the "high Court's counterweight":* Antonin Scalia, "Ruth Bader Ginsburg: The World's 100 Most Influential People," *Time*, April 16, 2015, https://
time.com/collection-post/3823889/ruth-bader-ginsburg-2015-time-100/.

33   *Lily Ledbetter Fair Pay Act of 2009:* "Ruth Bader Ginsburg," Academy
of Achievement, accessed September 17, 2021, https://achievement.org
/achiever/ruth-bader-ginsburg/.

33   *Ginsburg was a pillar of the Court's liberal block:* Robert Barnes and Michael
A. Fletcher, "Ruth Bader Ginsburg, Supreme Court Justice and Legal Pioneer for Gender Equality, Dies at 87," *Washington Post*, accessed September
17, 2021, https://www.washingtonpost.com/local/obituaries/ruth-bader-gins
burg-dies/2020/09/18/3cedc314-fa08-11ea-a275-1a2c2d36e1f1_story.html.

33   Weinberger v. Wiesenfeld *(1975):* Linda Greenhouse, "Ruth Bader Ginsburg,
Supreme Court's Feminist Icon, Is Dead at 87," *New York Times*, September 18,
2020, https://www.nytimes.com/2020/09/18/us/ruth-bader-ginsburg-dead.html.

34   *John was born at the Coco Solo:* "The Story of John Sidney McCain III," John
and Cindy McCain: Service to Country | JohnMcCain.com (blog), March 2,
2018, https://www.johnmccain.com/story/.

34   *Ever an independent spirit, McCain made it clear:* "McCain Addresses His
Alma Mater in Virginia," April 1, 2008, http://www.washingtonpost.com
/wp-dyn/content/article/2008/04/01/AR2008040101034.html.

34   *"to Baltimore and back many times.":* "Story of John Sidney McCain III."

35   *"I felt faithless, and couldn't control my despair":* Dan Nowicki, "John McCain
POW Recordings Revive Historic, Painful Episode," accessed August 24,
2021, https://www.azcentral.com/story/news/politics/azdc/2016/08/13/john
-mccain-pow-recordings-revive-historic-painful-episode/88547416/.

36   *savings and loan scandal:* "Is John McCain a Crook?," *Slate*, February 18, 2000,
https://slate.com/news-and-politics/2000/02/is-john-mccain-a-crook.html.

36   *"John, I'd be delighted to take it, but some of your colleagues might object":* Michael Lewis, "The Subversive," *New York Times,* accessed August 24, 2021,
https://www.nytimes.com/1997/05/25/magazine/the-subversive.html.

40   *"in our youth, our hearts were touched with fire":* Ben W. Heineman, Jr., "Justice Oliver Wendell Holmes and Memorial Day," *Atlantic*, May 30, 2011,
https://www.theatlantic.com/national/archive/2011/05/justice-oliver-wen
dell-holmes-and-memorial-day/239637/.

TWO: BECOMING THE AUTHOR OF YOUR OWN LIFE

43   *James Chaney, Andrew Goodwin, and Michael Schwerner:* Debbie Elliott,
"State Prosecutor Closes 'Mississippi Burning' Civil Rights Case," NPR,

June 21, 2016, sec. Law, https://www.npr.org/2016/06/21/482900192/state-prosecutor-closes-mississippi-burning-civil-rights-case.

45 *"Know thyself"*: Allyson Szabo, *Longing for Wisdom: The Message of the Maxims* (Allyson Szabo, 2008), 15.

45 *"The unexamined life is not worth living"*: Thomas G. West and Grace Starry West, "Plato's Apology of Socrates," in *Four Texts on Socrates: Plato's Euthypro, Apology, and Crito and Aristophanes' Clouds.*

45 *Plato explored the meaning of the Delphic maxim:* "Dialogues, vol. 5, Laws, Index to the Writings of Plato | Online Library of Liberty," accessed July 23, 2021, https://oll.libertyfund.org/title/plato-dialogues-vol-5-laws-index-to-the-writings-of-plato.

45 *"Managing Oneself" is still a must-read:* Peter F. Drucker, "Managing Oneself," Harvard Business Review, *Best of HBR 1999* (2005), https://www.csub.edu/~ecarter2/CSUB.MKTG%20490%20F10/DRUCKER%20HBR%20Managing%20Oneself.pdf.

45 *Candid feedback thus becomes essential:* Ibid.

46 *In his bestseller of 2017:* Ray Dalio, *Principles: Life and Work* (Simon & Schuster, 2017).

47 *"the omnipresent belief that the ideal self is gregarious, alpha and comfortable in the spotlight":* Susan Cain, *Quiet: The Power of Introverts in a World That Can't Stop Talking* (Crown, 2012), 4.

47 *mistaken belief from the Greco-Roman world:* Ibid., 3.

47 *As he wrote in his memoir,* In Love and War: James B. Stockdale and Sybil Stockdale, *In Love and War: The Story of a Family's Ordeal and Sacrifice During the Vietnam Years* (Harper & Row, 1984).

48 *"Patton is the best subordinate the American":* Drucker, "Managing Oneself," 4.

49 *Erving Goffman drew an analogy of actors onstage:* Erving Goffman, *The Presentation of Self in Everyday Life,* rev. ed. (Anchor Books, 1990).

50 *encouraging one's unique strengths builds confidence:* Laura Morgan Roberts et al., "How to Play to Your Strengths," *Harvard Business Review*, January 1, 2005, https://hbr.org/2005/01/how-to-play-to-your-strengths.

50 *CEO Tim Brown explains that it is essential to the firm:* Morten T. Hansen, "IDEO CEO Tim Brown: T-Shaped Stars: The Backbone of IDEO's Collaborative Culture," January 21, 2010, https://chiefexecutive.net/ideo-ceo-tim-brown-t-shaped-stars-the-backbone-of-ideoaes-collaborative-culture__trashed/.

51 *Jordan, who has repeatedly claimed that he was "cut":* Samantha Grossman, "A Myth Debunked: Was Michael Jordan Really Cut from His High-School Team?" TIME.com, accessed August 26, 2021, https://newsfeed.time

.com/2012/01/16/a-myth-debunked-was-michael-jordan-really-cut-from-his-high-school-team/.

51 *"I'm going to show you"*: Tom Huddleston Jr., "How Michael Jordan Became Great: 'Nobody Will Ever Work as Hard as I Work,' " CNBC, April 21, 2020, https://www.cnbc.com/2020/04/21/how-michael-jordan-became-great-nobody-will-ever-work-as-hard.html.

52 *"I don't do things half-heartedly"*: Ibid.

52 *he taped cardboard to the bottom of his glasses:* John McPhee, "A Sense of Where You Are," *New Yorker,* January 25, 1965, https://www.newyorker.com/magazine/1965/01/23/a-sense-of-where-you-are.

52 *[Churchill] is said to have rehearsed one hour for every minute:* Tom Vitale, "Winston Churchill's Way with Words," NPR, July 14, 2012, sec. History, https://www.npr.org/2012/07/14/156720829/winston-churchills-way-with-words.

52 *"Practice isn't the thing you do once you're good"*: Malcolm Gladwell, *Outliers: The Story of Success* (Little, Brown, 2008), 42.

53 *child prodigy "developed late"*: Ibid., 40–41.

53 *"They sounded like no one else"*: Ibid., 50.

53 *"Ten thousand hours is the magic number of greatness"*: Ibid., 41.

53 *"The people at the top don't work just harder or even much harder"*: Ibid., 40.

53 *"If I skip practice for one day, I notice"*: Daniel Coyle, *The Talent Code: Greatness Isn't Born. It's Grown. Here's How.* (Random House Publishing Group, 2009), 88.

54 *"Try again. Fail again. Fail Better"*: Samuel Beckett, "Worstward Ho," Samuel-Beckett.net, 1983, http://www.samuel-beckett.net/w_ho.html.

54 *Martha Graham has called "divine dissatisfaction"*: Agnes de Mille, *Martha: The Life and Work of Martha Graham* (Vintage Books, 1992), 264.

THREE: YOUR GATHERING YEARS

55 *As Erik Erikson has argued, it is difficult to move on:* Erik H. Erikson and Joan M. Erikson, *The Life Cycle Completed*, extended version (W.W. Norton, 1997).

56 *"your one wild and precious life"*: Mary Oliver, "The Summer Day."

62 *a majority of executives begin their careers:* James M. Citrin and Richard A. Smith, *The 5 Patterns of Extraordinary Careers: The Guide for Achieving Success and Satisfaction* (DIANE Publishing Company, 2005).

63 *"Everyone makes mistakes; just make sure you learn from them"*: Stephen J. Dubner, "Extra: Jack Welch Full Interview (Ep. 326)," Freakonomics (blog), accessed August 27, 2021, https://freakonomics.com/podcast/jack-welch/.

65 *Ike finished at the top of his class:* "Eisenhower Military Chronology," accessed August 8, 2021, https://www.nps.gov/features/eise/jrranger/chronomil1.htm.

65 *Congresswoman Pramila Jayapal took them under her wing:* Heather Caygle and Sarah Ferris, "Meet the Woman Mentoring Omar, Tlaib and Ocasio-Cortez," *Politico,* accessed August 8, 2021, https://politi.co/2Fsx53K.

65 *Pat Summitt left behind the winningest record:* "Pat Summitt, All-Time Winningest Division I College Basketball Coach, Dies: The Two-Way," NPR, accessed August 27, 2021, https://www.npr.org/sections/thetwo -way/2016/06/28/483612431/pat-summitt-legendary-tennessee-basketball -coach-dies-at-64.

66 *"When you sit in her office [as a player]":* Gary Smith, "Understanding How Pat Summitt Guided UT to Five Titles," Sports Illustrated Vault | SI.com, accessed August 8, 2021, https://vault.si.com/vault/1998/03/02 /eyes-of-the-storm-when-tennessees-whirlwind-of-a-coach-pat-summitt -hits-you-with-her-steely-gaze-you-get-a-dose-of-the-intensity-that-has -carried-the-lady-vols-to-five-ncaa-titles.

66 *sixty-two women who played for her:* "Coach Pat Summitt: 1952–2016," University of Tennessee Athletics, accessed August 27, 2021, https://utsports .com/sports/2017/6/20/coach-pat-summitt-1952-2016.aspx.

66 *"For four decades, she outworked her rivals":* "Statement by the President on the Death of Pat Summitt," whitehouse.gov, June 28, 2016, https://obama whitehouse.archives.gov/the-press-office/2016/06/28/statement-president -death-pat-summitt.

67 *"I wouldn't have gotten anywhere in the airline industry":* "3 Famous Billion-aires and Their Mentors," Bcombinator (blog), September 15, 2020, https:// bcombinator.com/3-famous-billionaires-and-their-mentors.

68 *35 percent for workers aged fifty-one to sixty:* Cynthia Emrich, Mark Livingston, and David Pruner, *Creating a Culture of Mentorship* (Heidrick and Struggles, 2017), https://doi.org/10.13140/RG.2.2.10649.11365.

68 *"There is a special place in hell for women who don't help each other":* Marianne Cooper, "Why Women (Sometimes) Don't Help Other Women," *Atlantic*, June 23, 2016, https://www.theatlantic.com/business/archive/2016/06 /queen-bee/488144/.

68 *twenty thousand agents had joined her company:* Alice George, "How Business Executive Madam C.J. Walker Became a Powerful Influencer of the Early 20th Century," *Smithsonian,* accessed August 27, 2021, https://www .smithsonianmag.com/smithsonian-institution/how-business-executive -madam-c-j-walker-became-powerful-influencer-early-20th-century -180971628/.

69 *"I am not merely satisfied in making money for myself":* "Madam C.J. Walker

Museum: Honoring Black Business Leaders," Madam Museum, accessed August 27, 2021, https://www.madamcjwalkermuseum.com.

69   *women are significantly under-"sponsored":* Herminia Ibarra, Nancy M. Carter, and Christine Silva, "Why Men Still Get More Promotions Than Women," *Harvard Business Review*, September 1, 2010, https://hbr.org/2010/09/why -men-still-get-more-promotions-than-women.

69   *compared to 13 percent of white people:* "Why You Need a Work 'Sponsor,'" NPR, December 3, 2012, sec. Race, https://www.npr.org/2012/12 /03/166402529/why-you-need-a-work-sponsor.

70   *Fortune 500 CEOs named James or Michael than there are Fortune 500 CEOs:* "Equileap_US_Report_2020.Pdf," accessed August 27, 2021, https://equileap .com/wp-content/uploads/2020/12/Equileap_US_Report_2020.pdf.

70   *research shows that people are more likely to hire candidates most similar:* Lauren A. Rivera, "Hiring as Cultural Matching: The Case of Elite Professional Service Firms," *American Sociological Review* 77, no. 6 (December 2012): 999–1022, https://doi.org/10.1177/0003122412463213.

70   *Having attended the same college or university or growing up in the zip code:* Drake Baer, "If You Want to Get Hired, Act Like Your Potential Boss," *Business Insider*, accessed September 21, 2021, https://www.businessinsider .com/managers-hire-people-who-remind-them-of-themselves-2014-5.

70   *women composed fewer than ten percent:* Gardiner Morse and Iris Bohnet, "Designing a Bias-Free Organization," *Harvard Business Review*, July–August 2016, https://hbr.org/2016/07/designing-a-bias-free-organization.

70   *these sponsors challenge preconceived notions and help pave the way:* Rosalind Chow, "Don't Just Mentor Women and People of Color. Sponsor Them," *Harvard Business Review*, June 30, 2021, https://hbr.org/2021/06/dont-just -mentor-women-and-people-of-color-sponsor-them.

72   *if you pursue a society with full, absolute equality:* James O'Toole, *The Executive's Compass: Business and the Good Society* (Oxford University Press, 1995).

73   *go up on a balcony and watch yourself on the dance floor:* Ronald A. Heifetz, *Leadership Without Easy Answers* (Harvard University Press, 2009).

73   *80 percent of our fellow citizens said we are spinning out of control:* Hart Research Associates and Public Opinion Strategies, "NBC News/Wall Street Journal Survey. Study #200266," June 28, 2020, https://www.document cloud.org/documents/6938425-200266-NBCWSJ-June-Poll.html.

74   *"No longer . . . should leadership be about":* Bill George, *Discover Your True North* (John Wiley & Sons, 2015), 3.

74   *"The longest journey you will ever take is the eighteen inches":* Ibid., 101.

74   *"Don't let the noise of others' opinions drown":* Steve Jobs, "Commencement

Address at Stanford University (2005)," *Stanford News* (blog), June 14, 2005, https://news.stanford.edu/2005/06/14/jobs-061505/.

75 *"Authentic leaders have discovered their True North"*: George, *Discover Your True North*, 8.

75 *"We have many selves"*: Herminia Ibarra, "The Authenticity Paradox," *Harvard Business Review,* January 1, 2015, https://hbr.org/2015/01/the-authenticity-paradox.

75 *Eisenhower said the head of an organization:* Fred I. Greenstein, "'The Hidden-Hand Presidency: Eisenhower as Leader,' a 1994 Perspective," *Presidential Studies Quarterly* 24, no. 2 (1994): 236.

76 *"Orson . . . you and I are the two best actors in the country"*: Conrad Black, *Franklin Delano Roosevelt: Champion of Freedom* (Public Affairs, 2012), 316.

76 *"No, Andrea, unhappy is the land that needs a hero"*: Bertolt Brecht, *Life of Galileo* (A&C Black, 2013), 68.

FOUR: SURVIVING THE FLAMING CRUCIBLE

78 *He could no longer walk*: Michael E. Ruane, "A Century Ago, Polio Struck a Handsome Young Politician—and Forged One of the Country's Greatest Presidents," *Washington Post*, accessed August 30, 2021, https://www.washingtonpost.com/history/2021/08/02/fdr-contracted-polio-100-years-ago/.

78 *killed or paralyzed tens of thousands in the United States each year:* CDC, "Polio Elimination in the United States," Centers for Disease Control and Prevention, July 23, 2021, https://www.cdc.gov/polio/what-is-polio/polio-us.html.

79 *His biggest failure, in his eyes, was his rejection:* "Harvard 1900—Clubs—The Franklin Delano Roosevelt Foundation," accessed August 16, 2021, https://fdrfoundation.org/the-fdr-suite/harvard-1900-clubs/.

80 *"although his legs remained withered, his spirit triumphed":*Ted Morgan, *FDR: A Biography* (Simon & Schuster, 1985), 258.

80 *eventually landed a 237-pound shark:* John Gunther, *Roosevelt in Retrospect: A Profile in History* (New York, Harper, 1950), http://archive.org/details/rooseveltinretro00gunt.

81 *several days aboard his presidential yacht in the Caribbean:* Doris Kearns Goodwin, "The Home Front," *New Yorker*, August 15, 1994, 40.

81 *Lend Lease and Churchill got his destroyers:* Black, *Franklin Delano Roosevelt.*

81 *swivel—not walk, swivel—across the stage:* Hugh Gallagher, "FDR's Cover-Up," *Washington Post*, January 24, 1982, https://www.washingtonpost.com/archive/opinions/1982/01/24/fdrs-cover-up-the-extent-of-his-handicap/9e3f26df-c0a4-4cb6-9852-754fd54d3cae/.

82 *has thousands of photos of Roosevelt:* "Image Thumbnails | Franklin D. Roosevelt Presidential Library & Museum," accessed August 26, 2021, http://

www.fdrlibrary.marist.edu/archives/collections/franklin/?p=digitallibrary
%2Fthumbnails&q=wheelchair.

82   *Franklin Roosevelt's ordeal provides the most clear-cut paradigm:* Doris Kearns
Goodwin, *Leadership in Turbulent Times* (Simon & Schuster, 2018).

83   *"Shattered in body, his sight and smell":* André Fribourg, *The Flaming Crucible: The Faith of the Fighting Men* (Macmillan, 1918), x.

84   *Coelho did become a writer and has published dozens:* "Paulo Coelho Biography," Paulo Coelho & Christina Oiticica Foundation (blog), accessed
August 31, 2021, https://paulocoelhofoundation.com/paulo-coelho/biogra
phy/.

84   *"When we least expect it, life sets us a challenge":* "Quotes from My Books,"
Paulo Coelho, June 30, 2017, https://paulocoelhoblog.com/2017/06/30/56408/.

84   *"You may not control all the events that happen to you":* Maya Angelou, *Letter
to My Daughter* (Random House, 2008), https://search-ebscohost-com.ezp
-prod1.hul.harvard.edu/login.aspx?direct=true&db=nlebk&AN=737699&s
ite=ehost-live&scope=site.

84   *"that certain people seem to naturally inspire confidence, loyalty, and hard work":*
Warren G. Bennis and Robert J. Thomas, "Crucibles of Leadership," accessed August 31, 2021, https://hbr.org/2002/09/crucibles-of-leadership.

85   *"One of the most reliable indicators":* Ibid.

86   *"Emotional occasions, especially violent ones, are extremely potent":* William
James, *The Varieties of Religious Experience: A Study in Human Nature* (Modern Library, 1902), 195.

86   *"impossible things . . . become possible":* Ibid., 236.

87   *"How dare the Taliban take away my basic right to education":* "The Nobel
Peace Prize 2014," NobelPrize.org, accessed August 31, 2021, https://www
.nobelprize.org/prizes/peace/2014/yousafzai/lecture/.

88   *On it she had inscribed the year "1918":* Doris Kearns Goodwin, *No Ordi-
nary Time: Franklin & Eleanor Roosevelt: The Home Front in World War II*
(Simon & Schuster, 2008), 377–78.

88   *"The soul that has believed":* Virginia Moore, "Psyche," *Saturday Review of
Literature*, 7, no. 1 (July 26, 1930).

FIVE: THE KEYS TO RESILIENCE

91   *"a large number of people show what's called post-traumatic growth":* Harvard
Business Review et al., *HBR's 10 Must Reads on Mental Toughness* (with
bonus interview "Post-Traumatic Growth and Building Resilience" with
Martin Seligman) (Harvard Business Press, 2017), 126.

91   *"they're stronger than they were before by psychological and physical measures":*
Ibid.

91   *"if it doesn't kill me, it makes me stronger"*: Friedrich Nietzsche, *Twilight of the Idols, or How to Philosophize with a Hammer* (Daniel Fidel Ferrer, n.d.).

91   *Thousands went through the resulting courses, reportedly with enthusiasm:* Rhonda Cornum, Michael D. Matthews, and Martin E. P. Seligman, "Comprehensive Soldier Fitness: Building Resilience in a Challenging Institutional Context," *American Psychologist* 66, no. 1 (January 2011): 4–9, https://doi.org/10.1037/a0021420.

91   *In the mid-nineties, all of the military branches were struggling:* "Recruiting and Retention in the Active Component Military: Are There Problems?," accessed August 15, 2021, https://www.everycrsreport.com/reports/RL31297 .html.

91   *"the Crucible":* Tony Perry, "Putting Marines Through a 'Crucible,' " *Los Angeles Times,* March 7, 1998, https://www.latimes.com/archives/la-xpm -1998-mar-07-mn-26377-story.html.

91   *the candidate becomes a marine:* Jim Garamone, "The Marine Corps Crucible," Military.com, March 31, 2021, https://www.military.com/join-armed -forces/marine-corps-crucible.html.

91   *army, navy, and air force saw continuing decline:* Perry, "Putting Marines Through a 'Crucible.' "

93   *"A second-class intellect but a first-class temperament":* "Author Reconstructs FDR's 'Defining Moment,' " NPR.org, accessed August 15, 2021, https:// www.npr.org/templates/story/story.php?storyId=5525748.

94   *"Adaptive capacity . . . is the essential competence of leaders":* Warren Bennis and Robert J. Thomas, "Crucibles of Leadership," *Harvard Business Review*, September 1, 2002, https://hbr.org/2002/09/crucibles-of-leadership.

94   *people who aged most successfully:* George E. Vaillant, *Adaptation to Life* (Harvard University Press, 1998).

95   *"My parents [would] turn in their graves to know":* Ida B. Wells, *Crusade for Justice: The Autobiography of Ida B. Wells* (University of Chicago Press, 2013).

95   *"the unsung heroine of the civil rights movement":* "Ida B. Wells: The Unsung Heroine of the Civil Rights Movement," *Guardian,* April 27, 2018, http:// www.theguardian.com/world/2018/apr/27/ida-b-wells-civil-rights-move ment-reporter.

95   *owner of the grocery store that was the heart of Memphis's Black community:* Wells, *Crusade for Justice*, 47.

95   *Her voice was so respected that "scores and hundreds":* " 'Fearless' Ida B. Wells Honored by New Lynching Museum for Fighting Racial Terrorism," *Washington Post*, accessed August 15, 2021, https://www.washingtonpost .com/news/retropolis/wp/2018/04/26/fearless-ida-b-wells-honored-by-new -lynching-memorial-for-fighting-racial-terror/.

95   *"opened my eyes to what lynching really was"*: Wells, *Crusade for Justice*, 64.

96   *the reporting techniques she pioneered in this effort*: Caitlin Dickerson, "Ida B.
      Wells, Who Took on Racism in the Deep South with Powerful Reporting
      on Lynchings," *New York Times*, March 8, 2018, sec. Obituaries, https://www
      .nytimes.com/interactive/2018/obituaries/overlooked-ida-b-wells.html.

96   *"There has been no word equal to it"*: Ida B. Wells, *The Red Record,* accessed Au-
      gust 15, 2021, https://www.gutenberg.org/files/14977/14977-h/14977-h.htm.

96   *Wells helped found the NAACP and the National Association of Colored Women*:
      "Woman Journalist Crusades Against Lynching (Educational Materials:
      African American Odyssey)," accessed August 15, 2021, https://www.loc
      .gov/exhibits/odyssey/educate/barnett.html.

97   *still others . . . have popularized it as "grit"*: American Public Media, "Angela
      Duckworth and the Research on 'Grit,' " accessed August 15, 2021, https://
      americanradioworks.publicradio.org/features/tomorrows-college/grit/an
      gela-duckworth-grit.html.

97   *the cancer was spreading*: "Rachel Carson's Silence," *Pittsburgh Post-
      Gazette,* accessed August 15, 2021, https://www.post-gazette.com/opinion
      /Op-Ed/2014/04/13/THE-NEXT-PAGE-Rachel-Carsons-silence/sto
      ries/201404130058.

97   *"wake in the night and cry out silently for Maine"*: Nancy Koehn, *Forged in
      Crisis: The Power of Courageous Leadership in Turbulent Times* (Simon &
      Schuster, 2017), 373.

97   *"reveal enough to give understanding"*: Ibid.

98   *"most revolutionary book since* Uncle Tom's Cabin*"*: Ibid., 426.

98   *"insects and diseases and vermin . . . inherit the earth"*: Ibid., 428.

98   *"we had felt no sadness"*: Ibid., 432.

98   *"Carson's moment of forging . . . from the precipice of despair"*: Ibid., 374.

98   *"Rachel Carson became one of the most important leaders"*: Ibid., 375.

99   *Plato and Aristotle had little application*: Forrest McDonald, foreword to *Cato:
      A Tragedy and Selected Essays* | Online Library of Liberty, by Joseph Addison,
      ed. Christine Dunn Henderson and Mark E. Yellin (Indianapolis: Liberty
      Fund, 2004), https://oll.libertyfund.org/title/henderson-cato-a-tragedy-and
      -selected-essays.

100   *"virtue in the sense of selfless"*: Ibid.

100   *he wandered into the philosophy area*: James B. Stockdale, *Stockdale on Sto-
      icism II: Master of My Fate* (Center for the Study of Professional Military
      Ethics, 2001).

100   *Stockdale wrote a stirring account*: James B. Stockdale, *Courage Under Fire:
      Testing Epictetus's Doctrines in a Laboratory of Human Behavior* (Hoover In-
      stitution, 1993).

100 *"is a noble philosophy that proved more practicable"* Ibid., 5.

101 *"those few were everywhere the best":* Stockdale, *Stockdale on Stoicism*, 237.

101 *"I flew at 500 knots":* Stockdale, *Courage Under Fire*, 7.

101 *Stockdale was the highest-ranking officer among the POWs:* Ibid., 12.

102 *"be reduced by wind and rain and ice":* Ibid., 8.

103 *"Look not for any greater harm":* Ibid., 13.

SIX: TURNING ADVERSITY INTO PURPOSE

104 *"The habits of a vigorous mind":* "Founders Online: Abigail Adams to John Quincy Adams, 19 January 1780" (University of Virginia Press), accessed August 16, 2021, http://founders.archives.gov/documents/Adams/04-03-02-0207.

105 *"those qualities . . . form the character of the hero and the statesman":* Ibid.

105 *At seventeen, he was corralled with other gay men:* Randy Shilts, *The Mayor of Castro Street: The Life & Times of Harvey Milk*, Stonewall Inn Editions 12 (St. Martin's Press, 1988).

105 *living in private with men while playing the role of a Wall Street financial analyst:* Ibid., 42.

106 *"Are you registered to vote?":* Ibid., 99.

106 *"You gotta give 'em hope":* "Transcript: Hear Harvey Milk's The Hope Speech," Museum of Fine Arts, Boston, accessed August 16, 2021, https://www.mfa.org/exhibitions/amalia-pica/transcript-harvey-milks-the-hope-speech.

106 *would not be broken until Elaine Noble was elected:* "Elaine Noble, Massachusetts, 1974 · Out and Elected in the USA: 1974–2004 Ron Schlittler. OutHistory: It's About Time," accessed August 19, 2021, https://outhistory.org/exhibits/show/out-and-elected/1970s/elaine-noble.

106 *"Milk Has Something for Everybody":* Shilts, *Mayor of Castro Street*, 79–80.

107 *he did win seventeen thousand votes:* Ibid., 88.

107 *he cut his hair:* Ibid., 90.

107 *a whopping five thousand people attended that first fair:* Ibid., 98.

107 *"If we in the gay community want others to help us":* Harvey Milk, Jason Edward Black, and Charles E. Morris, *An Archive of Hope: Harvey Milk's Speeches and Writings* (University of California Press, 2013), 126.

107 *The boycott worked:* Shilts, *Mayor of Castro Street*, 92.

107 *"We established a great amount of contacts":* Ibid., 42.

108 *advancing the rights of the gay community:* "Milk Foundation.Org: The Official Harvey Milk Biography," accessed August 16, 2021, https://milkfoundation.org/about/harvey-milk-biography/.

108 *Proposition 6 was shot down:* Ibid.

108 *The mayor of San Francisco was killed:* Ibid.

108 *Terminal 1 at the San Francisco airport is named after him:* "TIME 100 Persons of the Century," *Time*, June 6, 1999, http://content.time.com/time/magazine/article/0,9171,26473,00.html.

110 *Katharine was born during World War I:* "Katharine Graham," *Washington Post*, April 12, 2018, http://www.washingtonpost.com/brand-studio/fox/katharine-graham.

111 *having lunches with Harry Bridges:* Katharine Graham, *Personal History* (Knopf, 1997), Kindle location 1976.

111 *Philip was an "incandescent man":* David Halberstam, *The Powers That Be* (Open Road Media, 2012).

111 *despite a miscarriage and loss of a baby at birth:* Graham, *Personal History*, Kindle location 2808, 2809.

111 *"I was put on earth to take care of Phil Graham":* J. Y. Smith and Noah Epstein, "Katharine Graham Dies at 84," *Washington Post*, July 18, 2001, https://www.washingtonpost.com/wp-dyn/content/article/2005/08/04/AR2005080400963_5.html.

111 *Katharine was relegated to the sidelines:* Graham, *Personal History*, Kindle location 6915.

112 *One of Kay's friends described her as "patient Griselda":* Robin Gerber, *Katharine Graham: The Leadership Journey of an American Icon* (Portfolio, 2005), 33.

112 *the world she had known and loved had disappeared:* Graham, *Personal History*, Kindle location 6779.

112 *Katharine's share of company stock to his mistress:* Gerber, *Katharine Graham*, 57.

112 *his grave visible from Katharine's window:* Graham, *Personal History*, Kindle location 6862.

113 *"What I essentially did was to put one foot in front of the other":* Smith and Epstein, "Katharine Graham Dies at 84."

113 *"secretly wanted her to sell the* Post*":* Ben Bradlee, *A Good Life* (Simon & Schuster, 2011), 241.

113 *"got in the way of my doing the kind of job I wanted":* Graham, *Personal History*, Kindle location 8466.

113 *"When my husband died, I had three choices":* Smith and Epstein, "Katharine Graham Dies at 84."

114 *the key for a CEO getting started:* Jim Collins, *Good to Great: Why Some Companies Make the Leap . . . and Others Don't* (HarperCollins, 2001).

115 *"She has the guts of a cat burglar":* "Our Company | Graham Holdings Company," accessed August 16, 2021, https://www.ghco.com/historykgraham obituary/.

115 *They shared laughs over both stories:* Graham, *Personal History*, Kindle location 9356.

116 *John of the Cross, wrote a poem about an excruciating journey:* "The Dark Night of the Soul: Google Books," accessed August 16, 2021, https://www .google.com/books/edition/The_Dark_Night_of_the_Soul/B8tMAQAAM AAJ?hl=en&gbpv=1&pg=PR3&printsec=frontcover.

117 *"man will not merely endure: he will prevail":* "William Faulkner: Banquet Speech," accessed August 16, 2021, https://www.nobelprize.org/prizes/lit erature/1949/faulkner/speech/.

117 *"A man without a purpose is like a ship without a rudder":* "Famous Quote from Thomas Carlyle," Famous Quote From: (blog), accessed August 16, 2021, http://famousquotefrom.com/thomas-carlyle/.

117 *"If you don't know what your passion is":* "What I Know for Sure: Oprah Winfrey," accessed August 16, 2021, https://www.oprah.com/omagazine /what-i-know-for-sure-oprah-winfrey/all.

117 *"Many persons have a wrong idea of what constitutes true happiness":* Helen Keller, Helen Keller's Journal, 1936–1937 (Doubleday, Doran and Company, Inc., 1938), http://archive.org/details/helenkellersjour00hele.

118 *"Purpose endows a person with joy in good times":* "The Path to Purpose: Google Books," accessed August 16, 2021, https://www.google.com/books /edition/The_Path_to_Purpose/mx7Ds2MnnWQC?hl=en&gbpv=1&print sec=frontcover.

118 *must have a compelling mission and meet the highest standards of a profession:* "Good Work: Google Books," accessed August 16, 2021, https://www .google.com/books/edition/Good_Work/gforDaQFRSoC?hl=en&gbpv=1& printsec=frontcover.

119 *Grandma Moses began painting at seventy-eight:* "Grandma Moses (Anna Mary Robertson Moses) | Artist Profile," NMWA (blog), accessed August 16, 2021, https://nmwa.org/art/artists/grandma-moses-anna-mary-rob ertson-moses/.

SEVEN: LEARNING TO LEAD UP

126 *Marshall pulled him aside and acidly defended his men:* Benjamin Runkle, "When Marshall Met Pershing," War on the Rocks, October 3, 2017, https:// warontherocks.com/2017/10/when-marshall-met-pershing/.

126 *Pershing remembered that moment:* David Brooks, *The Road to Character* (Random House, 2015), 140.

127 *Marshall flatly rejected FDR's plan:* Kevin Baker, "America's Finest General," *Military History,* September 2011, https://www.marshallfoundation .org/marshall/wp-content/uploads/sites/22/2014/04/MarshallarticleMilitary History2011.pdf.

127 *Instead, FDR promoted him:* Ibid.

129 *"I've been a human answering machine"*: Rosanne Badowski and Roger Gittines, *Managing Up: How to Forge an Effective Relationship with Those above You* (Crown, 2003), xv.

129 *"Roseanne was . . . loyal, discreet, and forgiving"*: Ibid., xi.

129 *Acheson was born into an elite family:* "Dean Gooderham Acheson—People—Department History—Office of the Historian," accessed July 26, 2021, https://history.state.gov/departmenthistory/people/acheson-dean-gooder ham.

129 *"a little touch of Harry in the night"*: David McCullough, "Opinion | Clinton and Congress: A Touch of Harry in the Night," *New York Times*, December 2, 1994, https://www.nytimes.com/1994/12/02/opinion/clinton-congress-a-touch-of-harry-in-the-night.html.

129 *the platform was empty except for one man, Dean Acheson:* William E. Leuchtenburg, "New Faces of 1946," *Smithsonian,* accessed July 28, 2021, https://www.smithsonianmag.com/history/new-faces-of-1946-135190660/.

130 *George Washington called on Alexander Hamilton:* "Alexander Hamilton and His Patron, George Washington | American Experience | PBS," accessed July 28, 2021, https://www.pbs.org/wgbh/americanexperience/features /hamilton-and-his-patron-george-washington/.

130 *Abraham Lincoln brought two young men with him:* Joshua Zeitz, *Lincoln's Boys: John Hay, John Nicolay, and the War for Lincoln's Image* (Penguin, 2014), 2.

130 *Hay went on to become a leading statesman and secretary of state:* Ibid., 8.

130 *FDR had Louis Howe, Harry Hopkins, and Frances Perkins:* Frank Costigliola, "Broken Circle: The Isolation of Franklin D. Roosevelt in World War II," *Diplomatic History* 32, no. 5 (2008): 677–718, accessed July 28, 2021. http://www.jstor.org/stable/24915955.

130 *Harry Truman had George Marshall:* Walter Isaacson and Evan Thomas, *The Wise Men: Six Friends and the World They Made* (Simon & Schuster, 2012).

130 *For John F. Kennedy, it was his brother Bobby:* "Bobby Kennedy: Is He the 'Assistant President'? | Politics | US News," *US News & World Report,* accessed July 28, 2021, //www.usnews.com/news/articles/2015/06/05/bobby -kennedy-is-he-the-assistant-president.

130 *for Richard Nixon, it was Henry Kissinger:* Stephen Sestanovich, "The Long History of Leading from Behind," *Atlantic,* December 22, 2015, https:// www.theatlantic.com/magazine/archive/2016/01/the-long-history-of-lead ing-from-behind/419097/.

131 *highly successful corporate lawyers in Houston:* James A. Baker and Steve Fiffer, *Work Hard, Study . . . and Keep Out of Politics!* (Northwestern University Press, 2008), 4–7.

131   *"Work hard, study . . . and keep out of politics":* Ibid., 3–4.

131   *His family sent him to the best boarding schools:* Peter Baker and Susan Glasser, *The Man Who Ran Washington: The Life and Times of James A. Baker III* (Doubleday, 2020).

131   *Baker, age twenty, signed up for the marines:* Baker and Fiffer, *Work Hard*, 12.

131   *joined one of the most prestigious corporate law firms:* Ibid., 12–13.

131   *joined a country club in Houston, where he and George H.W. Bush:* Baker and Glasser, *Man Who Ran Washington*.

131   *In 1968, Jim's wife, Mary Stuart, contracted cancer:* Ibid., 46.

131   *the two eventually married in 1973:* Ibid., 60.

132   *Bush insisted they could cure both:* Baker and Fiffer, *Work Hard*, 17.

132   *accepted an offer to be number two at the Department of Commerce:* Ibid., 65.

132   *asked Baker to fill in for him at Ford White House meetings:* Ibid., 29.

133   *"the Miracle Man":* Baker and Glasser, *Man Who Ran Washington*, 79.

133   *Reagan swept the boards:* Ibid., 120.

133   *Reagan invited the man who had run two campaigns against him:* Ibid., 134.

133   *Reagan had his back on more than one occasion:* Ibid., 132.

133   *Meese became a member of the cabinet:* Ibid., 133.

134   *no match for Baker intellectually and organizationally:* Ibid.

134   *"the velvet hammer":* Ibid., 140.

134   *was not afraid of telling Baker hard truths:* Megan Rosenfeld, "The Fabulous Baker Girl," *Washington Post*, September 23, 1992, https://www.washingtonpost.com/archive/lifestyle/1992/09/23/the-fabulous-baker-girl/0b587b0c-da73-4d57-a6a2-215fd1e3fcc9/.

135   *"Prior Preparation Prevents Poor Performances":* Baker and Fiffer, *Work Hard*, 5.

136   *he guided the White House and Congress in overhauling Social Security:* "The Reagan Presidency," Ronald Reagan, accessed July 30, 2021, https://www.reaganlibrary.gov/reagans/reagan-administration/reagan-presidency.

EIGHT: LEADING YOUR TEAM

138   *Black Lives Matter was a nonprofit start-up created in 2013:* Victoria Capatosto, "A Brief History of Civil Rights in the United States," accessed August 1, 2021, https://library.law.howard.edu/civilrightshistory/BLM.

138   *"If you want to go fast, go alone":* "Patty Stonesifer—2005 UNICEF—Bill & Melinda Gates Foundation," accessed September 7, 2021, https://www.gatesfoundation.org/ideas/speeches/2005/06/patty-stonesifer-2005-unicef.

140   *identified five conditions that help a team flourish:* J. Richard Hackman, *Leading Teams: Setting the Stage for Great Performances* (Harvard Business Review Press, 2002), ix.

140   *featuring Haig and a headline calling him "The Vicar"*: George J. Church, "Alexander Haig: The Vicar Takes Charge," *Time*, accessed August 20, 2021, http://content.time.com/time/subscriber/article/0,33009,922441,00.html.

141   *"had clear protocols and chains of command for these kinds of threats"*: Abigail Tracy, "How Trump Gutted Obama's Pandemic-Preparedness Systems," *Vanity Fair*, accessed August 1, 2021, https://www.vanityfair.com/news/2020/05/trump-obama-coronavirus-pandemic-response.

141   *closed the NSC unit designed to protect the country*: Ibid.

142   *over 750,00 Americans have died from the pandemic*: "United States—COVID-19 Overview—Johns Hopkins," Johns Hopkins Coronavirus Resource Center, accessed August 20, 2021, https://coronavirus.jhu.edu/region/united-states.

142   *"The first responsibility of a leader is to define reality"*: Max De Pree, *Leadership Is an Art* (Crown, 2011), 11.

143   *In only nine days, he wrote his 1946 bestseller*: Emily Esfahani Smith, "There's More to Life Than Being Happy," *Atlantic*, January 9, 2013, https://www.theatlantic.com/health/archive/2013/01/theres-more-to-life-than-being-happy/266805/.

143   *He argued to other prisoners*: Viktor Emil Frankl, *Man's Search for Meaning: An Introduction to Logotherapy* (Beacon Press, 2006).

143   *the number who knew the actual purpose of the project*: "WWII's Atomic Bomb Program Was So Secretive That Even Many of the Participants Were in the Dark," *Washington Post*, accessed August 2, 2021, https://www.washingtonpost.com/science/wwiis-atomic-bomb-program-was-so-secretive-that-even-many-of-the-participants-were-in-the-dark/2019/10/31/8d92d16c-fb7e-11e9-8906-ab6b60de9124_story.html.

143   *he saw "a complete transformation" in their work*: "Los Alamos from Below: Reminiscences 1943–1945, by Richard Feynman," accessed August 2, 2021, http://calteches.library.caltech.edu/34/3/FeynmanLosAlamos.htm.

144   *twenty researchers to undertake a five-year study*: Jim Collins, *Good to Great: Why Some Companies Make the Leap . . . and Others Don't* (HarperCollins, 2001).

144   *"an individual who blends personal humility with intense professional will"*: Collins, *Good to Great*, 21.

144   *It sold 4 million copies*: Adam Bryant, "For This Guru, No Question Is Too Big," *New York Times*, May 23, 2009, https://www.nytimes.com/2009/05/24/business/24collins.html.

145   *"Get the right people on the bus"*: Ibid.

145   *Collins team cited the fifteen-year success of Wells Fargo*: Ibid.

145   *they had the "Right Stuff"*: Tom Wolfe, *The Right Stuff* (Farrar, Straus and Giroux, 2008).

145 *The Apollo program over the years employed a staggering 400,000 people:* "NASA—NASA Langley Research Center Contributions to the Apollo Program" (Brian Dunbar), accessed August 1, 2021, https://www.nasa.gov /centers/langley/news/factsheets/Apollo.html.

145 *Their calculations were so respected:* Margot Lee Shetterly, *Hidden Figures: The American Dream and the Untold Story of the Black Women Mathematicians Who Helped Win the Space Race* (HarperCollins, 2016), 217.

147 *a glowing account of great groups and how they collaborate:* Warren G. Bennis and Patricia Ward Biederman, *Organizing Genius: The Secrets of Creative Collaboration* (Addison-Wesley, 1997).

147 *"a dent in the universe":* Warren G. Bennis and Patricia Ward Biederman, *The Essential Bennis* (Jossey-Bass, 2009), 140.

147 *Xerox's Palo Alto Research Center:* Ibid., 143.

147 *Lockheed Martin's "Skunk Works":* Ibid., 140.

147 *The Bauhaus movement:* Ibid., 139.

147 *served as an incubator and a refuge for modern artists:* Ibid., 140.

148 *"a golden age of collaborative achievement for America":* Ibid., 140.

148 *"If you can dream it, you can do it":* Ibid., 150.

148 *Examples from the Edison quiz:* "Thomas Edison's Intelligence Test I American Experience I Official Site I PBS," accessed August 20, 2021, https://www .pbs.org/wgbh/americanexperience/features/thomas-edisons-intelligence -test/.

148 *"Why is a manhole cover round?"* Meghan Casserly, "Why Are Manholes Round? The 10 Toughest Interview Questions," *Forbes*, accessed August 20, 2021, https://www.forbes.com/sites/meghancasserly/2011/07/27/the -10-toughest-interview-questions/.

149 *they lost to Argentina:* Geoffrey Colvin, "Why Dream Teams Fail," *Fortune,* June 8, 2006, https://money.cnn.com/magazines/fortune/fortune_ar chive/2006/06/12/8379219/index.htm.

149 *"I'm not looking for the best players":* Gavin O'Connor, *Miracle* (Buena Vista Pictures, 2004).

149 *the U.S. team upset the Soviets:* "Miracle on Ice," 100 Greatest Moments, accessed August 1, 2021, https://www.amazon.com/100-Greatest-Moments /dp/B0779L7QQR.

150 *she then applied to work as an assistant field secretary of the NAACP:* Charles Payne, "Ella Baker and Models of Social Change," *Signs* 14, no. 4 (1989): 887, 888.

150 *Baker eventually moved away from the organization:* Ibid., 889.

150 *she was able to create the organization she had always dreamed of:* Ibid., 890–91

151 *"was as much against this nation's traditional Black leadership structure":* Mike

D'Orso and John Lewis, Chapter 6, "Nigras, Nigras Everywhere!" in *Walking with the Wind: A Memoir of the Movement* (Simon & Schuster, 1998), 98–118.

151 *Baker fostered what has been referred to as "group-centered leadership":* Ibid., 892.

151 *"organizing people to be self-sufficient":* Ibid., 347.

152 *the "leaderless" designation discounts the multitude of leaders:* NPR Staff, "The #BlackLivesMatter Movement: Marches and Tweets for Healing," NPR, June 9, 2015, https://www.npr.org/2015/06/09/412862459/the-blacklivesmat ter-movement-marches-and-tweets-for-healing.

152 *decentralized organizations can also respond more quickly to changing dynamics:* Joshua Keating, "The Leaderless Black Lives Matter Protests Are the Future of Politics.," accessed August 20, 2021, https://slate.com/news-and -politics/2020/06/george-floyd-global-leaderless-movements.html.

NINE: THE ART OF PUBLIC PERSUASION

154 *He copied from both, studying and reciting lines:* David W. Blight, *Frederick Douglass: Prophet of Freedom* (Simon & Schuster, 2018).

154 *"Every opportunity I got I used to read this book":* Frederick Douglass, *Narrative of the Life of Frederick Douglass, an American Slave* (Pub. at the Antislavery office, 1845), 39.

154 *He was drawn not only to the moral tales in the* Orator: "The Book That Taught Frederick Douglass and Abraham Lincoln How to Speak," New England Historical Society (blog), August 22, 2020, https://www.newen glandhistoricalsociety.com/the-book-that-taught-frederick-douglass-and -abraham-lincoln-how-to-speak/.

155 *the two would meet for the first time thirty-three years later:* Frederick Douglass and C. W. Foster, "Lincoln and Frederick Douglass—With Malice Toward None: The Abraham Lincoln Bicentennial Exhibition | Exhibitions— Library of Congress," web page, February 12, 2009, https://www.loc.gov /exhibits/lincoln/lincoln-and-frederick-douglass.html.

155 *Frederick Bailey had changed his name to Frederick Douglass:* Douglass, *Narrative of the Life*, 112.

155 *each spoke for ninety minutes and on a single subject:* "Lincoln-Douglas Debates | Summary, Dates, Significance, & Facts," *Encyclopaedia Britannica,* accessed August 4, 2021, https://www.britannica.com/event/Lincoln-Doug lass-debates.

155 *Curious people walked as many as nine hours to hear them:* Graham A. Peck, "New Records of the Lincoln-Douglas Debate at the 1854 Illinois State Fair: The Missouri Republican and the Missouri Democrat Report from Springfield," *Journal of the Abraham Lincoln Association* 30, no. 2 (2009): 25–80.

156   *spoke for only thirty-nine and thirty-eight minutes respectively:* Jiachuan Wu, et al., "Graphic: Presidential Debate Topic Tracker," NBC News, accessed August 20, 2021, https://www.nbcnews.com/politics/2020-election/first -presidential-debate-2020-topics-graphic-n1241389.

156   *educator Neil Postman captured the sentiments of his day:* Neil Postman, *Amusing Ourselves to Death: Public Discourse in the Age of Show Business* (Penguin, 2006).

156   *Isocrates was the father of oratory:* S. E. Smethurst, "Supplementary Paper: Cicero and Isocrates," *Transactions and Proceedings of the American Philological Association* 84 (1953): 262–320, https://doi.org/10.2307/283414.

156   *over time he developed a reputation for his own speaking:* "Isocrates | Greek Orator and Rhetorician," *Encyclopaedia Britannica,* accessed August 5, 2021, https://www.britannica.com/biography/Isocrates.

156   *rallied Athenians to resist the expansion of nearby Macedonia:* "Demosthenes | Greek Statesman and Orator," *Encyclopaedia Britannica,* accessed August 5, 2021, https://www.britannica.com/biography/Demosthenes-Greek-states man-and-orator.

156   *Lincoln liked to quote from Pericles:* "The Greeks at Gettysburg: An Analysis of Pericles' Epitaphios Logos as a Model for Abraham Lincoln's Gettysburg Address," accessed August 5, 2021, https://projects.iq.harvard.edu /persephone/greeks-gettysburg-analysis-pericles-epitaphios-logos-model -abraham-lincolns-gettysburg-0.

157   *He proclaimed there is no such thing as a red America or a blue America:* "Barack Obama's Keynote Address at the 2004 Democratic National Convention," PBS NewsHour, July 27, 2004, https://www.pbs.org/newshour/show/barack -obamas-keynote-address-at-the-2004-democratic-national-convention.

158   *"I can call spirits from the vasty deep":* William Shakespeare, *Henry IV, Part 1* (Folger Shakespeare Library, n.d.), https://shakespeare.folger.edu/shake speares-works/henry-iv-part-1/.

158   *Kennedy was also a great fan of Churchill's:* Barbara Maranzani, "Inside John F. Kennedy's Lifelong Admiration of Winston Churchill," Biography, accessed August 5, 2021, https://www.biography.com/news/john-f-kennedy -winston-churchill.

158   *Churchill was not a brilliant student:* Winston Churchill, *My Early Life: 1874–1904* (Simon & Schuster, 2010), 14.

158   *He did more than memorize speeches:* Ibid., 17.

158   *wound up at Sandhurst only upon his third try:* Martin Gilbert, *Churchill: A Life* (Rosetta Books, 2014).

158   *He was posted overseas as a junior military officer:* Roy Jenkins, *Churchill: A Biography* (Macmillan, 2001).

158 *Churchill also became a voracious reader:* Ibid., 24.

158 *Churchill read the debates:* Gilbert, *Churchill*, 67.

158 *began to read extensively among the English classics:* Jenkins, *Churchill*, 26.

159 *At twenty-six, he won his first seat in Parliament:* Gilbert, *Churchill*, 135.

159 *he remained before the public eye for nearly sixty years:* "History of Sir Winston Churchill—gov.UK," accessed August 5, 2021, https://www.gov.uk/govern ment/history/past-prime-ministers/winston-churchill.

159 *"Churchill mobilized the English language and sent it into battle":* "Quotes FAQ," International Churchill Society, March 1, 2009, https://winston churchill.org/resources/quotes/quotes-faq/.

159 *"none is so precious as the gift of oratory":* "America's National Churchill Mu-seum | Sir Winston Churchill's Speeches," accessed August 20, 2021, https:// www.nationalchurchillmuseum.org/winston-churchills-speeches.html.

159 *"Insist on yourself; never imitate":* Ralph Waldo Emerson, *Self-Reliance and Other Essays* (Sanage Publishing), Kindle edition, 48.

159 *That triggered deep passions in Lincoln:* Ronald C. White, *A. Lincoln: A Biog-raphy* (Random House Publishing Group, 2009), 205.

159 *he felt he had to get into the streets with them:* Clayborne Carson, "MLK, the Reluctant Civil Rights Leader," CNN, January 20, 2014, https://www.cnn .com/2014/01/20/living/martin-luther-king-identity/index.html.

160 *"This is the real me":* Gerald Eugene Myers, *William James: His Life and Thought* (Yale University Press, 2001), 49.

160 *he traveled third class across his native land for a year:* "1915–16: A Tour of the Homeland," *Hindustan Times,* September 30, 2019, https://www.hindu stantimes.com/india-news/1915-16-a-tour-of-the-homeland/story-NcyhMn 8NEZiAp5m6OQplfL.html.

161 *speaking in front of an audience:* "America's Top Fears: Public Speaking, Heights and Bugs," *Washington Post*, accessed August 20, 2021, https:// www.washingtonpost.com/news/wonk/wp/2014/10/30/clowns-are-twice -as-scary-to-democrats-as-they-are-to-republicans/.

161 *she compared public speaking to standing naked in front of an audience:* Rosa-lind Russell and Chris Chase, *Life Is a Banquet* (Random House, 1977). 211.

162 *it became one of the seven basic liberal arts:* "Liberal Arts," *Encyclopaedia Bri-tannica,* accessed August 5, 2021, https://www.britannica.com/topic/liberal -arts.

163 *there are three main elements of oratory:* Mortimer J. Adler, *How to Speak, How to Listen* (Simon & Schuster, 1997).

163 *"When persuasion is the end, passion also must be engaged":* George Campbell, *The Philosophy of Rhetoric* (Harper & Brothers, 1851).

163 *to be the world's greatest horseman:* Thomas K. McCraw, *Prophet of Innovation:*

Joseph Schumpeter and Creative Destruction (Harvard University Press, 2009), 4.

164   *every good speaker should have the calm confidence of a Christian with four aces up his sleeve:* Mark Twain, *Early Tales and Sketches, Volume 1: 1851–1864* (University of California Press, 1979), 368.

164   *He loved to tell stories:* Kathleen Hall Jamieson, *Eloquence in an Electronic Age: The Transformation of Political Speechmaking* (Oxford University Press, 1990).

164   *he recalled the heroes who gave their last full measure:* "Inaugural Addresses of the Presidents of the United States: from George Washington 1789 to George Bush 1989," Text (Washington, D.C.: U.S. Government Printing Office, 1989), accessed August 5, 2021, https://avalon.law.yale.edu/20th_century/reagan1.asp.

164   *defines a figure of speech:* "Figure, n.," in OED Online (Oxford University Press), accessed August 5, 2021, http://www.oed.com/view/Entry/70079.

165   *"We couldn't do it without TV":* Richard Reeves, *President Kennedy: Profile of Power* (Simon & Schuster, 1994), 326.

166   *"You really felt like you were connecting to him and to his campaign":* Jennifer Aaker and Victoria Chang, "Obama and the Power of Social Media and Technology," Stanford Graduate School of Business Case No. M-321, https://www.gsb.stanford.edu/faculty-research/case-studies/obama-power-social-media-technology, accessed July 2021, 7.

166   *His team built a grassroots network of supporters:* Ibid., 2.

166   *Obama was able to bring in 6.5 million digital donations:* Ibid., 2.

167   *she officially launched a challenge to the fourth-ranking Democrat:* Charlotte Alter, "Inside Rep. Alexandria Ocasio-Cortez's Unlikely Rise," *Time*, accessed September 7, 2021, https://time.com/longform/alexandria-ocasio-cortez-profile/.

168   *she will deliver a witty retort on there":* "Analysis I AOC Just Played 'Among Us' on Twitch. Over 400,000 People Came to Watch," *Washington Post*, accessed August 9, 2021, https://www.washingtonpost.com/politics/2020/10/22/aoc-just-played-among-us-twitch-over-400000-people-came-watch/.

168   *"The way we grow our presence is by being there":* Devin Dwyer, "Alexandria Ocasio-Cortez's Twitter Lesson for House Democrats," ABC News, accessed September 7, 2021, https://abcnews.go.com/Politics/alexandria-ocasio-cortezs-twitter-lesson-house-democrats/story?id=60443727.

169   *"commanded a weekly radio audience of 90 million":* Albin Krebs, "Charles Coughlin, 30's 'Radio Priest,'" *New York Times*, accessed September 7, 2021, https://www.nytimes.com/1979/10/28/archives/charles-coughlin-30s-radio-priest-dies-fiery-sermons-stirred-furor.html.

169 *"The art of communication is the language of leadership"*: Jim Paymar, "Speak Like a Leader," *Forbes*, accessed August 9, 2021, https://www.forbes.com /sites/jimpaymar/2012/02/02/speak-like-a-leader/.

TEN: WHEN JOURNEYS CONVERGE

174 *they could not stir the nation into action:* Robert Coles, *Lives of Moral Leadership: Men and Women Who Have Made a Difference* (Random House Trade Paperbacks, 2013), 20.

174 *to make things happen in the halls of Congress:* Ibid., 22–25.

174 *Kennedy arranged for the team to testify before Congress:* Ibid., 26.

174 *a tour of the poorest communities in Mississippi and West Virginia:* Ibid., 44.

175 *"You learn what's ahead through the living of it":* Ibid., 52.

176 *the board graciously granted her a three-month sabbatical:* Mary S. Hartman, *Talking Leadership: Conversations with Powerful Women* (Rutgers University Press, 1999), 52.

177 *twenty-one-page PowerPoint:* Tessa Stuart, "What the Democratic Party Can Learn From Stacey Abrams' Success in Georgia," *Rolling Stone*, December 20, 2020, https://www.rollingstone.com/politics/politics-features/stacey -abrams-georgia-senate-races-2020-election-1097107/.

177 *"800,000 unregistered people of color":* Stacey Abrams, *Lead from the Outside: How to Build Your Future and Make Real Change* (Picador, 2018), Kindle location 1043.

178 *"I'm nothing special":* Ibid.

ELEVEN: HOW LEADERS LOSE THEIR WAY

187 *"Man is conceived in sin and born in corruption":* Robert Penn Warren, *All the King's Men* (Houghton Mifflin Harcourt, 2006), 235.

188 *he won a job at another prestigious institution:* Michael Rothfeld, "The Rise and Fall of Rajat Gupta," *Wall Street Journal*, October 24, 2012, https:// online.wsj.com/article/SB10001424052970203400604578075291193560764 .html.

188 *he became the first CEO of the firm born outside the United States:* Ibid.

188 *opening offices in twenty countries, doubling the number of partners, and increasing revenues by 230 percent:* Walter Kiechel, "The Tempting of Rajat Gupta," *Harvard Business Review*, March 24, 2011, https://hbr.org/2011/03 /the-tempting-of-rajat-gupta.

188 *served in advisory capacities at numerous business schools:* Rothfeld, "Rise and Fall."

189 *Gupta engaged in serious insider trading:* "Rajat Gupta Pleads Not Guilty in Insider Trading, Released on $10 Mn Bail," *Economic Times*, accessed

August 9, 2021, https://economictimes.indiatimes.com/news/international
/rajat-gupta-pleads-not-guilty-in-insider-trading-released-on-10-mn-bail
/articleshow/10505219.cms?from=mdr.

189   *an investment that allegedly reaped gains and loss avoidance totaling $23 mil-
lion:* "SEC Files Insider Trading Charges Against Rajat Gupta," accessed
August 9, 2021, https://www.sec.gov/news/press/2011/2011-223.htm.

189   *He spent nineteen months in jail:* "Ex-McKinsey Chief Gupta Says He Was in
Solitary for Weeks in U.S. Jail," Reuters, March 26, 2019, sec. Banks, https://
www.reuters.com/article/us-crime-gupta-prison-idUSKCN1R70XR.

189   *His net worth seemed well over $100 million:* Peter Lattman, "Rajat Gupta's
Wealth in Spotlight at Trial," *Business Standard India,* June 3, 2012, https://
www.business-standard.com/article/economy-policy/rajat-gupta-s-wealth
-in-spotlight-at-trial-112060302002_1.html.

190   *Dante wrote of penitents required to carry slabs of stone on their backs:*
"The Project Gutenberg EBook of The Divine Comedy, Hell, by Dante
Alighieri," accessed August 11, 2021, https://www.gutenberg.org/files
/1001/1001-h/1001-h.htm.

191   *Elizabeth Holmes drops out of Stanford at age seventeen:* Ken Auletta, "Blood,
Simpler," *New Yorker,* December 7, 2014, https://www.newyorker.com
/magazine/2014/12/15/blood-simpler.

191   *could face a twenty-year sentence: U.S. v. Elizabeth Holmes, et al.,* February 26,
2019, https://www.justice.gov/usao-ndca/us-v-elizabeth-holmes-et-al.

191   *He was then charged with fraud and went to prison:* Anne Gearan, "Three
Years Later, Aramony Scandal Still Hurts United Way," AP NEWS, accessed August 11, 2021, https://apnews.com/article/8d91ad96f55046e2bebc3
e55feb6996d.

191   *He is forced to resign when accused of being at the center of a sex scandal:*
David K. Li, "Jerry Falwell Jr. Is Suing Liberty University after His Forced
Resignation over Sex Scandal," NBC News, accessed August 11, 2021,
https://www.nbcnews.com/news/us-news/jerry-falwell-jr-suing-liberty
-university-after-his-forced-resignation-n1245258.

192   *"The rock of democracy will founder":* "These 5 Qualities Define Good Leadership, According to a Presidential Historian," Aspen Institute, October 26,
2018, https://www.aspeninstitute.org/blog-posts/these-five-qualities-define
-good-leadership-according-to-a-presidential-historian/.

192   *she had him fired:* Donald Regan: 1918–2003 // Reagan's Staff Chief Stung
by Iran-Contra," *Tampa Bay Times,* accessed August 11, 2021, https://www
.tampabay.com/archive/2003/06/11/donald-regan-1918-2003-reagan-s-staff
-chief-stung-by-iran-contra/.

192   *"as long as you don't care who gets the credit":* "Oval Office," accessed

August 11, 2021, https://www.reaganfoundation.org/library-museum/perma
nent-exhibitions/oval-office/.

193   *inspired Schultz to ensure that baristas at his Starbucks:* Carmine Gallo,
"How Starbucks CEO Howard Schultz Inspired Us to Dream Bigger,"
Forbes, accessed August 11, 2021, https://www.forbes.com/sites/carmine
gallo/2016/12/02/how-starbucks-ceo-howard-schultz-inspired-us-to
-dream-bigger/.

193   *President Obama chose to sit at the same desk:* "Treasures of the White House:
'Resolute' Desk," White House Historical Association, accessed August 11,
2021, https://www.whitehousehistory.org/photos/treasures-of-the-white
-house-resolute-desk.

194   *he accused them of rash, even reckless imprudence:* David Halberstam, *The Best
and the Brightest* (Random House Publishing Group, 2002).

194   *Some fifty-six thousand Americans perished in that war:* "Vietnam War U.S.
Military Fatal Casualty Statistics," National Archives, August 15, 2016,
https://www.archives.gov/research/military/vietnam-war/casualty-statis
tics.

196   *"We need leaders of inspired idealism":* "American Rhetoric: Teddy
Roosevelt—The Right of the People to Rule," accessed August 11, 2021,
https://www.americanrhetoric.com/speeches/teddyrooseveltrightpeople
rule.htm.

196   *"A prince . . . must imitate the fox and the lion":* Niccolò Machiavelli, *The
Prince* (Branden Books, 2002), 103.

197   *subtitled a positive biographical work on FDR:* James MacGregor Burns, *Roosevelt: The Lion and the Fox (1882–1940)* (Open Road Media, 2012).

197   *"We want a decent, just, caring, and compassionate president":* Thomas A. Cronin and Michael A. Genovese, *The Paradoxes of the American Presidency* (Oxford University Press, 1998), 9.

199   *"He must know when to dissemble, when to be frank":* Charles de Gaulle, *The
Edge of the Sword* (Criterion Books, 1960), 104.

200   *"he has lost his greatest strength":* Michael Beschloss, *Mayday: Eisenhower,
Khrushchev, and the U-2 Affair* (Open Road Media, 2016), 252.

200   *"No one's going to give you power":* Nancy Carroll, "Nancy Pelosi's Legacy as
One of the Most Important People in History," accessed September 22, 2021,
https://www.usatoday.com/story/opinion/2021/04/16/nancy-pelosi-house
-speaker-book-susan-page-power-american-history/7231734002/.

200   *"Every prime minister must be a good butcher":* Haynes Johnson, "Nixon
Stirs All the Old Memories," *Washington Post,* May 5, 1977, https://www
.washingtonpost.com/archive/politics/1977/05/05/nixon-stirs-all-the-old
-memories/6d3e39ce-70e1-409d-84e5-1e72a0e17253/.

TWELVE: LEADING THROUGH A CRISIS

201 *Conditions were harsh:* History.com Editors, "Nelson Mandela Writes from Prison," History, accessed August 12, 2021, https://www.history.com/this -day-in-history/mandela-writes-from-prison.

201 *"You have no idea of the cruelty of man against man":* Jill Smolowe, "Nelson Mandela: 1918–2013," People.com, accessed August 12, 2021, https://people .com/archive/nelson-mandela-1918-2013-vol-80-no-26/.

202 "It matters not how strait the gate": Poetry Foundation, "Invictus by William Ernest Henley," Poetry Foundation (Poetry Foundation, August 11, 2021), https://www.poetryfoundation.org/, https://www.poetryfoundation .org/poems/51642/invictus.

202 *Churchill paraphrased the last two lines in a speech bucking up Parliament:* "Captain of Our Souls," International Churchill Society, November 30, 2016, https://winstonchurchill.org/resources/quotes/captain-of-our-souls/.

202 *President Clinton said that Mandela consoled him through conversations about its message:* "How Mandela Helped Clinton Survive Scandal," *Guardian,* June 21, 2004, http://www.theguardian.com/world/2004/jun/21/usa.inter views.

202 *President Obama quoted the poem in a memorial service:* "Nelson Mandela Memorial: Barack Obama's Speech in Full | CNN Politics," CNN, December 10, 2013, https://www.cnn.com/2013/12/10/politics/mandela-obama-re marks/index.html.

202 *John Lewis liked to repeat the poem:* Grace Hauck and Natalie Allison, "12-Year-Old Tybre Faw Met His Hero Two Years Ago; He Read John Lewis' Favorite Poem at His Funeral," *USA Today,* accessed August 12, 2021, https://www.usatoday.com/story/news/nation/2020/07/30/john-lewis -funeral-tybre-faw-reads-invictus-poem-honors-hero/5545602002/.

203 *"There is no easy walk to freedom anywhere":* "Nelson Mandela: No Easy Walk to Freedom," accessed August 12, 2021, http://www.columbia.edu/itc /history/mann/w3005/mandela01.html.

203 *"He stays behind the flock, letting the most nimble go out ahead":* Nelson Mandela, *Long Walk to Freedom* (Back Bay Books; Hachette Book Group, 1995), 22.

203 *They settled upon an acronym, VUCA:* "Who First Originated the Term VUCA (Volatility, Uncertainty, Complexity and Ambiguity)?—USAHEC Ask Us a Question," accessed August 12, 2021, https://usawc.libanswers .com/faq/84869.

205 *"using every form of profanity he'd ever heard":* "Character Above All: Harry S. Truman Essay," accessed August 12, 2021, https://www.pbs.org/news hour/spc/character/essays/truman.html.

205 *"learned two vitally important things about himself"*: Ibid.

205 *at the bottom of a grave marker, he found this inscription:* Jack Valenti, *This Time, This Place: My Life in War, the White House, and Hollywood* (Crown, 2007), Kindle location 744.

207 *Napoleon would work through half a dozen scenarios:* "Napoleon on Strategy," Strategic Thinking, accessed August 12, 2021, http://www.strategybydesign .org/napoleon-on-strategy.

207 *he was instructed to first steer his raft toward a farmhouse downriver:* Geoffrey C. Ward, "Before He Became a Saint," *New York Times*, October 22, 1995, https://www.nytimes.com/1995/10/22/books/before-he-became-a-saint .html.

208 "In time of peril, like the needle": Herman Melville, *White-Jacket: Or, The World in a Man-of-War* (Harper & Brothers, 1850). 173.

209 *"Constitutionally, gentlemen, you have the president"*: Richard V. Allen, "When Reagan Was Shot, Who Was 'in Control' at the White House?," *Washington Post,* March 25, 2011, shttps://www.washingtonpost.com/opinions/when -reagan-was-shot-who-was-in-control-at-the-white-house/2011/03/23/AF JlrfYB_story.html.

211 *"You don't know Americans the way I do"*: History.com Editors, "FDR Commits to Biggest Arms Buildup in U.S. History," History, accessed August 12, 2021, https://www.history.com/this-day-in-history/roosevelt-commits-to -biggest-arms-buildup-in-u-s-history.

211 *we weren't building fifty thousand planes a year:* United States Army Air Forces Office of Statistical Control, Army Air Force Statistical Digest: World War II 1945), http://archive.org/details/ArmyAirForcesStatistical DigestWorldWarII.

212 *"The American people are slow to wrath"*: "December 3, 1901: First Annual Message | Miller Center," October 20, 2016, https://millercenter.org/the -presidency/presidential-speeches/december-3-1901-first-annual-message.

212 *federal intelligence agencies had failed to imagine the magnitude of the threat:* "National Commission on Terrorist Attacks Upon the United States," accessed August 12, 2021, https://govinfo.library.unt.edu/911/report/911 Report_Exec.htm.

212 *New Orleans wasn't prepared for a Hurricane Katrina:* Pam Fessler, "Why Wasn't New Orleans Better Prepared?," NPR, September 2, 2005, sec. Katrina & Beyond, https://www.npr.org/templates/story/story.php ?storyId=4829443.

212 *"The captains of finance and the public stewards of our financial system ignored warnings"*: Mark Memmott, " 'Human Action and Inaction' Caused 2008 Financial Crisis, Report Concludes," NPR, January 27, 2011, https://www

.npr.org/sections/thetwo-way/2011/01/27/133269668/human-action-and-in action-caused-2008-financial-crisis-report-concludes.

213 *American lives were lost to COVID in the Trump era:* Steffie Woolhandler et al., "Public Policy and Health in the Trump Era," *Lancet* 397, no. 10275 (February 20, 2021): 705–53, https://doi.org/10.1016/S0140-6736(20)32545-9.

213 *the average white household has almost eight times the amount of wealth:* "The Black-White Wealth Gap Left Black Households More Vulnerable," accessed September 22, 2021, https://www.brookings.edu/blog /up-front/2020/12/08/the-black-white-wealth-gap-left-black-households -more-vulnerable/.

213 *the life expectancy gap between Black and white Americans grew to five years in 2020:* Paola Scommegna and Mark Mather, "COVID-19 and Other Risk Factors Widen the Black-White Life Expectancy Gap | PRB," accessed September 22, 2021, https://www.prb.org/resources/covid-19-and-other-risk -factors-widen-the-black-white-life-expectancy-gap/.

214 *"One of the main responsibilities of leadership":* Max H. Bazerman and Michael Watkins, *Predictable Surprises: The Disasters You Should Have Seen Coming, and How to Prevent Them* (Harvard Business School Press, 2004). 1.

214 *failed attack on the World Trade Center in 1993 alerted leaders to its vulnerabilities:* History.com Editors, "World Trade Center Is Bombed," History, accessed August 12, 2021, https://www.history.com/this-day-in-history /world-trade-center-bombed.

216 *every single victim who made it to a hospital survived:* "The Key to Saving More Lives in a Mass Violence Incident," EMS1, accessed August 12, 2021, https:// www.ems1.com/ems-products/incident-management/articles/the-key-to-sav ing-more-lives-in-a-mass-violence-incident-1GPkseQwc6Qm4haF/.

216 *"The track record of U.S. commissions is decidedly mixed":* Jordan Tama, "Congress May Appoint a Commission to Investigation the Capitol Riot. Three Factors Affect Whether These Work," accessed September 7, 2021, https:// www.washingtonpost.com/politics/2021/01/19/members-congress-want -commission-investigate-capitol-invasion-heres-when-these-work/.

216 *an all-volunteer military grew out of a Nixon-appointed commission:* Ibid.

217 "It matters not how strait the gate": VADM James B. Stockdale, "Stockdale on Stoicism II: Master of My Fate," n.d., 18.

THIRTEEN: BOOSTER ROCKETS

219 *"I am not going to follow a course which will allow anyone to write a comparable book about this time":* Robert F. Kennedy, *Thirteen Days: A Memoir of the Cuban Missile Crisis* (W. W. Norton, 2011), 97.

220 *"We went eyeball to eyeball":* "TWE Remembers: Eyeball to Eyeball and the

Other Fellow Just Blinked (Cuban Missile Crisis, Day Nine)," Council on Foreign Relations, accessed August 13, 2021, https://www.cfr.org/blog/twe -remembers-eyeball-eyeball-and-other-fellow-just-blinked-cuban-missile -crisis-day-nine.

220 *published a highly influential study of different models of decision-making: Essence of Decision: Explaining the Cuban Missile Crisis* (Boston: Little, Brown, 1971), 30

220 *"shifted from the simple question of what to do now to the harder question":* Richard E. Neustadt, *Thinking in Time: The Uses of History for Decision Makers* (Simon & Schuster, 2011), 14.

221 *remember that Philip II of Macedon hired Aristotle to tutor his son Alexander:* "Aristotle—World History Encyclopedia," accessed August 13, 2021, https://www.worldhistory.org/aristotle/.

221 *Jefferson kept his first collection at his home in Albemarle County:* "Founders Online: From Thomas Jefferson to John Page, 21 February 1770" (University of Virginia Press), accessed August 13, 2021, http://founders.archives .gov/documents/Jefferson/01-01-02-0023.

221 *The 6,487 volumes became the foundation of the library Congress has today:* "Jefferson's Library—Thomas Jefferson | Exhibitions—Library of Congress," April 24, 2000, https://www.loc.gov/exhibits/jefferson/jefflib.html.

221 *John Adams gave his collection . . . to his community in Quincy:* "Adams, John (1735–1826) Library," accessed August 13, 2021, https://www.bpl.org/archi val_post/adams-john-1735-1826-library/.

221 *Lincoln, as we know, was not well schooled but he'd taught himself to read:* Ethan Anderson, "Lincoln: Shakespeare's Greatest Character," National Endowment for the Humanities, accessed November 12, 2021, https://www .neh.gov/blog/lincoln-shakespeares-greatest-character.

222 *Teddy Roosevelt was voracious, consuming as many as a book a day at the White House:* Jeremy Anderberg, "Teddy Roosevelt's 10 Rules for Reading," Book Riot (blog), January 30, 2014, https://bookriot.com/teddy-roosevelts -10-rules-reading/.

222 *TR led a spirited discussion of the book, which he had read overnight:* Edmund Morris, *The Rise of Theodore Roosevelt* (Random House Publishing Group, 2010), xxxiii.

222 *"Not every reader is a leader, but every leader is a reader":* "Truman Quotes," Truman Library Institute (blog), accessed August 13, 2021, https://www .trumanlibraryinstitute.org/truman/truman-quotes/.

222 *When he was a teenager, his mother gave him a multivolume book:* "Truman Home Study Book List—Harry S Truman National Historic Site (U.S.

National Park Service)," accessed August 13, 2021, https://www.nps.gov/hstr /learn/historyculture/truman-home-study-book-list.htm.

222   *he spent seven years behind a mule on his small family farm:* Robert H. Ferrell, *Harry S. Truman: A Life* (University of Missouri Press, 2013).

222   *Truman also knew that if he recognized, there was a danger that Marshall would quit:* "Recognition of Israel | Harry S. Truman," accessed August 13, 2021, https://www.trumanlibrary.gov/museum/ordinary-man/recognition-of-israel.

223   *To his credit, Marshall stuck by his president:* David McCullough, *Truman* (Simon & Schuster, 2003). 736.

223   *he devoured books, from Hemingway to Faulkner to Fitzgerald:* Jim Mattis and Bing West, *Call Sign Chaos: Learning to Lead* (Random House Publishing Group, 2019), 5.

223   *a marine is given a new list of books to read relevant to his new responsibilities:* "Commandant's Professional Reading List (Foundational)," MCA (blog), accessed August 13, 2021, https://mca-marines.org/blog/resource/comman dants-professional-reading-list/.

223   *he delved back into the history of the nations and the cultures where his marines would fight:* Mattis and West, *Call Sign Chaos*, 43.

223   *Mattis had a personal library filled with seven thousand books:* "Defense Secretary James Mattis' Extraordinary Reading Habits," accessed August 13, 2021, https://www.cnbc.com/2018/09/13/defense-secretary-james-mattis -extraordinary-reading-habits.html.

223   *"If you haven't read hundreds of books, you are functionally illiterate":* Mattis and West, *Call Sign Chaos*, 42.

225   *"Writing is not the simple transfer of fully formed intellectual inventory from brain to paper":* Sidney Harman, *Mind Your Own Business: A Maverick's Guide to Business, Leadership and Life* (Crown, 2003), xii.

227   *"Gentlemen . . . why don't you laugh":* Merrill D. Peterson, *Lincoln in American Memory* (Oxford University Press, 1995), 97.

227   *"Well, for land sake, you are the homeliest man I ever saw":* Richard Carwardine, *Lincoln's Sense of Humor* (SIU Press, 2017), 45.

227   *"But if you want someone to get the job done, ask a woman":* "Thatcher's Thoughts from a Life in Politics," AP News, accessed August 14, 2021, https://apnews.com/article/db88dbafc70b46f2a286a343105b472d.

227   *"All things considered, I would rather be in Philadelphia":* Del Quentin Wilber, "When Reagan Was Shot, Country Rallied Around, but He Hadn't Spent Months Downplaying Assassins," *Los Angeles Times*, October 2, 2020, https:// www.latimes.com/politics/story/2020-10-02/when-reagan-shot-country-ral lied-he-hadnt-spent-months-downplaying-assassins.

228 *"I want you to know that also I will not make age an issue of this campaign"*: "Debate Between the President and Former Vice President Walter F. Mondale in Kansas City, Missouri," accessed August 14, 2021, https://www.reaganfoun dation.org/ronald-reagan/reagan-quotes-speeches/debate-between-the-presi dent-and-former-vice-president-walter-f-mondale-in-kansas-city-missouri/.

229 *"Let us spend two days there"*: Con Coughlin, "Marrakesh: Where Churchill and Roosevelt Played Hookey," *Telegraph*, February 4, 2016, https://www .telegraph.co.uk/travel/destinations/africa/morocco/marrakech/articles /Marrakesh-where-Churchill-and-Roosevelt-played-hookey/.

230 *"I feel like a sultan. You may kiss my hand, my dear"*: Ibid.

231 *it is an engineering concept—a search for equilibrium—that has proven impossible:* "Speed Dial: Warren Bennis," Bloomberg.Com, September 23, 2010, https:// www.bloomberg.com/news/articles/2010-09-23/speed-dial-warren-bennis.

231 *One season might be heavily devoted to work projects:* Olga Khazan, "Give Up on Work-Life Balance," *Atlantic*, May 30, 2019, https://www.theatlantic .com/health/archive/2019/05/work-life-balance/590662/.

232 *"Work, work, work is the main thing"*: "Abraham Lincoln's Advice to Lawyers," accessed August 14, 2021, http://www.abrahamlincolnonline.org/lin coln/speeches/law.htm.

234 *Lamar Alexander is another public leader who has demonstrated an integrated life:* Lamar Alexander, *Six Months Off: An American Family's Australian Adventure* (Morrow, 1988).

EXECUTIVE SUMMARY: 20 KEY TAKEAWAYS

237 *leadership today must be exercised "inside out"*: Nancy Koehn, *Forged in Crisis: The Power of Courageous Leadership in Turbulent Times* (Simon & Schuster, 2017), 4.

243 *"If there are many leaders, you can't compromise a movement and you can't kill it"*: Charlotte Alter, *The Ones We've Been Waiting For: How a New Generation of Leaders Will Transform America* (Penguin, 2021), 119.

EPILOGUE: ANSWERING THE CALL

245 *"Let the word go forth from this time and place"*: "Our Documents—Transcript of President John F. Kennedy's Inaugural Address (1961)," accessed July 19, 2021, https://www.ourdocuments.gov/doc.php?flash=false&doc=91&page =transcript.

246 *Jimmy Carter, was still studying at the Naval Academy:* "Jimmy Carter's Naval Service—About Us—The Jimmy Carter Presidential Library and Museum," accessed July 19, 2021, https://www.jimmycarterlibrary.gov/about _us/naval_service.

246 *Kennedy took a strap from the man's life jacket*: Hersey, "John F. Kennedy's

Story of Survival," *New Yorker*, accessed July 19, 2021, https://www.new yorker.com/magazine/1944/06/17/survival.

246 *George H.W. Bush included in his inaugural parade a replica of the Avenger aircraft:* Rene Sanchez and Fern Shen, "New President Charms Throngs Along America's Main Street," *Washington Post,* January 21, 1989, https://www.wash ingtonpost.com/archive/politics/1989/01/21/new-president-charms-throngs -along-americas-main-street/b277e78a-ff85-4c7c-9f71-908baaccedf7/.

246 *he was one of the youngest U.S. pilots shot down over the South Pacific:* "Bush, George H. W.," accessed August 18, 2021, http://public1.nhhcaws.local/re search/histories/biographies-list/bios-b/bush-george-h-w.html.

246 *Some 16 million Americans served in uniform, nearly 40 percent of whom were volunteers:* Jonathan E. Vespa, "Those Who Served: America's Veterans from World War II to the War on Terror," n.d., 18.

247 *Brokaw concluded that they were "the greatest generation":* Tom Brokaw, *The Greatest Generation* (Random House, 1998).

249 *resistance movements led by the young have mobilized the largest crowds in history:* Larry Buchanan, Quoctrung Bui, and Jugal K. Patel, "Black Lives Matter May Be the Largest Movement in U.S. History," *New York Times*, July 3, 2020, https://www.nytimes.com/interactive/2020/07/03/us/george -floyd-protests-crowd-size.html.

250 *somewhere between 3 and 5 million protestors participated in the Women's March:* Ibid.

252 *The civil rights protests of the 1960s drew far more Black Americans than whites:* Amanda Barroso and Rachel Minkin, "Recent Protest Attendees Are More Racially and Ethnically Diverse, Younger Than Americans Overall," Pew Research Center (blog), accessed August 18, 2021, https://www.pewresearch .org/fact-tank/2020/06/24/recent-protest-attendees-are-more-racially-and -ethnically-diverse-younger-than-americans-overall/.

252 *Millennials now occupy thirty-one seats in the House and one in the Senate:* "Which Generations Have the Most Members in the 117th Congress? | Pew Research Center," accessed August 18, 2021, https://www.pewresearch.org /fact-tank/2021/02/12/boomers-silents-still-have-most-seats-in-congress -though-number-of-millennials-gen-xers-is-up-slightly/.

253 *Ashoka partners up with some three hundred nonprofits around the world:* "Home | Ashoka | Everyone a Changemaker," accessed August 18, 2021, https://www.ashoka.org/en-hu.

253 *it now has 64,000 alumni serving fifty regions across the country and has expanded abroad:* "Learn More about Teach for America's Nationwide Impact," accessed August 18, 2021, https://www.teachforamerica.org/what-we-do/impact.

253 *KIPP Foundation,, which has some 270 charter schools and 160,000 students*

and alumni: "KIPP's Structure | Learn How KIPP Public Charter Schools Are Structured," KIPP Public Charter Schools, accessed August 18, 2021, https://www.kipp.org/schools/structure/.

253 *Echoing Green has provided early funding for almost a thousand social innovators:* "Echoing Green Kicks Off Work Supported by Racial Equity Philanthropic Fund," Echoing Green, February 11, 2021, https://echoinggreen .org/news/echoing-green-kicks-off-work-supported-by-racial-equity-phil anthropic-fund/.

255 *calls to the young to embrace a life "greater than one's own self-interest":* John McCain and Stan McChrystal, "Expand Opportunities for Young Americans to Serve Their Country," CNN, August 10, 2015, https://www.cnn.com/2015/08/10 /opinions/mccain-mcchrystal-national-service-legislation/index.html.

255 *AmeriCorps affiliates volunteered millions of hours to keep communities afloat:* David Gergen and Caroline Cohen, "Opinion: This Program Puts People to Work Serving America. Now It's Going to Jump in Size," CNN, accessed August 18, 2021, https://www.cnn.com/2021/03/17/opinions/americorps -stimulus-national-service-gergen-cohen/index.html.

255 *a bridge between volunteers and community*: E. J. Dionne and Kayla Meltzer Drogosz, "United We Serve?: The Debate over National Service," Brookings (blog), November 30, 1AD, https://www.brookings.edu/articles /united-we-serve-the-debate-over-national-service/.

258 *"It is not the critic who counts":* "Address at the Sorbonne in Paris, France: 'Citizenship in a Republic' | The American Presidency Project," accessed August 18, 2021, https://www.presidency.ucsb.edu/documents/address-the -sorbonne-paris-france-citizenship-republic.

259 *President Nixon read the same passage in his resignation speech:* "Roosevelt's Lessons for Nations Across Generations," accessed August 18, 2021, https://www .lowyinstitute.org/the-interpreter/roosevelt-s-lessons-nations-generations.

259 *LeBron James puts "Man in the Arena" on his shoes before a game:* "LeBron James Is the 'Man in the Arena,'" https://www.cleveland19.com, accessed August 18, 2021, https://www.cleveland19.com/story/38385477/lebron -james-is-the-man-in-the-arena.

259 *Miley Cyrus has a passage tattooed on her forearm:* Jen Chaney, "Miley Cyrus Is Now Tattooing Presidential Quotes on Herself," *Washington Post* (blog), July 11, 2012, https://www.washingtonpost.com/blogs/celebritology/post /miley-cyrus-is-now-tattooing-presidential-quotes-on-herself/2012/07/11 /gJQA9PGedW_blog.html.

260 *they were soon nicknamed Patience and Fortitude:* "The Library Lions," New York Public Library, accessed August 18, 2021, https://www.nypl.org/help /about-nypl/library-lions.

Acknowledgments

A central theme of this book is that leadership scholars have largely moved away from a Great Man theory of history. Individual leaders are still indispensable, of course, but it has become increasingly clear that to "get big things done" these days, a leader also needs creative collaboration.

That was certainly my experience in pulling together this book: it has been a collaborative effort right from the start, with many minds and pens contributing. It has also come with a welcome surprise.

As in the past half century of our marriage and parenthood, my wife, Anne, was once again an invaluable partner, providing a steady stream of ideas and edits; she is the most cultured member of our foursome. We are proud that our son Christopher and daughter Katherine are both engaged in public service, as are their spouses and kids. Their families provided lots of insights into the challenges of younger generations.

I am also deeply grateful to those who have partnered in creating and then building the Center for Public Leadership at the Harvard Kennedy School; our work together has been a wonderful training ground for me. The Center is in great hands today with the stewardship of Dean Doug Elmendorf, our new co-directors, Deval Patrick and Hannah Riley Bowles, and our new executive director Ken Himmelman. I am thankful not only to the faculty and staff but also to our donors whose generosity has funded nearly 1000 fellowships for students, enabling them to pursue advanced degrees: Les and Abigail Wexner, Mort Zuckerman, Glenn Dubin, David Rubenstein, Bill George, Sheila C. Johnson, the Leon and Debra Black family, Louis Bacon, Alan Gleitsman, and the government of the UAE. We can all take pride in nearly one thousand fellowships they have financed.

In exploring how one becomes a great leader, I drew heavily upon longtime masters in the field: Warren Bennis, John Gardner, Deborah Rhode, Peter Drucker, James MacGregor Burns, and Richard Hackman. Some of those have died in recent years. I miss them all, especially Warren, a dear friend. Fortunately, a number of others have emerged as key players in leadership studies, starting with Bill George, Jim Collins, Iris Bohnet, Walter Isaacson, Amy Edmondson, Generals Mattis and McChrystal, Admiral Dana Borne, Rosabeth Moss Kanter, Ron Heifetz, Marshall Ganz, and Barbara Kellerman. Most are featured in these pages, especially Bill George, whose work on authentic leadership is reshaping the field.

In my view, historians and biographers are also a rich source for understanding leadership. Pick up any book by Doris Kearns Goodwin or Nancy Koehn or Jon Meacham, Jill Lepore, Fred Logevall, Drew Faust, Garry Wills, Michael Beschloss, Barbara Tuchman, Stephen Ambrose, or Arthur Schlesinger Jr., and you will find key lessons. And powerful writing. Happily, all except Tuchman, Ambrose, and Schlesinger, are still with us but their work lives on, too.

I could go on by describing social scientists whose work has also influenced my views—luminaries like Joe Nye, Joseph Campbell, Erik Erikson, Martin Seligman, Howard Gardner, Iris Bohnet, and Susan Cain—but I want to save room for the big surprise of this project:

what a grand role would be played in creating this volume by the very generations who should lead this country into the future.

My appreciation of their promise began taking root a quarter century ago when I began college teaching, discovered students with serious talent, and decided to hire two graduates a year for help—one my research assistant, the other my executive assistant. In each case, I proposed an informal pact: if you will give me two years working by my side, I will help you open doors to the world. I had no idea how much they would become partners and then companions for life.

They are the ones who got me off my duff a few years ago, persuading me to write this book. Michael Zuckerman, Blythe Riggan, Jamie Piltch, Greg Honan, and Emma Dolson were the chief initiators; each has gone on to a rewarding life. Michael became editor of the *Harvard Law Review*, clerked for Justice Sotomayor, and then went to work for a nonprofit on penal reform in Ohio. Blythe is now enrolled at the UNC Law School in Chapel Hill. Jamie had his choice of topflight law schools: Harvard, Yale, or Stanford. He chose Yale (a wise choice, says this Yale alum). Greg earned a master's degree from the Kennedy School and now helps to manage With Honor, a nonprofit encouraging military veterans of both parties to run for Congress. After leaving my team, Emma headed up strategic partnerships at CPL and now works as the chief operating officer of a research advisory firm in Washington, D.C. (You can find brief profiles for members of "Team Gergen" on my website.)

Of great import, they discovered Caroline Cohen, who recently graduated from Harvard College with high honors and a prize for her writing. Since joining our team, Caroline has been an extraordinary partner, magical in pulling together research, bandying ideas, and turning words into print. I came to rely upon her sound judgment and wise discernment on a daily basis. Without her, the book might never have appeared. Happily, Lia Janzer joined up, too, a year ago. She came from graduate studies at the London School of Economics, where she excelled. Lia is rapidly developing into another star.

I would be remiss not to acknowledge as well the wonderful team at Simon & Schuster who helped make this book a reality—in addition to other notable advisors. Stuart Roberts, my editor, has provided a guiding hand throughout this process, as has his Editorial Assistant Awura Ama Barnie-Duah. I should also thank Associate Director of Publicity Larry Hughes, Marketing Director Stephen Bedford, and Publisher Dana Canedy. Two special coaches have been Bob Barnett and Aileen Boyle. I have relied upon Bob's wise advice for decades, and this book was no different. This has been the second time I have been lucky enough to work with Aileen; she was a terrific outside adviser helping me navigate the world of book publishing.

Frankly, even with the talent who came aboard, I wasn't certain that our team could pull off a respectable showing. As I had learned much earlier, tackling a book can be a daunting enterprise. Churchill said it well: "Writing a book is an adventure. To begin with it is a toy and an amusement. Then it becomes a mistress, then it becomes a master, then it becomes a tyrant. The last phase is that just as you are about to be reconciled to your servitude, you kill the monster and fling him to the public."

To my delight, our little team performed far above expectation. All of those young people working by my side underscore just how promising the young are these days. They are the ones who deserve credit for making this book a creative collaboration; they are the ones who turned it into an adventure. And they are the ones who should give the rest of us more faith in the future of our democracy. The mistakes are all mine.

Index